Science of Whole Person Healing

Organized by

Friends of Health

Co-Sponsored by
Alternative Therapies in Health and Medicine
Arizona State University, CRESMET Program
The Chopra Center
Citizens for Health
National Foundation for Alternative Medicine
Penn State University, STS Program
The Rodale Institute
The Samueli Institute
TAI Sophia Institute
University of Arizona, Program in Integrative Medicine
Wisdom Media

Science of Whole Person Healing

Proceedings of the First Interdisciplinary International Conference

Volume 1

Rustum Roy, Editor

iUniverse, Inc.
New York Lincoln Shanghai

Science of Whole Person Healing
Proceedings of the First Interdisciplinary International Conference

iUniverse, Inc.

For information address:
iUniverse, Inc.
2021 Pine Lake Road, Suite 100
Lincoln, NE 68512
www.iuniverse.com

ISBN: 0-595-30153-3

Printed in the United States of America

CONTENTS

Volume I

Volume II

PREFACE

Rustum Roy
Conference Chair

This collection of research papers was generated at the First International Conference on "The Science of Whole Person Healing," held in Bethesda, Maryland on March 28-30th, 2003.

In opening the conference, as Chair, I made the following points. There are today literally a dozen major and another dozen minor conferences in the area of what is otherwise called by a variety of names, often including CAM (Complementary and Alternative Medicine). This conference was distinctive among those in several ways, including the introduction of a more comprehensive name for the field—*Whole Person Healing*.

The origin, leadership, and goals

The conference was conceived of by the Science Advisory Committee—a group of high-level research scientists and physicians, who have studied the field in depth for years—of Friends of Health (FOH), a non-profit organization. While the CAM-WPH (Complementary and Alternative Medicine—Whole Person Healing) movement is sweeping the nation, it was clear that the scientific community and physicians were simply not being exposed to the excellent science and new research opportunities in the field. This "bridge to science," which is one of FOH's major goals, clearly would be greatly helped by such a conference.

One of our goals was to collect the national and international leaders of the CAM-WPH movement and have the audience exposed to magisterial reviews of each of their fields. Another parallel goal was to capture the latest advances in research by CAM-WPH practitioners—as in any normal scientific meeting.

The interdisciplinary nature of the conference

One of the distinctive characteristics was that the attendees constituted a highly interdisciplinary group, which included:

- The consumers of healthcare: all citizens;

- Pioneer physicians within the medical establishment;
- Leaders of research in a dozen ancestral practices;
- Adventuresome scientists, acting like scientists—open to the really new;
- Sponsors: Friends of Health and its allies, universities;
- Program managers from federal research agencies;
- Legislators and/or their staff representing the people.

Internationally acclaimed physicists, engineers, chemists, and biologists were mixed with equally distinguished physicians. One great success of the conference was the fact of bringing together the enormous range of different CAM-WPH practitioners to learn of each other's advances. This also enabled the scientists (not involved with any of the practices) to identify possible common threads of theory or manifestations.

Reassertion of the true nature of science

In a climate where theories, current paradigms, and projections into the far future have become the warp and woof of medical research, the reassertion of facts, well-established, observed repeatedly and in different locations, as the *only* basis for science, is an absolute requirement. Only thus could one avoid the criticism of science voiced by one of the most perceptive Americans of all time, Mark Twain:

> *There is something fascinating about science. One gets such wholesale returns of conjecture out of such a trifling investment of fact.*

Scattered throughout the printed program were the primordial principles of science, espoused by the organizers, expressed by scholars throughout the ages. These pithy assertions, which together make our epistemological position clear, included the following:

> *Nor again must we in all matters alike demand an explanation of the reason why things are what they are; in some cases it is enough if the fact that they are so satisfactorily established. This is the case with first principles; and the fact is the primary thing—it is a first principle. And principles are studies—some by induction, others by perception, others by some form of habituation, and also others otherwise; so we must endeavor to arrive at the principles of each kind in their natural manner, and must also by careful to define them correctly.*
> -Aristotle in *Nichomachean Ethics* I, vii. 17-22

A good scientist has freed himself of concepts and keeps his mind open to what is.

-Lao-Tze, s.27

You will observe with concern how long a useful truth may be known and exist, before it is generally received and practiced on.

-Benjamin Franklin

If there is anything [that] human history demonstrates, it is the extreme slowness with which the academic and critical mind acknowledges facts to exist [that] present themselves as wild facts, with no staff or pigeon-hole, or as facts [that] threaten to break up the accepted system.

-William James (1900 Philosopher/Psychologist)

Science seems to me to teach in the highest and strongest manner the great truth which is embodied in the Christian conception of entire surrender to the will of God. Sit down before fact as a little child, be prepared to give up every preconceived notion, follow humbly wherever and to whatever abysses Nature leads, or you shall learn nothing. I have only begun to learn content and peace of mind since I resolved at all risks to do this.

Thomas H. Huxley, in a letter to Charles Kingsley,
author and clergyman

Regrettably, much of *contemporary* science—denying the grand tradition of successful science, engineering, and technology—has raised (often) transient paradigms to the status of religious dogma. So much so that one of the great mathematician/philosophers of our time wrote fifty years ago:

The universe is vast. Nothing is more curious than the self-satisfied dogmatism with which mankind at each period of its history cherishes the delusion of the finality of its existing modes of knowledge. Skeptics and believers are all alike. At this moment scientists and skeptics are the leading dogmatists. Advance in detail is admitted: fundamental novelty is barred. This dogmatic common sense is the death of philosophical adventure. The universe is vast.

Alfred North Whitehead in *Essays in Science and Philosophy*

Structure of the conference and the Proceedings Volume

Plenary

The morning and afternoon presentations were all invited talks by experienced, distinguished physicians and scientists. They were all presented in plenary sessions, explicitly to help the inter-discipline and inter-community exchange among and within the different communities listed above.

Tell-and-Show

The evening presentations consisted of the submitted papers. The structure was one developed in the Chair's field of materials science, called "Tell-and-Show" sessions. The authors each present in very short statements (sometimes three minutes, but in our case, ten minutes) their most interesting results, and why the audience may wish to learn more. At the end of all the reports, there is a poster or display session, where the audience may get further detailed information from the authors via posters, devices, and displays.

Sequence of topics

An important part of the structure of the conference is our utter dedication to facts, to data. Hence, we started with a series of papers on a wide variety of data on a very wide range of procedures, starting with the effects of human intention on deformation of materials, or the pH of water, to qigong healing of paralyzed patients given up on by modern medicine, to "psychic surgery" in Brazil.

However, it is not accurate to assume that there are no theoretical models for such data. Just as the effects predicted by quantum mechanics could not be explained by classical physics and required a paradigm change, so also it is obvious that major theoretical hypotheses, such as operating in multi-dimensions, will be real options to be considered. Three or four different models were presented.

The "why" of this conference: Lower-cost healing, beyond the biochemical straitjacket

All current reports on the state of the U.S. healthcare system record that only something radically new can rescue it from disaster. The present *costs* affiliated with the act of healing, curing, relief of pain, are obviously unsustainable, even for a decade. Long before any other unsustainable practice meets the apocryphal immovable object, the healthcare system will meet physical reality, beyond the reach of palliative political or economic manipulation.

Any objective observer of the variety of extraordinary, even astounding, examples of healing reported from all over the world, including our own country, seems to be totally ignored by the mainstream media who usually are eager to find extraordinary occurrences. This is inexplicable, except by the hypothesis that those who write for the media (educated in an academic establishment perfectly described by Mark Twain, Ben Franklin, and Alfred North Whitehead in the quotes above) simply have come under the dogmatic hegemony of the so-called "scientific medicine" establishment, with very little in the way of scientific credentials, and locked into a model of the body-only, and that as a biochemical-only system.

How else can one explain that while all the world's leaders are often cured by CAM-WPH providers, the media *never* report on it? Thus, Richard Nixon, whose phlebitis had obviously defeated the very best efforts of western medicine, through the good offices of the Japanese Prime Minister, had to import a special yoga instructor from India to finally restore him to health. How is it that Deng Xiao Peng used Dr. Yan Xin, the greatest of present-day qigong masters, for his ailments, and George W.H. Bush respected him enough to invite him to the White House on five separate occasions.

In a shrunken world, why does not our media report that in Brazil, a psychic healer/trance surgeon called Joao de Deus has been healing literally a million people a year for 20 years? Here is the case where thousands upon thousands of surgeries have been conducted in open halls with video cameras constantly rolling, where in breast or neck or thigh surgeries, there is zero pain, no anesthesia, no bleeding, and no sepsis. Even if the media do not report it, how is it that N.I.H. or some health foundation does not have an institute, even perhaps a whole program, dedicated to researching and importing this discovery into the U.S.

We believe that for all these reasons, this conference will join with other conferences focusing on CAM-WPH practices to help bring such lower cost, less dangerous, healing practices to the people. Moreover, this is entirely consistent with our commitment to championing science in its rightful place. I have described my view of that place in my book, "Experimenting with Truth" (Pergamon Press, 1982). Simply put, it is that Science is exquisitely accurate and very powerful at the detail level, whereas our values, our commitments, and our beliefs are the only ways to define our own Big Picture. The two approaches are of complementary and immense value together in the healing of whole persons.

Correcting Medical Mistakes That Cause Thousands of Needless Deaths

Henry J. Heimlich, MD, ScD

The Heimlich Institute
311 Straight Street
Cincinnati, OH 45219
e-mail: heimlich@iglou.com

Abstract

Thousands of people die needlessly because of mistaken concepts in medicine. For decades, leading medical organizations taught backslaps should be used for choking victims; yet every study showed backslaps drive choking objects deeper and tighter into the airway, causing death. Similarly, asthmatics and drowning victims die because of blocked airways. Accepted resuscitation protocols ignore this blockage. If everyone understood the same simple technique—the Heimlich maneuver—they use to save choking victims, can save asthmatics and drowning victims, thousands of lives could be saved each year.

Since the onset of the AIDS health crisis, a vast amount of effort has been spent on finding a drug cure for HIV infection. Drugs have provided only temporary improvement in HIV-infected patients. The virus, however, remains viable in the brain, and other organs drugs cannot penetrate, and becomes resistant to drugs. Consequently, individuals are being infected with drug-resistant HIV. The co-chair of the 2002 Barcelona AIDS conference said, "We need to treat the immune system. With antiretroviral therapy, we have reached the roof."

Currently, malariotherapy is the only treatment for HIV patients having the potential to control the AIDS pandemic; furthermore, it is a low cost therapy. Malariotherapy increases production of cytokines that strengthen the immune system, offering the possibility to overcome HIV throughout the body. Malariotherapy's scientific basis and safety is clearly established. Treating HIV patients with malariotherapy increased their CD4 cells to normal levels which,

1

without any further treatment, persisted for two years, during which the patients remained clinically well. Further investigation of malariotherapy for HIV is warranted.

Today, it has been proven that thousands of people, many of them children, are dying needlessly from asthma attacks, heart attacks and drowning. Recent changes in lifesaving methods are being taught to relatively small groups by first aid organizations. Until the word is spread to the entire public, these unwarranted deaths will continue. Furthermore, the current misconception that drugs can cure a virus, offers false hope to millions of AIDS sufferers. One of the important adverse effects of this is the spread of drug resistant strains of HIV. Perhaps there will be a drug that one day can cure HIV infection, but this goal has not yet been reached.

Asthma

Every year, more than 5000 Americans, many of them children, die during asthma attacks. In 1995, Hillary, a four-year-old child, diagnosed with asthma, suffered a severe asthma attack. Her mother applied the Heimlich maneuver and, within a minute, the child was able to breathe normally. The Heimlich Institute has received other reports of the Maneuver stopping asthma attacks.

As described by the National Institutes of Health, asthma attacks constrict breathing tubes (bronchi), which are then blocked by mucous plugs. The victim can breathe in, but cannot breathe out. Trapped air distends the lungs. Victims die because they can neither breathe in or out. They also cannot inhale medication.

A Heimlich maneuver, performed gently on one's self, or by a bystander, presses the diaphragm upward, diminishing the volume of the chest cavity, which compresses the lungs, expelling trapped air. This air flow may carry away mucous plugs and enable the asthma victim to resume normal breathing. Additionally, use of the Maneuver once or twice a week to expel mucus from the lungs in order to prevent asthma attacks is being studied. Those using the Heimlich maneuver for asthma should do so under a physician's care and be properly trained in use of the Maneuver.

Heart Attacks

CPR (CardioPulmonary Resuscitation) consists of mouth-to-mouth and pressing on the chest. Mouth-to-mouth is a complex procedure. For almost thirty years the American Heart Association has been teaching the public to perform CPR for heart attack victims. Throughout those decades, no study was done to determine whether CPR was saving lives or causing deaths.

On May 25, 2000, a 7-year study by the University of Washington, in Seattle, was reported in the prestigious *New England Journal of Medicine* and by the *Associated Press* [1]. The study found that 911-operator instructions for using mouth-to-mouth for heart attacks increases the number of deaths. Only 10% of those given mouth-to-mouth and chest compressions, survived to discharge from the hospital. Nearly 15% receiving chest compressions alone recovered and were discharged from the hospital.

Two months after the Seattle study appeared, the American Heart Association (AHA) *Guidelines 2000*, published in its journal, *Circulation*, instructed emergency telephone operators to omit teaching mouth-to-mouth for heart attack victims [2]. 911 operators are instructed to teach callers, faced with a heart attack victim, to use only chest compressions. In addition, AHA instructions no longer require rescuers to use mouth-to-mouth for heart attacks. In fact, they warn that mouth-to-mouth blows air into the stomach, not into the lungs, and this causes vomiting with aspiration of vomit. The AHA also states that the exchange of saliva with mouth-to-mouth has caused tuberculosis, herpes, and meningitis, and there is fear of spreading AIDS and hepatitis.

Drowning

Drowning victims die because their lungs fill with water, blocking the airway. They choke to death on water. Until 1961, manual methods of emergency resuscitation were used for drowning. These techniques include the Schaefer prone-pressure method (with the victim lying face down, press intermittently on the back of the lower chest), rolling the victim over a barrel, draping the victim face down in a jackknife position over the rescuer's shoulder and jogging, or over the back of a trotting horse. These methods caused intermittent elevation of the diaphragm, compressing the lungs, expelling water and ventilating the victim—in effect crude Heimlich maneuvers [3]. For four decades the American Red Cross taught rescuers to use CPR—blow air into a drowning victim's mouth. No study ever showed that doing mouth-to-mouth without first removing the water from the lungs saved drowning victims.

A 1982 University of Pittsburgh study experimentally proved four Heimlich maneuvers clear the water from the lungs, enabling air to get into the lungs and allow victims to breathe [4]. Four Heimlichs take ten seconds to perform and anyone can do them. The Red Cross adopted the Heimlich maneuver for drowning victims in their 1995 manual *First Aid Fast* [5]. In a five-year study, conducted 1995-2000, 32,000 lifeguards were trained to use the Heimlich maneuver as the first step to resuscitate unconscious, non-breathing drowning victims. 97% of the victims survived with full recovery [6]. University studies, using CPR, reported 50%-60% of such drowning victims died [7-9].

Lifeguards are taught to use the Heimlich maneuver to clear the lungs of water. Every year, however, more than 1,000 children die of drowning at home—in toilets, bath tubs, pails of water, and pools. In 18 states, drowning is the leading cause of accidental death for children under five years old. First to respond in the home is a parent or babysitter, many of whom attempt to use only CPR. Media articles frequently report CPR was used by rescuers before children died of drowning.

Many of the 284 million Americans know the Heimlich maneuver. Reports of 911 operators successfully instructing callers how to perform to the Maneuver to save choking victims show that it is easily taught. The public must learn: To save drowning victims, perform the same Heimlich maneuver you would for a choking victim. Use the lying down (supine) position for adult victims. Repeat until water no longer flows from the mouth. Proceed with CPR if warranted.

Treating HIV by Strengthening the Immune System

The journal *Science*, June 28, 2002, reports, "HIV has become increasingly resistant to existing drugs, and transmission of these resistant strains is on the rise...virus hides out in various reservoirs in the body that would take decades of treatment to empty." They quote Gatell, co-chair of the 2002 Barcelona AIDS conference: "We need to treat the immune system. With antiretroviral therapy, we have reached the roof."

A pandemic similar to AIDS, was, after the failure of drugs, eradicated a little over 25 years ago by stimulating the immune system. Scientific facts indicate that this treatment, malariotherapy, can be effective against HIV/AIDS.

Drugs or antibiotics, which cured early stages of syphilis, were ineffective against neurosyphilis—syphilis of the brain. There appeared to be a "blood-brain barrier," which prevented medications from effectively reaching brain tissue. Spirochetes, therefore, persisted in the brain, causing progressive neurological damage. Death occurred one to four years after the onset of symptoms. Spontaneous acute febrile diseases were known to sometimes cure neurosyphilitics, but attempts to induce them by injection of bacteria failed due to the body's resistance to the organisms. In 1918, Wagner Jauregg reported that malariotherapy cures neurosyphilis, for which he was awarded the 1927 Nobel Prize in Medicine. In addition to treating neurosyphilis by inducing malaria, examples of using one disease to prevent another include cowpox to prevent smallpox and Sabin live polio vaccine.

Malariotherapy consists of intravenous injection of 10 ml of screened blood obtained from malaria patients. After 10-12 fevers, approximately three weeks, the malaria is cured with drugs. *Plasmodium vivax* was preferred due to its toleration by patients and ease of cure, which persists today. *Plasmodium falciparum* was successful but requires closer patient observation.

The reason for malariotherapy's success in treating neurosyphilis was unknown, but was attributed to the malarial fevers (hyperthermia). Some patients were cured, however, even when the malaria did not produce high fevers, and production of fever by mechanical means (fever cabinets) did not achieve the same success as malariotherapy. Scientists, therefore, speculated that an immune reaction was taking place. However, modern immunological knowledge was unavailable at that time.

Malariotherapy was extremely safe during the more than five decades it was successfully used to treat neurosyphilis. In a 1984 review, Chernin (Harvard School of Public Health) [10] states: "…malariatherapy was less expensive and produced clinical improvement more frequently and more rapidly than did the best of drug treatments…the contraindications to malariatherapy, and there were some, must have been carefully observed because records of treatment-related deaths or extreme disability are few relative to the thousands of patients treated…It is not hard to imagine the almost certain fate of the thousands of paretics (neurosyphilitics) who would have sickened horribly and died but for malariatherapy." There is no known report of induced malaria not being cured and malaria was never spread from hospitalized patients.

It is surprising that few doctors today are aware of malariotherapy, which was used internationally for almost 60 years. During that period, United States Public Health Service laboratories, Johns Hopkins Hospital, Horton Laboratory in Epsom, England, and others, provided malarial blood to hospitals throughout the world. Tens of thousands of neurosyphilitics were successfully cured. By 1975, malariotherapy had eradicated neurosyphilis. New cases did not develop since early stages of syphilis were cured by antibiotics.

HIV and the Immune System

As we all know, HIV-infection weakens patients' immune systems by outstripping the ability of the body's CD4 immune cells to respond to the virus. This effect of HIV infection results in decreased ability of the body's immune system to respond to secondary infections that prove fatal. Restoration and preservation of the immune system are crucial elements for the successful clinical management of HIV infection [11].

Drug therapies attempt to restore the immune system by inhibiting viral reproduction. HIV, however, mutates and becomes resistant to drugs, enabling the virus to multiply. Since HIV invades the brain, as evidenced by AIDS dementia, inadequacy of drug treatment may, also, be due to the "blood-brain barrier," recognized in the treatment of neurosyphilis.

In contrast, the immune system is able to adapt to changes in viruses and eradicate them throughout the body. Immunobased approaches to treating HIV-infection focus on directly strengthening the immune system.

Malaria and the Immune System

In the late 1980's, I became aware of a number of scientific studies which reported that malaria causes the immune system to increase production of a variety of immune substances. These substances include interleukins and interferons (IFN- [12,13], IFN- [12-16], IL-6 [16,17], IL-2R [15, 18-23], and sCD8 [15,24]). Since then, many other studies have confirmed that malaria stimulates the production of a great variety of immune substances. Strengthening the immune system, rather than the fever, is most likely the basis for the success of malariotherapy in treating neurosyphilis.

Since malaria has been proven to boost the immune system, this treatment, therefore, has the potential to overcome a host of life-threatening diseases, including cancer. In 1986, the Centers for Disease Control (CDC) offered to obtain malarial blood for the Heimich Institute to treat cancer patients using malariotherapy. Robert L Kaiser, Medical Director, Division of Parasitic Diseases, Centers for Disease Control wrote to Dr. Heimlich, "...we will be pleased to assist in providing appropriate strains of Plasmodium Vivax (malaria) and in helping you establish the necessary technology."

The immunostimulative effect of malaria logically has potential benefit for restoring the immune system of HIV patients. It is feasible that malariotherapy can produce immune substances in HIV infected patients in sufficient quantities to overcome the virus throughout the body.

Confirmation of this possibility came in a study reported at the 1990 International AIDS Conference in Florence which provided positive evidence of the beneficial effect of malaria infection on children with AIDS [25]. Studies were carried out in a children's hospital in Kinshasa, Congo, overseen by the U.S. Centers for Disease Control (CDC). The authors reported, "Among 112 children with symptomatic HIV infection, 41 (37%) had associated malaria....None of the 41 children with malaria and AIDS died, all recovered from their malaria. However, of the remaining 71 children with AIDS without malaria, 25 (35%) died."

Of course, before treating HIV patients with malariotherapy, strong evidence was needed that it would be safe to induce malaria in an HIV patient whose immune system was impaired. In 1991, the U.S. CDC studied 587 children in the same children's hospital in Kinshasa, Congo [26]. Two hundred sixty, aged 5 to 9 months, had been born to HIV seropositive mothers and 327 of the same age had been born to seronegative mothers. 271 children developed *Plasmodium falciparum* malaria and were treated with a standard regimen of oral quinine. The CDC concluded: "No significant differences were found in the incidence, severity, or response to therapy of malaria between children with progressive HIV-1 infection and the seronegative controls...No evidence was found to suggest that malaria has any role in accelerating the rate of progression of HIV-1 disease.... there is no adverse clinical or epidemiological association between these two important public health problems." Other studies also confirm that malaria does not effect HIV patients adversely [27-30].

In addition, three independent studies of malarial regions in Venezuela [31], Indonesia [32] and the Philippines [33] showed that people had HIV-type antibodies, but there was no AIDS. AIDS did exist in nearby non-malarial areas. The studies were carried out by researchers from the University of Nebraska and two U.S. Navy Medical Research teams.

NIH researchers reported the beneficial effect of injecting recombinant interleukin-2 (IL-2) in HIV patients [11]. They showed that, in HIV patients with CD4 cell counts greater than 200 cells/mm^3, IV infusions of IL-2, in combination with zidovudine (AZT) was followed by an increase in CD4 cells. CD4 cell counts subsequently diminished, but CD4 production was stimulated repeatedly with bimonthly infusions of IL-2. Such intravenous infusions of recombinant IL-2, however, caused severe secondary reactions. Note, as stated earlier, that IL-2 is produced naturally in malaria infected patients.

Malariotherapy for HIV Infected Patients

A clinical study of malariotherapy in eight HIV-positive males, ages 23-40, was carried out in collaboration with a Chinese public health agency, using *P. vivax.* HIV infection was confirmed by ELISA and Western blot testing. Following cure of the malaria, these patients have been monitored with CD4 counts and health examinations for two years. There were no complications.

Initial CD4 counts ranged from 269 to 1868. In seven patients, two years after malariotherapy was completed, the CD4's were from 570 to 2063 with fluctuations between those figures during the two years of follow-up. All those patients were in good health. One patient, clinically well, died of unrelated causes 15 months post-malariotherapy. These results and the evidence cited above confirm malariotherapy is safe and can be effective for HIV infected patients. Malariotherapy is the only treatment, to date, that caused the CD4 count to increase for a two-year period after a single course of treatment. No further treatment of any kind was required to maintain this increase.

Physicians in Africa also determined that malaria increases the CD4 cell counts in HIV infected patients. They reported: "We are in fact extremely excited about the expected trials and Dr. Alberts has done some preparatory work. He had a look at the CD4 counts of patients who were known HIV positive and had contracted plasmodium falciparum and those that didn't. It actually confirms your (Dr. Heimlich's) preparatory trials. Their CD4 count was raised. I think we should start with the trials as soon as possible…"

These studies and prior research by the CDC and others, cited above, confirm that malariotherapy is safe for HIV patients, just as it was for treatment of thousands of neurosyphilis patients over nearly six decades. Following malariotherapy in our HIV positive patients, CD4 cell counts increased and remained at normal levels for two years, during which time they have been clinically well. Treatment of additional HIV-positive patients is contemplated on a larger scale. Viral loads were not available during this preliminary study, but will be included in the future to determine the status of the HIV. It is apparent that the cost of malariotherapy is minimal and it is readily accessible.

Conclusion

The mind set in medical treatment has led to thousands of deaths by unwarranted assumptions and ignoring basic facts. We frequently read of asthmatics who die during severe attacks. Children die as a result of drowning, because their airways are blocked with water. Both asthmatics and drowning victims die because of blocked airways. But existing resuscitation protocols ignore this blockage. If everyone understands that the same simple technique—the Heimlich maneuver—they use to save a choking victim can be used to save asthmatics and drowning victims, thousands of lives could be saved each year.

A similar situation exists for the AIDS pandemic. Drug therapies for HIV attempt to inhibit viral replication in order to restore the immune system. The virus, however, remains viable in the brain and other organs that drugs cannot penetrate and becomes resistant to the drugs. Consequently, drugs have provided only temporary improvement in HIV infected patients

Malariotherapy increases production of cytokines, strengthening the immune system, in order to overcome the virus throughout the body. For more than 50 years, from 1918 to 1975, malariotherapy was used in the United States and throughout the world to treat and eradicate neurosyphilis, syphilis of the brain. As reported from the Harvard School of Public Health, malariotherapy was proven to be safe and effective.

Recent studies by the U.S. Centers for Disease Control and others report that there is no adverse clinical or epidemiological association in HIV patients who also have malaria. This finding confirms the safety of malariotherapy when used in HIV-infected patients. In a related study no children with AIDS and malaria died, and all recovered from their malaria; 35% of children with AIDS, without malaria, died in the same period of time. Our preliminary studies, treating eight HIV infected patients with malariotherapy, increased or maintained normal levels of CD4 immune cells during the two years they were followed, and the patients remained clinically well during that period.

HIV infection causes a gradual fall in CD4 cells, eventually leaving patients susceptible to fatal diseases. The increase in CD4 cells following three weeks of malariotherapy indicates restoration of the patient's immune system. Sustained increase of CD4 cells to normal levels for two years after receiving malariotherapy, without any further treatment, and the fact that those HIV patients remained in good health, suggests that the virus may have been controlled. Further tests and followup will determine whether the virus has been eradicated.

Malariotherapy is the only treatment for HIV patients today with the potential to control the AIDS pandemic and at low cost. Malariotherapy's scientific basis and safety is clearly established. Collaboration between countries will greatly enhance the development and evaluation of this treatment. The Heimlich Institute is prepared to participate in the establishment and course of such programs.

Details of our studies and references can be found at

References

1. Hallstrom A, Cobb L, Johnson E, Copass M (2000) New Eng J Med 342:1546
2. American Heart Association, International Liaison Committee on Resuscitation (2000) Circulation 102 [8 Suppl]:I-1
3. Heimlich HJ. (1981) Ann Emerg Med 10:476
4. Werner JZ, Safar P, Bircher NG, Stezoski W, Scanlon M, Stewart RD (1982) Anesthesiology 57 [suppl. 3A]:A81.
5. American Red Cross (1995) Drowning. In:First Aid Fast. Mosby Lifeline, St. Louis, p 15
6. Ellis & Associates. 1995-1999 Drowning resuscitation statistics. Available at: www.jellis.com
7. Biggart MJ, Bohn DJ (1990) J Pediatr 117:179
8. Quan L, Wentz KR, Gore EJ, Copass MK (1990) Pediatrics 86:586
9. Elam JO, Ruben AM, Greene DG (1960) JAMA 174:13
10. E Chernin (1984) J Parasitol 70:611
11. JA Kovacs, M Baseler, RJ Dewar, et al. (1995) N Engl J Med 332:567
12. A Rhodes-Feuillette, G Jaureguiberry, JJ Ballet, et al. (1985) J Interferon Res 5:159
13. A Rhodes-Feuillette, M Bellosguardo, P Druilhe, et al. (1985) J Interferon Res 5:169
14. SJ Slade, J Langhorne. (1989) Immunobiology 179:353
15. R Harpaz, R Edelman, SS Wasserman, MM Levine, JR Davis, MB Sztein. (1992) J Clin Invest 90:515
16. RN Mshana, J Boulandi, NM Mshana, J Mayombo, G Mendome (1991) J Clin Lab Immunol 34:131
17. P Kern, CJ Hemmer, J van Damme, H-J Gruss, M Dietrich (1989) Am J Med 87:139
18. P Ringwald, F Peyron, JP Vuillez, JE Touze, J Le Bras, P Deloron (1991) J Clin Microbiol 29:2076
19. PG Kremsner, GM Zotter, H Feldmeier, et al. (1990) J Infect Dis 161:1025
20. Josimovic-Alasevic, H Feldmeier, K Zwingenberger, et al. (1988) Clin Exp Immunol 72:249
21. P Deleron, JP Lepers, P Coulanges (1989) J Clin Microbiol 27:1887
22. P Nguyen-Dinh, AE Greenberg (1988) J Infect Dis 158:1403
23. EM Riley, P Rowe, SJ Allen, BM Greenwood (1993) Clin Exp Immunol 91:495

24. PG Kremsner, U Bienzle (1989) J Infect Dis 160:357
25. F Davachi, L Kabongo and K Nagule (1990) [abstract W.A. 1291]. Proceedings of the VI International Conference on AIDS, Florence, 1990.
26. AE Greenberg, W Nsa, RW Ryder, et al. (1991) New Eng J Med 325:105
27. Müller, R Moser (1990) Trans Roy Soc Trop Med Hyg 84:336
28. RH Morrow, RL Colebunders, J Chin (1989) AIDS 3 [suppl 1]:S79
29. AF Fleming (1990) Trans Roy Soc Trop Med Hyg 84 [suppl. 1]:1
30. SB Lucas (1990) Trans Roy Soc Trop Med Hyg 84 [suppl.1]:34
31. DJ Volsky, YT Wu, M Stevenson, S Dewhurst, F Sinangil, F Merino, L Rodriguez, G Godoy (1986) New Engl J Med 314:647
32. RL Anthony, GB Jennings, A Sie, S Ratiwayanto, MJ Bangs (1993) Am J Trop Med Hyg 48:230
33. CG Hayes, JP Burans, RB Oberst (1991) J Infect Dis 163:257

WHOLE PERSON HEALING:

The Irresistible Tidal Wave in Healthcare and a New Threshold for Science

Rustum Roy*
Evan Pugh Professor Emeritus of the Solid State, Pennsylvania State University
Professor Emeritus of Science, Technology, and Society, Pennsylvania State University
Distinguished Professor of Materials, Arizona State University
Visiting Professor of Medicine, University of Arizona
Chair, Friends of Health

102 MRL
University Park, PA 16802
Email: rroy@psu.edu.

Abstract

First, we present the rationale for the use of the term *Whole Person Healing* (WPH) as, by far, the most desirable term to describe this emerging field. It describes *accurately* its relation to medicine, science, technology, and use of the range of practices and techniques which are challenging the mainstream Western medical practices.

Next, we describe the reason for the sudden acceptance of WPH in the U.S. It is located first in the very poorly-known failures, not only of the socio-politico-economic healthcare system, but in the failure of the system in scientific terms of international outcomes comparisons, total harm done, and resistance to scientific innovations. Combined with the emerging power of globalization, this has led to the "tidal wave" previously also called CAM (Complementary and Alternative Medicine).

Highlights are then presented of the current status of selected successful traditional healing methods (each developed over centuries from several countries). Several striking examples reported in this conference are included. These traditional procedures are now being validated by the most sophisticated Western methods, and clearly offer extraordinary opportunities, for both much lower-cost healing, and also new openings for basic science.

Finally, we argue the case that the irrefutable data contradict only the self-imposed limits of the contemporary mainstream paradigm of science, but offer the first opportunity since quantum mechanics for a new and enlarged paradigm to incorporate all the data. Likewise, Whole Person Healing obviously accommodates the best of modern western medicine, along with the best of ancestral empirical learnings about wellness.

Introduction

The very name of the "movement" away from reductionist western medicine has been evolving rapidly over the last 10-15 years. Starting as *Alternative Medicine*, its practitioners objected, saying they were not the "alternative" to anything. Next, *Complementary Medicine* appeared, and soon Prof. Andrew Weil, a major pioneer of the field, introduced the term *Integrative Medicine*, which is a great improvement. However, events intervened, as the National Institutes of Health (N.I.H.) named its new center the "National Center for Complementary and Alternative Medicine (NCCAM)", thereby making CAM the easiest label to use. However, since we believe that language is profoundly important, the committee decided to try to install slowly, but surely, a much more *accurate* term which reflects what we really mean to encompass. That term is *Whole Person Healing* (WPH).

Replacing the axiom

We start with the reductionist implications of the titles allopathic/western/scientific medicine. Current allopathic medicine practice has the implicit implication that the person (patient) is merely a body. For all practical purposes, P(erson) = B(ody). The presenting symptoms heard by the typical physician never include the chorus of personal, family, and community issues, which affect the patient greatly. They certainly do not include religious or spiritual practices, and rarely are the mental states recorded. In practice, the reductionism has become even narrower. The body is treated, largely as a chemical entity, which is treated by adding chemical or biological agents—medicines—largely in pill or injection form. We exclude surgery here, which was also an ancient practice, now greatly advanced by the great skills of *engineers* (with no connection to any kind of "medicine"). Furthermore, it is accurate to say that for all intents and purposes, western medical practice has simply forgotten, or never really understood, that even in bodily form, the human is also a complex *electromagnetic* system. Its focus has been nearly exclusively on a biochemical approach. If this reality were actually accepted, the treatment options would obviously reflect it, but such interventions are virtually non-existent or extremely rare. This single, simple, and obvious fact alone immediately points to the limited potential of the allopathic biochemical approaches.

The axiom of *all* other healing systems the world over—including the Western family practice model until, let us say, 1950 or World War II—is that:

$P \neq B$. This is clearly wrong. Instead:
P(erson) = B(ody) + M(ind) + S(pirit).

Moreover, the B, M, and S components are intimately mixed in the person, and highly interactive with each other. One can hardly expect that two systems based on such radically different axioms would come up with similar treatments.

Importance of the spiritual dimension, and re-integrating death into life

Other axioms where the two systems differ include the acceptance in *all* ancestral practices that death is an unavoidable natural property of all living systems. And death is *not* always the enemy to be fought off at any, and all, costs. Hence, preservation of life is *not* a primary goal of the WPH system. Improving the quality of life of the whole person replaces it. This is in part, of course, caused by the first axiom that P = B + M + S, and the affirmation by the WPH adherents that attention to the Spirit aspect of the person is as important, if not more so, than the Body alone, and indeed that the Spirit persists in various ways after death.

The assertion of the mutually interactive nature of B, M, and S also immediately implies that one can access the body via the mind and/or spirit, and vice versa. Thus, "mind-body medicine" and "spiritual healing" are corollaries of the axiom. On the basis of vast bodies of data on mind-body and spiritual healings of the body, there is hardly any competition between the two sets of axioms. Hence, the crucial importance of the term *whole person* in describing the new paradigm.

We turn then to *healing* as distinct from *medicine*. Healing is obviously the same desired goal of a visit, whether to an experienced shaman or a research physician. And healing includes much more than even curing: etymologically, it is linked to restoring a sense of wholeness and wellness. The term *medicine* is used for both the agent required for cure—as a pharmaceutical, antibiotic, or a natural herbal product—and also for the "medical system." The origin of the term *alternative medicine* arose no doubt in connection with the simple-minded idea of substituting, say, a natural herb for a synthetic product. That is obviously a very, very minor part of the difference in the two systems. Another key paradigmatic—if over-generalized—difference is that, by and large, western high-tech medicine is built on attacking the invading hosts of viruses, bacteria, or malignant cells; whereas WPH approaches tend to emphasize building up the body's own defenses and its immune system. Thus, *prevention*—whether by stress relief in meditation, exercise, diet—is central to WPH approaches, although recently (belatedly) high-tech medicine is also turning to essentially similar prevention practices, as *part* of its armamentarium. From the resistance to hand-washing in the 19th Century, to the very slow pace of the medical establishment in vigorously pushing for exercise and diet control in contemporary obese America, certainly championing of prevention ends up as a WPH advantage. This is all the more surprising, since the greatest triumph of the overall "western high-tech medicine"—the increase in longevity—owed most of it to prevention. Again, it must be emphasized, this was achieved via good civil engineering, and not medical curing at all, via the access to pure water and sewage systems. (See Footnote 1)

Western medicine has treated the healing vector as a one-way-street process. The WPH axiom posits a much more robust, two-way interaction between healer and patient. This is, of course, likely via all three channels: body and mind (by conversation and discussion), and spirit (by the belief system) of both healer and patient. (See chapter by Wayne Jonas in this volume for much data on this point.)

Footnote 1

In the plenary address to the conference, and in this paper, I present the overview of the field. I make several allusions to research data without providing references because, rather than repeat references in specific fields, I simply refer the reader to the speakers in this conference who provide both the references and much more detailed context in the different fields I have selected.

These interactions between healer and patient, and the absolute need to look much deeper and wider than the body, are hardly new. After all, it was Hippocrates who instructed his disciples, *"It is more important to know the person who has the disease, than the disease the person has."* Moreover, all the research shows that the intervener (healer) is an active part of the system. Another key learning is that the intervener can be yourself, which opens up the possibility that self-healing can be a very important part of all healing.

It is quite inexplicable how the medical establishment totally failed to see the enormous significance of the extensive data on "placebo" effects. While this is changing slowly, the establishment appears unwilling to understand that what is at stake in these data (see Jonas paper) is the fundamental demolition of the underpinning of the reductionist paradigm. In its own terms, it has become obvious that *belief is the single most important healing pill in the universe.*

Among the empirical data, which point to the compete rout of the current ruling paradigm of P = B, is the sudden return of the role of spirituality, even in healing. In the triumphal days of western medicine in the 1970s and 80s, the idea that "spiritual healing" could be part of the M.D. curriculum, and hospital services would have appeared ridiculous, and the proponents of such a view would have been (and were) ridiculed for decades (for example, as in the treatment of Mary Baker Eddy and Christian Science) without any attempt at examining the data in the normal processes of science.

Yet today, as a measure of the change, we note that:

1.   70 percent of medical schools in the U.S. offer courses in spiritual healing.
2.   The most influential physicians among the public, such as Deepak Chopra, make compelling cases for it on national television programs and in best-selling books.
3.   Spiritual healers flourish on national television aimed principally at the conservative sector of our society.
4.   Internationally, the work of spiritual healers such as Joao de Deus and other psychic surgeons in Brazil and the Philippines are finally being permitted on U.S. television.
5.   Dean Ornish presents unimpeachable data on the importance of love and intimacy on survival rates, as well as in his diet and small-group attendance program. When questioned by Sen. Harkin in a hearing as to which was more important, the witness, one of Ornish's patients, stated he could not diet without the support and intimacy of the group.

In books, papers, magisterial reviews of the field, and in this conference, Larry Dossey has established the scientific reality of spiritual healing, even from long distances by detailed analysis of the data, with a thoroughness that has not even been challenged.

It is clear, therefore, that the battle for the paradigm is over. P ≠ B. Rather, P = B + M + S.

Hence, Whole Person Healing is being positioned as the new globally acceptable paradigm, in many ways much more friendly to science, and certainly more friendly to physics, electricity, magnetism, and technological innovation with its emphasis on *continuously lowering costs*. The major development phase of transferring this knowledge to the public and its elected representation is now the main goal.

Why the WPH tidal wave?

Failure of the reductionist model

Had the United States (or at least the western, reductionist part of it) been successful in meeting the personal health needs of the population, the penetration by the "foreign," "unscientific" (indeed generally maligned with terms such as "weird") WPH practices we are dealing with here would have been relegated to the museums and use by cultists in the hollows of Appalachia. But in spite of a total monopoly on the media, in spite of a $100 billion/year R&D budget in advertising, the dominant reductionist model has lost in the "free market." The WPH approach has captured a dominant market share of users among "red-blooded," highly-educated Americans, and continues to increase this market share. This is the "tidal wave" to be described below. Meanwhile, it is time for scientists to pay attention to the dangers and the opportunities as this competition plays out.

In spite of the culturally mandated bow to national pride by every politician enshrined in the mantra, "We (the U.S.) have the best medical system in the world," the facts are nearly the opposite. Table I presents (in tabular form to make its reproduction easy) the facts we have to face, and which moreover will continue to drive, especially as the WTO enforces even a freer market, even more in the WPH direction. These outcome measures are obviously carefully thought through, by appropriate experts, including those from the U.S. and Europe, as appropriate for making international comparisons. *The data are hardly ever mentioned in scientific circles discussing medical research*, in hearings on the N.I.H. budget, for example. In the world of "hard" science and technology, our scientific research has led to dominance in consumer acceptance (television, computers, internet, etc.) and dramatic *lowering* of costs. This is exactly the opposite in the biochemical medicine field.

Table I

B. Starfield. *Journal of the American Medicine Association*, Vol. 284(4), 483-485 (July 26, 2000).

Is U.S. health really the best in the world?

No! The fact is that the U.S. population does not have anywhere near the best health in the world. Of 13 countries in a recent comparison, the United States ranks an average of 12th (second from the bottom) for 16 available health indicators.

Countries in order of their average ranking on the health indicators (with the first being the best) are:

Japan, Sweden, Canada, France, Australia, Spain, Finland, the Netherlands, the United Kingdom, Denmark, Belgium, the United States, and Germany.

Rankings of the United States on the separate indicators are:

13th (last) for low birth weight percentages
13th for neonatal mortality and infant mortality overall
11th for post-neonatal mortality
13th for years of potential life lost (excluding external causes)
11th for life expectancy at 1 year-old for females, 12th for males
10th for life expectancy at 15 years-old for females, 12th for males
10th for life expectancy at 40 years-old for females, 9th for males
7th for life expectancy at 65 years-old for females, 7th for males
3rd for life expectancy at 80 years-old for females, 3rd for males
10th for age-adjusted mortality

These data are confirmed by WHO, using very different indicators, which ranks the U.S. 15th among 25 industrialized countries.

In fairness to the system, it must be noted that the U.S. and Europe provide to its wealthier citizens access to both the most sophisticated technologies, analytic tools, surgical apparatus, and devices that modern *engineering* provides and some of the most skilled diagnosticians and surgeons in the world. For emergency care, and the extension of breathing life for the wealthier minority, the political mantras could be accurate.

In addition to the failure of the reductionist system to live up to the false advertising by its politicians, there are much more serious *technical* failures, which are amazing for a *technological* enterprise, never been directly addressed. It is even more remarkable for a country where its biggest technology (medicine) departs so radically from the national corporate technological goals of "zero defects" and "5 sigma" and "6 sigma" quality control. (Ref. 1, which includes many other related references, is part of a special issue with several papers devoted to this same topic.)

If one simply lists the number of Americans who die due to medical interventions of one kind or other, one finds the following:

1. Some 110,000 persons per year die due to drug interactions. A much larger number are seriously harmed.
2. Some 75,000 (+/-25,000) die each year due to medical mistakes.
3. Well over 20 percent of hospital stays are caused as a result of the hospital stays.

Thus, one can see that the U.S. medical system as a whole kills some 250,000 persons every year. We immediately insert the caveat that *in no way* does this reflect on the competence, intentions, or caring concerns of the millions of individuals doctors, nurses, and other staff. Yet, the medical system itself is the third leading cause of death, and clearly in normal N.I.H. strategic planning, deserves to have a separate National Institute all to itself.

In addition to these failures, we must add a list of socioeconomic outcome failures:

- The entire system from payers—insurance companies, hospitals, doctors, prescription payment, patient satisfaction—is in total disarray and will be radically changed in a decade.
- The doctor dissatisfaction is as great as the patient dissatisfaction.
- N.I.H. research contributes zero to lowering costs or improving the system.

These are not the opinions of radical fringe groups. In his Presidential Address to the American Association for the Advancement of Science just before this conference in 2003, one of the nation's senior neuroscience researchers and former editor of *Science*, Floyd Bloom, used the following terminology: "A problem of major proportions…is the imminent collapse of the American health system." He calls it the "crisis in medical care (which) cannot be ignored." He refers to much of the excellent science being done, but suggests that this gives scientists the "delusions of success." [2]

Indeed, when one considers the fact that the N.I.H. budget has been doubled recently to some $30 billion per year, it is amazing that no body of scientists in N.I.H. in charge of the nation's *health* (as in its title) have started a crash program to ameliorate, if not reverse, this alarming trend.

Data on the WPH tidal wave

The newly aroused public, disaffected by their experiences of the two-minute intake sessions with their doctors, armed with education via the television and internet, by the 1980s had started to investigate the whole range of WPH modalities. Most importantly, they experienced and experimented with them, whether it was the local yoga master, the massage therapist, the visiting Reiki practitioner, or Andrew Weil's website (which receives 5 million hits each month). Citizens, with a substantial women's majority, felt empowered to do something about their health. They learned about the dangers of too much mercury in fish, and not enough antioxidants, and soon discoursed on good and bad cholesterol. They championed organic foods—for some good reasons, and some not so good. The very important fact, for personal and national policy, is that they became what every democracy wants—interested and educated consumers. The most significant fact for both the reductionist medical community and national policy planners is that the judgment of these aroused, not by slogans, but by interested involvement, is that more WPH is the way they will go.

The summary of the data on the WPH "invasion," from the now-classic Eisenberg paper in JAMA, are very well-known (see Table II). Those numbers are now five or six years old. The trend lines from the last report of rapid increase show no sign of changing. Newspaper accounts since in different parts of the country indicate that in some states, over 60 percent of the populace utilize WPH practitioners. When you observe from Table II that a very large part of these costs are borne out-of-pocket (not by insurance), one can easily imagine what will happen, albeit slowly—as the insurance coverage of these modalities becomes as widespread as the more expensive high-tech version. On such a newly-leveled playing field, the market share of traditional high-tech medicine for primary care could slip to one-third or one-quarter of visits by American citizens.

Table II
The Meteoric Rise of Whole Person Healing

D.M. Eisenberg et al. *Journal of the American Medicine Association,* Vol. 280: 1569-75 (November 1998).

	1990	1997
Use of any one of 16 alternative therapies	33.8%	42.15%
Visiting any A.T. provider	36.3	46.3
Disclosed to physician	39.8	38.5
Percentage paying out of pocket	64	58.3
Total visits to A.T.	427 (x 10^6)	629 (x 10^6) [*] *47% increase*
Expenditures for A.T. services Total expenditure for A.T. Out of pocket (for services)	$14.6 B	$21.2 B 27.0 [†] 12.2 [‡]

[*] This number exceeds total visits to U.S. primary care physicians
[†] Exceeds total out-of-pocket for all hospitalizations
[‡] Comparable to total out-of-pocket expenditures for all U.S. physician services

Further, insofar as cost factors are absolutely certain to drive trends in the near future, the lower costs of WPH, especially avoiding expensive MRI and CAT Scan-type diagnostics, and the placing of greater responsibility on the patient, emphasizing prevention, will be another factor pushing the tidal wave even higher. And perhaps the most important factor for lowering costs will be the (slow) acceptance of a very different attitude to death.

Research costs are another major factor favoring WPH. The roughly $30 billion taxpayer annual investment in N.I.H., plus roughly twice that from industry, has been shown to have had little effect on the health status of Americans (see above data). For all the weekly breakthroughs advertised, not critically analyzed and reported, by the media, they have amounted to only marginal improvements in outcomes in incidence or overall cure rates in major diseases since the polio vaccine. Moreover, the pharmaceutical industry, using human need and despair as unique motivators, has been able to operate at three times higher margins than the average U.S. technology by emphasizing not really innovative research, but mainly by aggressive marketing to doctors, and huge advertising directly to consumers..

The WPH beachhead for minor research funding is now established in the NIH-NCCAM. While funded at roughly $150 million/year for next year, it is obviously only a token investment at one-half of one percent of the federal funds allocated to high-tech, high-cost medicine. Again, with healthcare costs looming ever larger with policy makers, this factor alone will finally tilt the balance even further in the direction of WPH.

Role of science in the WPH tidal wave

We list below, as a summary, the status of the relevant facts in the juxtaposition of the "tidal wave" growth of WPH against what had been for—and *only* for—some decades, an intellectual monopoly of the healing/medicines industry. Points 1-3 recap what has been said above, and we will then move on to points 4-7.

1.   **The discovery and acceptance of WPH proceeds apace.**
2.   **Reductionist (body-only) medicine is in *total* disarray.** All their claims against WPH for 50 years have been shown to be utterly worthless.
    a. 25 years ago, the nation could be made to scoff at acupuncture, even after it was used for anesthesia for the surgery of James Reston (*NY Times* editor) in Peking.
    b. Today, there are 15,000 licensed acupuncturists in the U.S.
    c. As late as 15-20 years ago, qigong practitioners in San Francisco could be jailed! Now they are repeat guests at the Bush Sr. White House.
    d. A majority of the better-educated public has accepted and embraced WPH. There is no going back.
    e. The "sickcare" system is in near collapse on every front (costs rose 14 percent last year).
    f. The politicians and the public are seeing through the pill-pusher mentality. ABC's Peter Jennings runs an hour-long special on primetime.
3.   **WPH, previously functioning as isolated, tiny, "cult-like" movements, has started to get into a collaborative federation of ancestral practices.**
4.   **Research data is challenging the old paradigm.**
    a. More cheating scandals
    b. Challenge to Hormone Replacement Therapy

    c. Challenge to mammography

    d. Vioxx Celebrex scandal: Historic impact on all science publications

    e. Sham arthroscopic surgery works as well as real surgery

5. **Laboratory high-tech research data supporting WPH keeps piling up.** Some spectaculars:

    a. fMRI approach confirms reality of acupuncture meridian system.

    b. P.E.T. studies on placebo effect show the same

    c. Belief is as good as arthroscopic surgery

    d. Columbia University study supports reality of the effects of prayer on fertilization of in-vitro human eggs

6. **Scientific empirical data on extraordinary healings have been demonstrated routinely (effects of human intention on humans—not rats!) all over the world, including the U.S.**

    a. Surgery without pain, bleeding, or sepsis (in spite of no sterilization) on hundreds of thousands over decades

    b. Instant wound healing

    c. Paralysis improvement in seconds/minutes

7. **Effects of human intention on non-living matter.**

    a. Excellent data from leading scientists worldwide on material deformation

    b. Structure of water revolutionized, confirming plausibility of WPH practices

In spite of the fact that the scientific research budgets are some 1000 times larger, the major spectacular results where WPH challenges the conventional model, research always appears to support WPH. Indeed, in points 4 and 5 above, I have tried to assemble a kind of balance sheet in a possible hypothetical contemporary confrontation between WPH and medical establishment science.

We start with item 4: fraud and cheating. The science establishment, within which I live—as a 30-year member of the National Academy of Engineering and a leader of one of its more recently successful major branches, materials science—is immersed in one of its periodic bouts with a major cheating scandal (the Schon affair at the world's leading laboratory, Bell Labs). This is relevant to this discussion because this paranoia—*within* mainstream science—about "cheating" is projected on to all innovations *outside* the establishment, where in fact the "cheating" has *never* been shown to be involved in any major case. Fraud does occur, but largely in the heartland of science, and via the best peer-reviewed journals.

As a science policy analyst, I have pointed out that science as a part of human society should expect, and has indeed experienced, probably the same percentage of cheating as in any other profession. It is absolutely certain that the WPH world has a certain percentage of snake-oil salespersons making exaggerated claims and selling nostrums. In a tiny industry, quality control is no doubt much poorer than in major industries. The flip side of this fact is that as quality control improves in herbs and supplements, their track record will become even more attractive to consumers. It is equally certain that the best-established pharmaceutical companies are doing the same with respect to exaggerated claims. The difference is that, due to the TV and media advertising, the latter affects 1000 times more people, while the scientists too often focus their criticisms on the former.

The Vioxx-Celebrex scandal has been largely hushed up in medical science circles. It is much more significant than the Schon affair for three reasons. First, it was surfaced not by the science community, but by the *Washington Post* and the *Wall Street Journal*. Second, it affected *millions* of citizens at *billions* of dollars cost, not merely the hurt pride of a few hundred scientists. Third, it has caused a major change in behavior of *all* scientists worldwide submitting papers to the dozen most prestigious journals, since each of us must now sign a declaration of no conflict of interest. This makes it all the more remarkable, that while hundreds of pages and weeks of very high-level committee members' time have been devoted to the Schon affair, which will pass on with no noticeable impact on the daily lives of 99.999 percent of citizens, the Vioxx-Celebrex affair was ignored in the news sections, but caused an appropriately major behavioral change affecting *all* scientists wishing to publish in the same "premier journals!"

In just the past year or so, major, medically-established, FDA-approved, used by tens of millions, procedures have been either disproved or so severely challenged that their use is no longer automatic. Certainly, hormone replacement therapy (HRT) is one such procedure. The routine use of mammography is another, not quite as clear-cut a case. However, both of these should help us appropriately temper our certainty that all established, widely-accepted, and widely-used medical procedures are unambiguously valuable.

The demonstration of the fact that the value of arthroscopic surgery may largely be a response of "belief" or "meaning" of the procedure, should raise among scientists profound questions, even about something as "objective" as surgery. These are not cases from remote areas of Tibet. It is essential for the medical science community to come to terms with what this means. The papers by Jonas and Moorman (in this volume) give compelling data with other examples to prove that in surgery, impressive equipment and high-tech names like "laser," act as catalysts for belief, which in turn makes the procedure (or its absence) equally effective.

Against this litany of major society-affecting challenges to the reductionist paradigm system, let us now contrast some of the remarkable wins for WPH. Under point 5, we list some spectacular and unchallenged "wins" for WPH. In many of these, we find that the highest-tech instruments when applied, add explanations and plausibility to what are the already scientifically established facts of tradition on the basis of empirical data. Modern science, it must be emphatically pointed out, is not discovering these procedures, or making them scientific (!!), it is confirming what other cultures discovered by solid empirical science thousands of years ago.

a. The Cho et al. proof in the Proceedings of the National Academy of Science [3] on the validity of the existence of the acupoint in the right foot toe for the visual cortex started a whole round of fMRI work establishing that western analytical tools could confirm what had long been established by empirical science in Asia some thousands of years ago. (See paper by Joie Jones in this volume.)

b. fMRI and PET scan studies likewise confirm the power of "belief." The positron emission tomography study in Stockholm's Karolinska Institute shows that a "placebo" procedure produced the same changes in the brain scan as the pharmaceutical painkiller, injected into patients. [4a]

c. This power of "belief" is the most difficult for some scientists to believe in. [4b] But the recent study showing that a sham surgery with all the white coats, anesthesia, and bandaging produces the same effects as arthroscopic knee surgery is an extraordinarily powerful demonstration of the principle that belief, consciousness, or the spiritual dimension has healing powers. The Jonas and Moorman data on the "absolute" role of "meaning response" (i.e. belief) all apply here.

d. A very recent triple-blind study led by a team from Columbia University, and conducted over distances of several thousand miles, provided data that appear to establish that teams of people praying for a desired outcome (in this case, the implanting of in vitro human eggs and subsequent birth of a healthy child) could have a major favorable and measurable effect on acceptance of prayer as a contributor to healing. [5]

A thundering silence, and no scientific experimentation, emanates from the usual personalities paid to write skeptical comments (to make some scientists more comfortable in their prejudices) on any of these rather significant reports (which are reported in peer-reviewed journals of the stature of *Science* and *Nature*). But these data are only the tip of the iceberg, and still are partial concessions to the ruling paradigm as to how healing occurs via the body according to in the reductionist paradigm described earlier.

There are, in addition, however, thoroughly well-established data to satisfy *any* level of scientific rigor based on data and facts which do not fit that reductionist paradigm, indeed which constitute a Popperian falsification thereof. I have chosen to highlight but three of these sets of data. Each of these is covered in more detailed talks by Norman Don, Howard Hall, and Effie Chow in their respective chapters.

a.   There exist in Brazil at least a few hundred practitioners of "trance surgery" or "psychic surgery." Perhaps the best-known of these is Joao de Deus of Abadiana, a remote town near the capital Brasilia. Joao de Deus works in a modest clinic in which he and his staff have had upwards of 15 million patients over two decades. Several books and a myriad of videotapes record everything everyday. For our purposes, the *least* extraordinary of his practices are his daily surgeries performed on 200 or 300 patients taken, ad seriatim, from the crowded waiting rooms. Using unsterilized instruments, he makes incisions, e.g. across a woman's breast, excises a tumor, sometimes huge one-pound masses from a man's thigh, with his bare hands. After simple suturing, he sends the patient with attendants to rest for a few hours. What radically contradicts the western paradigm is the continually repeated demonstrations of:
    - The absence of pain, although absolutely no anesthesia is ever used;
    - The absence of bleeding, in spite of huge cuts;
    - The absence of sepsis in hundreds of thousands of cases, over decades, although not sterilization procedures are used.

National television crews of a half-dozen countries have recorded and aired programs on his work. In the U.S., not one major program has been shown. Many prominent Americans, from Congresspersons to movie stars, have visited his clinic. Perhaps most radical of all: Joao charges nothing! Free-will donations may be made to the clinic.

As noted, there are many similar healers in Brazil and also in the Philippines. My own explanation is that this is an example of the power of *collective* belief. Brazil, a deeply religious culture, has vested in this tradition—the belief that it can bring about healing by practices such as these. And it is the belief that confers on the practice the extraordinary powers that it displays. No culture that wants to call itself scientific can avoid examining this mass of data and presenting its own hypothesis to explain the fact. (See chapter by Norman Don.)

b.   We turn next to a parallel example of the cultures of belief. This time in Sufi practices in Iraq. To select only one example of many, it is only practiced as the *demonstration* of the power of belief. Adepts pass skewers, 6-10 mm in dimension, through both cheeks, walk around, even talk and discuss the matter, and then remove the skewer with a rapid pull out. Again, there is no anesthesia, no pain, no bleeding, no sepsis, and the wound heals in a few seconds.

After observing Prof. Howard Hall's videotapes made in Iraq, colleagues in Cleveland who were skeptical asked how why it was not demonstrated in the U.S. Prof. Hall obliged. He arranged for a colleague from the Middle East to come to the clinic in Cleveland, Ohio, where the entire process was conducted with a CBS television crew in attendance. Moreover, the young physics professor with the skewer in his mouth had X-rays, CAT scans, and all his bodily functions measured throughout the event. The simple-minded skeptics who have earlier talked loudly about cheating, parlor tricks, and sleight-of-hand (or mouth?) are again reduced to a deafening silence when confronted *by data*. Most interestingly, Prof. Hall, of Case Western Reserve University, has visited with, been instructed by, and connected to, the master, and has demonstrated the same instant wound healing *on himself* in front of audiences in the U.S.

c.   The third example is the enormous body of demonstrated achievements of Chinese medicine over the last few millennia (of which acupuncture is but one manifestation or epi-phenomenon). In very broad Western terms, one may subdivide all of Qigong (which can very roughly be translated as "energy" or "vital force" management) into three parts:
1.   "Balance" of yin and yang maintenance by gentle practices. The Tai Chi exercises are the best-known manifestation.
2.   Healing or rebalancing via acupuncture, via other qigong direction by masters.

3.   "Martial" arts, or performance enhancement, where the energy (qi) is channeled into bodily expressions.

In this conference and Proceedings, qigong practices were/are described by these speakers outside the special subset dealing with acupuncture. Dr. Phil Shinnick, dealing with the performance enhancement (3, above) and Drs. Yoshiaki Omura and Effie Chow about amazing western paradigm-breaking healings. Dr. Omura, inventor of the so-called bi-digital O-ring test, presented here but a small selection of an incredible series of medical phenomena which are being demonstrated—yet amazingly ignored—not in the high Himalayas, but in New York City. My own studies of these data convince me that we have in these phenomena some extremely potent tools both for "cure" and "diagnosis." His usage of a simple laser to carry a signal on which is "imprinted," say, integrand 5β-1, to scan the six major organs or chakras, to locate "disease." This is all accomplished in 2 minutes, with about 30 minutes required for a more precise diagnosis. Such qigong methods could totally revolutionize the costly diagnosis time and cost of western medicine. In addition, Omura's work is very nicely complementary to western medicine—as are many other such procedures. Thus, he can direct the delivery of a particular pharmaceutical to a particular site, multiplying its effectiveness many fold.

Another example which challenges the body-only paradigm is the ability of Qigong masters to restore a very large degree of physical and mental ability to children and adults who are cerebral palsy or paralysis victims. Dr. Effie Chow demonstrated such a "healing" of a 60 year old white male in front of a large audience of professionals, doctors, scientists, etc., during a San Francisco conference in November 2002. The patient, with complete records on his condition from the VA hospital, was confined to a wheelchair and had been unable to perform any function for himself for months. In five minutes, his dsystonorrhic was stopped for the first time in months. The next day, in less than 30 minutes of attention from Dr. Chow, he was able to walk around the ballroom, walk up the steps of the podium, and whisk Dr. Chow around in a short dance.

Since then, Dr. Chow, in the Indianapolis University Hospital, has treated a senior political executive, who had been given up by its researchers to a vegetative state. In less than two weeks, with no drugs, no injections, no special potions, he was chatting at breakfast with his children. (See details in her paper.)

What these three examples prove, beyond any shadow of a doubt, to any scientist acting as scientists must, willing to examine the data, is that:

- There are healing processes which cannot possibly be squeezed into the western body-only paradigm. Hence, **that paradigm must now be discarded.**
- Some of these processes are correlated with the presence of strong belief systems, belief in the possibility in the healer, and also on the part of the patient or experimenter.

Interaction of intention with non-living matter

Finally, we come to the most elegant test of the existence of forces which transcend the body-only (matter-only) paradigm, but do not involve as complex a system as the human being as the recipient. The details and complete references are found in the papers by Houck and Robertson in this volume.

The first example is the three decade long work of Prof. John Hasted, head of the physics department, Birkbeck College, University of London. He has conducted hundreds of detailed experiments over two decades on the interaction of "human intention" on the deformation of a wide variety of solid materials. The exhaustive set of data are recorded in the book, "The Metal Benders." [6] While Uri Geller was *one* of the persons who provided the "intention" for Prof. Hasted's research, the attribution of the process to Uri Geller is like saying that there can be no basketball without Michael Jordan. Kids play basketball, kids bend spoons, albeit not as well as talented adults. Indeed, the most robust data supporting the field is that it is so common and easy to observe and duplicate—albeit just as in basketball, not with the prowess of Michael Jordan.

The scientific tests for this phenomenon have been met a thousand times over. It has been replicated tens of thousands of times. It has been repeated in many countries and continents, by many totally independent scientists and engineers. In France, Prof. Charles Crussard of the Pechiney Company, one of the country's leading metallurgists, in charge of the work on the Concorde, obtained extensive data parallel to those in London. In the U.S., Jack Houck, a senior engineer with Boeing, has kept the world's most meticulous set of data outside the laboratory setting on the same phenomenon.

While material deformation by human intention is not healing humans, it is clearly the place where a reductionist might begin to enter this complex field. It is certainly as close to WPH as experiments on rats are. It is truly extraordinary that in 20 years since the phenomena has been established beyond any challenge, no agency has pursued this truly revolutionary scientific opportunity. It is perhaps a confirmation of Alfred North Whitehead's description of the danger of dogmatism in science: *"Advance is permitted; fundamental novelty is barred."*

The importance of water

In the healing of humans, it is easy to see why water should figure prominently, since we are 70 percent water. Yet again, it is truly extraordinary that the reductionist paradigm healers have so neglected the really scientific study of water. They have made the most naïve assumptions about the most important single material to all of human health, possibly several orders of magnitude more so than the human genome project.

Several different groups of WPH champions have recognized the powerful role of water and its manipulability. Among these are the Ayurvedic tradition of water therapy, the western water treatments in spas, the variety of water (even urine) based therapies, and of course, the entire school of homeopathy.

The naiveté of the reductionist-science paradigm within medicine is best manifested in the absurdly oversimplified concept that if the concentration of the homeopathic additive is lowered by successive dilution to less than Avogadro's number, *it can have had no effect on the water*. True believers in the old paradigm are so threatened by new data that, as demonstrated by the editor of *Nature*, John Maddox, some establishment scientists are so unsure of themselves that they have to take along a compliant magician of modest talents (in disguise!) to check on the work of a senior scientist in Paris. Not only was the literature on the structure of water neglected, but the data from a dozen of the world's *leading* magicians on the effects created by Geller, who assure the scientists that whatever Geller does has nothing to do with "magic."

Reading the literature on the *structure*, not the composition, of water would have saved the embarrassment. Indeed, in the same college as John Hasted, Prof. J.D. Bernal, a prominent figure in British science, and a prominent one especially with relation of science to society, had written of the complexity of the water structure in the 1930s, and its similarity to SiO_2 structures. The minimum facts, which eluded generations of the critics of homeopathy, are known to undergraduates in materials science and solid state physics. A foreign substrate, a seed, can change the *structure* of even a solid growing in contact with it, *without transmitting any composition whatsoever*. Hence, key structural *information* is transferable with zero compositional transfers, i.e. far "beyond" the Avogadro limit!

Of course, this basic fact hardly proves the case for homeopathic healing, but it makes short shrift of the major line of criticism. Indeed, the next generation of research must involve examining the role of epitaxy, of "succussing" (involving substantial pressures), of nanobubbles, etc., all on the *structure* of the water, and the capacity to "freeze" that structure in. A recent review by Roy, Tiller, and Bell treats the topic in detail. [7]

The intersection of these data with the mainstream paradigm of science

The progress of "fundamental" science is very uneven in time. Derek de Solla Price has clearly shown that most such "basic" science, i.e. scientific laws and concepts which apply to the widest ranges of natural phenomena, started from real world observations, applications, and technology [8]. The most recent advance in such basic science—the development of quantum mechanics—may be the best exception. Yet it is now 75 years old. Since then, applied science and technology have exploded into enormous whole new realms, but no new basic principles have been found. And this in spite of the fact that, for the first time in human history, thousands of persons have been funded with time, money, and the most sophisticated equipment to look exclusively for such new basic scientific principles. Yet there have been no such new principles found. For the last twenty years or so, a few senior distinguished scientists, such as Victor Weisskopf, former head of M.I.T.'s physics department and Director General of CERN, concluded that "the basic principles of the atomic world are known, and no additional law or principle is necessary in order to explain the phenomena of the atomic realm, including the existence and development of life." [9]

The Weisskopf case seems to have been justified by history, except for the very last phrase. While humanity has seen the most extraordinary developments in technologies of transportation, communication, information, and new sciences applicable to parts of the whole of the knowledge of nature, there has been no paradigm-breaking equivalent to the arrival of quantum mechanics. Indeed, Hans-Peter Duerr, successor to Einstein and Heisenberg in the directorship of the same Max Planck Institute, makes the key contention—as in this conference—that most scientists have not faced up to the truly radical implications of quantum mechanics itself, which could perhaps accommodate some of the phenomena being observed in WPH.

The data we have presented here have a unique characteristic in connection with the normal Kuhnian patterns of the evolution of science. These are not new data. These observations have been around for millennia. Indeed, modern reductionist science grew up around these data, and refused to deal with them because they didn't fit their evolving paradigm. We often use this strategy in normal science: avoid the data that don't fit. This is not at all bad, as long as it notes the exceptions. That's the problem. This goes back, to the dominance of the Newtonian approach to science, getting directly to the abstract principle and designing experiments only on the basis of that theory. "Theory-based science" soon became in practice, "all science must be theory-based." This social-intellectual dominance can explain the exclusion of huge amounts of data in all science, but not in engineering, where exceptions are valuable. In a recent article, Ribe and Steinle [10] have clearly shown that such parts of modern science have thrived by a very different approach. The archetypal figures include Faraday and Goethe and Edwin Land. Labeled the "exploratory experimentation" approach, this route has obviously proved to be very fruitful.

It is clear that WPH research fits very comfortably into the "exploratory experimentation" approach, especially in developing the new theory of the *interaction* of life with all "non-living systems." Within that term, one encompasses both the material world of inorganic, organic, and biological matter (body), and the reality of mind and spirit.

New theoretical approaches, which give normal weight to the rich trove of empirical, scientific data, will no doubt have a wide open field for the next several years (see papers by Tiller and Duerr in this volume).

Acknowledgements

The author wishes to acknowledge the financial support for 55 years by the Office of Naval Research and the Defense Advanced Research Projects Agency, of his fundamental and applied work in materials research, which supported the science base for the extension into related fields.

References

1. Roy R (2002) "Science and Whole Person Medicine: Enormous potential in a new relationship," Bull. S.T.S. 22[5]: 374-390
2. Bloom FE (2003) "Science as a way of life: Perplexities of a physician-scientist," Science 300: 1681-1685
3. Cho ZH, Chung SG, Jones JP, et al (1998) "New findings of the correlations between acupoints and corresponding brain cortices using fMRI," Proc. Nat. Acad. Sci. 95:2670-2673

4. de la Fuente-Fernandez R, et al (Aug 10 2001) "Expectation and dopamine release: Mechanism of the placebo effect in Parkinson's disease," Science 293[5532]: 1164-66

5. Mosely JB et al (2002) "A controlled trial of arthroscopic surgery for osteoarthritis of the knee," N. Engl. J. Med. 347: 81-88

6. Cha KY, Wirth DP, Lobo RA (Sept 2001) "The Columbia fertility-and-prayer study," J. Reproductive Med. 46[9]: 781-7

7. Hasted J (1981) The Metal-Benders. Routledge, Kegan, Paul, London.

8. Roy R, Tiller WA, Bell I (in preparation) "The structure of water: A contemporary analysis."

9. de Solla Price D (May 1983) "Sealing wax and string: A philosophy of the experimenter's craft and its role in the genesis of high technology," Sarton Lecture, AAAS meeting.

10. Weisskopf V and others (1981) In: Roy R (ed) Experimenting with truth. Pergamon Press, Oxford, p 27

11. Ribe N, Steinle F (July 2002) "Exploratory experimentation: Goethe, land, and color theory," Phys. Today, 43-49.

CHOW MEDICAL QIGONG:

A Holistic Body/Mind/Spirit Approach to Rehabilitation and Total Health

Dr. Effie Poy Yew Chow
President, Ph.D., R.N., Lic.Ac. (CA), Dipl.Ac. (NCCAOM)
Qigong Grandmaster
EAST WEST ACADEMY OF HEALING ARTS
San Francisco, California 94131
www.eastwestqi.com

"Each person carries his own doctor inside him. They come to us not knowing that truth. We are at our best when we give the doctor who resides within each patient a chance to go to work."

Albert Schweitzer

"Giving individuals the power to determine and manage their own health and destinies is the secret of true healing."

Effie Poy Yew Chow

I am delighted and honored to be part of this first Science of Whole Person Healing Conference. Thank you very much Rustum for being the inspirational person and the organizer of this wonderful event. The title of my program is *"Chow Medical Qigong—A Holistic Body/Mind/Spirit Approach to Rehabilitation and Total Health"*. I shall begin by describing Chow Integrated Healing System or Chow Medical Qigong, presenting some case samples and then describe generally Qigong and interspersed with some demonstrations.

First though, before I proceed, I would appreciate if all of you would stand, say hello and meet the person next to you on both sides, in front of and behind you. Now, as I prescribe in my book Miracle Healing from China, Qigong, at least eight hugs a day and three belly-aching laughs a day, please give the people you've touched hugs and laughter. (Everyone did so with happy laughter)

Well how does that feel? (Everyone proclaims with laughter…wonderful) Thank you, you may sit down and if at anytime you need a hug, go ahead and get a hug, promise? (Everybody responded yes/okay!)

The Chow Integrated Healing System (The Chow System) or Chow Medical Qigong is a system's approach that I developed with much experimentation. It is a pragmatic system that combines modern Western health practices, ancient Traditional Chinese Medicine, and my own original concepts of a total integrated approach to health of the body, mind, and spirit along with nature. Qigong in Traditional Chinese Medicine (TCM) is the basic underlying component of The Chow System based on the classic Chinese theory that a powerful energy system exists in the body, and that energy (Qi) flows through known energy pathways. The pathways are referred to as channels, or meridians. The Qi system is as direct as the respiratory and nervous systems. If Qi patterns are disrupted by emotional distress, environmental exposures, or any number of factors, a person becomes susceptible to disease. When this disruption of energy is rebalanced, health is restored.

In this integrated approach, a person's body, mind, and spirit are one, interacting with people, the immediate environment, and the Universe. Clients play a central role in their therapy. Fitness and preventive health are emphasized and stress and tension often are seen as common precursors to disease. Another concept is that all true healing originates from a higher power, and that effective healing occurs only when a healer or practitioner has facilitated the flow of Qi from this higher source.

The Concepts of the Chow Integrated Healing System is comprised of many important components, theories, and principles. As a summary, ten of the most important basic concepts for initial practice are:

1. Get at least eight hugs a day, and be "in touch"
2. Get at least three Belly-Aching-Laughs-A-Day
3. Maintain a positive mental attitude
4. Maintain proper posture and breathe with the diaphragm (not the chest)
5. Meditate daily
6. Good nutrition, supplements, and perhaps herbs
7. Practice the right type of exercise—Qigong exercises
8. Be at peace with yourself and others
9. Live the Qi energy concept
10. Give and receive lots of love

Before presenting the cases I would like to briefly demonstrate the power of Qi in Chow Qigong. I would like two volunteers. You select and appoint the first one...the biggest and heaviest and strongest person here. And the second person can be of any stature. These demonstrations are to illustrate for you some of the operating principles and the reasons why Chow Qigong is getting results where all else have failed. Most of my clients are in that category where they have tried "everything" with no results.

The first demonstration: With the first person I will demonstrate the use of Qi and breath. He weighs 200 pounds and I weigh approximately 115. (I pushed him aggressively confronting him with no results and everybody laughed.) This exercise reflects what you do in real life: if you push and shove and confront, you won't get anywhere. How many of us live that way? Use confrontation only as a last measure. Pushing him the second time, I use the Qi and breath when he says ready. So I proceeded to gently push him with Qi and breath moving him more than 20 feet to against the wall (everybody laughed and cheered). How many would like your life to be this way...getting what you want always? (Everybody agreed). This is just an indication of what you can do when you can manage, control and discipline Qi and this is what I create in healing.

The second demonstration: the person puts up his arms and hands to forehead height with the strong hand on top and elbows straight. I tested how strong he is by pushing down on his hands. He was very strong. I then emitted Qi from the back of the room affecting the person's energy, then tested samples of people from each side of the room. When Qi was emitted and the target person was weak or strong, everyone else tested likewise. So this theory in turn demonstrates that everyone affects everyone around them and that we are all one. This has a very emotional and spiritual impact. This example of Qi energy discipline demonstrates how Chow Qigong can get such remarkable results as in the case samples that I shall present now. Yes, everyone can learn to do what I do. It demands good teaching and a good student.

My case samples are the following:

Case #1: Bill G. 82 years young. Three massive strokes and one seizure with severe brain damage and comatosed.

Case #2: Nicholas T. 6 years old. Brain damaged at birth, cerebral palsy, diabetes.

Case #3: Hope S. 82 years young. Fibrosarcoma Grade II. 23 year survivor.

Case #4: Bill T. 62 years young. Dystoniccorea, wheelchair dependency for 12 years. Stroke May 2002, prognosis, never walk again.

Case #1: Bill G. 82 years young. Three massive strokes and one seizure with severe brain damage and comatosed.

In February 2003, I was invited by Tom, the son of Bill, with cooperation the Indianapolis University Medical Center which has one of the top neurology divisions in the country. We had full cooperation of the medical staff and it was a joy to work with them. The following is what transpired.

February 1, 2003—Chinese New Year of the Ram and the day of Columbus Shuttle Disaster. Bill had 3 massive strokes and 1 seizure resulting in massive brain damage of parietal, temporal and cerebral, comatose, no speech, no response to light, speech, nor

other stimuli. Involuntary movement of limbs. On intravenous and gastric feeding, catheter, and had involuntary bowel movement. Had atrial fibrillation, elevated temperature, and left hemiplegia. Had CAT scan, MRI.

With all tests, physician's prognosis was that it was likely that he would never ever walk again, nor hear, see or talk properly nor ever eat by mouth.

February 12, 2003—Began Chow Medical Qigong at the Indianapolis University Medical Center. 1st therapy session with Chow Medical Qigong Bill regained full cognizance—upon request and slight assistance, turned head, moved arms and legs 6 times each. Sat in high fowler's position with eyes opened and smiling.

Feb. 13. 2nd therapy session—transferred with light assistance to chair for one hour

Feb. 14. 3rd therapy session—walked 18 feet with light assistance

Feb. 15. 4th therapy session—walked 120 feet with almost no assistance

Feb. 16-19. Continued progress with fine motor skills, catheter removed, to toilet, writing though not clearly legible, reading the newspaper, magazines on occasions, walked 400 feet, increasing skills of ADL e.g. brushing teeth with guidance, puts on own glasses, uses kleenix to wipe mouth, etc..

Feb. 21. He was transferred to a Nursing Rehabilitation Home.

3rd week Found it was more advantageous for his progress by going home, to restaurant, shopping, etc. Secured doctor's order for home visitation and outings

Began sipping fluid and taking bits of food. Socializing with family, other residents.

5th week Ate first pureed lunch! But he was still officially on NPO.

The staff at both the University Medical Center and the Nursing Rehabilitation Home were extremely cooperative with prescribing what we requested for expediting his recovery even though it was a highly unusual circumstance for them. The physicians were using terms in their rounds with their residents and interns such words as "striking", remarkable", "unbelievable" progress since Chow Qigong therapy!

I thank them all for their cooperation and courage to step out of their usual "box".

Case #2: Nicholas T. 6 years old. Brain damaged at birth, cerebral palsy, diabetes.

He is a "sage" trapped in a challenged body.
-6 years old boy
-born with brain damage of unknown origin
-cerebral palsy
-no voluntary movement
-no sound
-lie with no movement
-cannot sit
-head-drop
-diabetes

Family sought world-over for treatment—no results

The Institute for Human Potential—helped with communication facilitation, but not physically

January 2002: Began Chow Medical Qigong (CMQ) Therapy-referred by his physician.

1st visit Chow Medical Qigong

Outcome: rolled with assistance 40times and Arm and leg bend exercises 30 times

Had 3-4 therapy sessions per month—one session 3 hours

Total number of sessions 45 sessions

Results and Progress: Continues.

Can hold head up 85% of time
Can sit up with only 2 fingers on shoulder to balance for count of 230
Can stand and walk with assistance
Making much sounds
Speaks inconsistently about 12 words
Writes with communication facilitation, beautiful poetry and philosophy.
These are two samples of his poetry and writings unedited:

How can Goodness come out of the events of September 11, 2001

How We Can Be At Peace:

I think we as a nation have much work to do to be closer to God, not in a Biblical sense, but in a spiritual sense. We are all too busy, too caught up to listen to our inner selves. This is where all the inner power lies.

It lies within us. It is so important to listen to out inner power and strength.

This is magnificent, this power and strength is the most advanced way of knowing God.

Instead, we look outward for answers. Don't we know? Haven't we learned that the right thinking…and the right answers come from our own inner power?

the events of this tragedy can be avoided if we as a people, as a collective conscience learn to meditate, be in nature, and pray. Pray for love and divinity…no matter who is our metaphorical God. This is my almighty wish! Love from Nicholas.

5 years of age.

Rare Beauty

I saw a rare beauty called a tree,
It enveloped me.
I think it is divine.
I wish I could spend more time.
It is not always going to be there.
This is why I want to be with it

all that I can.
A tree of such rare beauty makes me
want to be a magician who

can grant a final wish.
Once who can grant me a departure

to the Land of Oz.
There, trees are full of monkeys and beauty.
There, monkeys become mentors to the trees.
I believe I will become a monkey.

3 years of age.

Case #3: Hope S. 82 years young. Fibrosarcoma Grade II. 23 year survivor.

Hope was lucky to be alive after emergency surgery. A large cancer had caused a perforation of her small intestine. Facing certain death, she applied healing methods of The Chow System, and is still alive and free of cancer twenty-three years later at 82 years of age.

Hope was sixty-two when she nearly died in 1981. The first sign of trouble was the sudden onset of abdominal pain and fever. At the time she was working in a small village in the Northwest Territories of Canada. Immediate surgery found a large cancer measuring eight inches in diameter in its largest area. Bowel contents were oozing into the abdominal cavity causing a life threatening infection (peritonitis).

Surgical removal was impossible because of the extent of the cancer. The bowel leak was sealed, drains placed, the abdomen closed, and Hope was given huge doses of antibiotics. The diagnosis was fibrosarcoma (Grade II), a form of cancer generally treated with irradiation, but unresponsive to other treatments.

After recuperating for a month, Hope was told she was going to die; she would be lucky if she lived two more years. She was not a candidate for irradiation therapy because of the location of the cancer. In desperation, her doctors recommended a trial of chemotherapy, but told her in advance it probably wouldn't work. Hope started the toxic treatment and experienced the usual side effects of nausea, vomiting, weight loss, and hair loss. Periodic CAT scans were not encouraging. After five months of chemotherapy her oncologist wrote in her medical record, "I don't believe chemotherapy will help this lady," and the treatment was stopped.

Hope always had been receptive to alternative approaches. At this point two friends who had taken a 100 hour course from Dr. Chow encouraged her to practice qi balancing exercises centered around Chow Qigong. Hope (her real name and a good name for this story) was looking for something like this to come along, and was receptive. There were many more things she wanted to do in her life, and she didn't want a "little cancer problem" to upset her plans. Hope was a very positive-minded person with a good sense of humor.

She practiced Chow Qigong diligently which included other measures such as diet, meditation, etc. and her miracle began to happen. When she began Qigong her abdomen was so swollen with cancer she looked six months pregnant. Over the next four months her abdomen shrank, CAT scans showed a steady reduction in the size of the cancer, and she began to feel like life might be worth living again.

At this point her friends asked what she would like to do more than anything else. She said she wanted to visit with friends at her alma mater in Berkeley, and on the East coast, John Hopkins University. Not long before, she thought she would never be able to see her old friends again. She took the trip, knowing it would be therapeutic.

When Hope returned to the clinic for a follow up exam (four months after beginning routines of The Chow System), a CAT scan showed that the original cancer mass had disappeared, but a suspicious mass remained in the left kidney. The kidney was removed surgically, but no evidence of cancer was found.

Hope still had little energy, and was fearful the cancer would return. In October, 1982, she began Dr. Chow's intensive training course to perfect her energy balancing practices, and much more. Classes were spread out over several months, but at the end she felt so much better she was able to go back to work full time.

Twenty three years have now passed since Hope's recovery. She is cancer free and enjoying good health. In contrast to most people who are looking for a quick fix for their health problems, she faithfully practices the Chow Qigong principles and exercises that cured her and continue to keep her healthy. She is well aware that she needs to do so to keep the cancer from returning.

At 82, she is very active, owns and runs a bed and breakfast place, a small apple orchard producing apple cider and dried apple, and traveling over the world.

Case #4: Bill T. 62 years young. Dystoniccorea, wheelchair dependency for 12 years. Stroke May 2002 prognosis, never walk again.

A male client from the Veteran's Adminstration (VA), wheelchair dependent for 12 years, a hospital administrator for 27 years, Vietnam shell shocked…result of experimental medication developed severe dystonicchorea symptoms, eg. non-stop constant motion of arms and body severely since 1992. He had a brain operation May, 2002 which caused a stroke and total dependency upon the wheelchair. Two weeks before he came to the 5th World Congress on Qigong, November 2002, his doctor and physiotherapist told him he would never walk again and ordered a power wheelchair for him. At the Congress, he and his caretaker from the VA came to Chow Qigong workshop on Sunday….3 minutes of Chow Qigong he sat very still relatively free of the dystoniccorea symptoms and after 8 minutes of Chow Qigong he got up, walked and encircled me in his arms and danced me around, then walked the perimeters of the large room. He also walked for the first time up the steps onto the stage, after the presentation he got up and again danced me on the stage laughing heartily!!!! You can imagine the reaction from the audience! There were tears, cheering and applause. Subsequently I had him get down by himself to the floor from the wheelchair, do some movement and rolling, and then got up by himself back into the wheelchair. Since that Sunday he continues to be mobile. We have a short video on this if you wish to see it.

Bill T. at the 5th World Congress on Qigong (November, 2002) Testimony—

Speech delivered by David as seen in the videotape.

I don't know if I can say anything more than what you just saw right there. (as Bill walked up the 5 steps to the stage!)

1963 left the military for chronic depression and was given an experimental drug.

1982 he stopped taking it and was suffering from dystoniccorea. A debilitating disease that causes involuntary reflexive movement. In 1992 his symptoms became full blown requiring full medical care, full treatment, full home-care. February, 2002, Bill received from the San Francisco VA hospital a series of surgeries called "deep brain implant". What they did was insert two electronic instruments in his brain and two power packs one side of his chest to remove the involuntary movement so he can sit in his chair. In second operation they clipped a blood vessel in his brain and he stroked out.

In May of 2002, he had no movement, no feeling on his complete right side and he was "aphasic". In June 2002, we sent him to Palo Alto Brain Damage Treatment Center where he came back not quite how he was before his physical therapy. Two weeks at his physical therapy appointment his physical therapist said 'Bill we're gonna have to put you in a powered wheelchair, you'll never walk again." It was hard for me to take, Bill's a friend of mine, I saw him regularly at the hospital but for Bill it was a crushing blow. About a week ago I was given an invitation to this Congress and I am a disabled veteran from Desert Storm and I wanted to come for my own benefit but I thought (Bingkun Hu, Dr. Hu over there who was the one that got me started on Qigong about 6 years ago) maybe this can help Bill. Well, Bill came in yesterday and spent about 3 minutes with Dr. Chow and for the first time since I've known him, which is 1998/1997, he sat completely still. I've never seen that before, never. *Sigh* He had movements so outrageous he couldn't hold glasses, he was completely involuntary. In fact, he now tried to make himself do that again (imitate his jerking waving motions) and he can't even remember how he did it. Three minutes with this lady (pointing to Dr. Chow) right here, he sat completely still, I've never seen that before and today we went to her workshop. After working with a group of people she spent a little bit of time (8 minutes) with Bill *sigh* he walked from his chair to the center of the room and began to dance step with her! *applause*

I got tears in my eyes, that was pretty moving. I thought enough for now let's go home. Then she said let's make sure he gets practice of this so he walked by himself the full length of the conference room, again I was astounded. She asked me if I wanted to get up here and talk about it. I was pretty interested and I wrote all these notes which I haven't been able to read, not once. But besides all that, *snicker* I see Bill asking me "you sure you want to do this?" Folks, um, you know this is not a paid announcement, I am just stunned! *applause*. His wife is arriving for the first time to the United States at the end of this month and they were married and I've seen the video tapes. He was standing in a Cambodian ceremony and you do a lot of standing. He was using crutches and two strong men were holding him upright. When he gets to see his wife, he gets to greet her standing. Bill, what a blessing these two days have been.

Just as an aside, I was a veteran in Desert Storm, I had heart surgery in 1992. They went into my back so they cut the whole left side trapezius muscle group which is my power side. I have no strength in my left side and arm. And I have 25% nerve degeneration. After my surgery I was put on 500mgm darvoset, a pain medication…since then I had not run out. I have taken increased and stronger dosage and now I'm on what is called Oxycontin, a Time Release pain medication. As a test after I saw Dr. Chow yesterday at the workshop, I stopped taking my medication last night just to see what happens when I came back to her workshop and I still haven't taken any. I can feel that effect, but folks, when I came today I reached down automatically with my left hand to pick up my gym bag, something I trained myself not to do a long time ago…for 10 years, I have never been able to do this…(he picked up his heavy gym bag up high to show everyone, then dropping it and continued to raise both arms up in the air saying that he do that for 10 years) *applause*. Thank you.

(Before getting off the stage, Bill grabbed the surprised Dr. Chow and danced with her up on the stage to whistles, cheers and tears! And walked down the stairs to his wheelchair.)

What is Qigong?

Qigong (pronounced "chee-gung") is a five thousand-year-old traditional form of Chinese energy exercise and healing for the body, mind, and spirit in harmony with nature. It is a system for improving and maintaining health as well as to help cure disease. The basic aim is to bring the body into a state of balance and self-regulation. Qigong is an ancient philosophical system of harmonious integration of the human body with the Universe. It is an art and science that plays an active role in protecting and strengthening health, preventing and treating diseases, resisting premature senility, and prolonging life. Qigong has succeeded akin to a miracle where all else has failed. Ancients referred to Qigong as the method to "eliminate diseases and prolong life." Qigong is the modern pinyin spelling, but also is written as Chi Kung, Qi Gong, and Chi Gung, among others. It is pronounced "chee-goong."

Qigong is derived from two words. "Qi" is the term used in Traditional Chinese Medicine for our vital breath, life force or energy. The concept has no direct counterpart in Western culture. It is roughly the equivalent of "Bioenergy" (living energy), or electromagnetic energy. This "living energy" is the vital life force that permeates all nature. It is the force in our bodies that controls our biochemistry and all other functions and behavior. This concept is at the core of most every aspect of Chinese culture, including art, architecture, philosophy, sports and science.

"Gong: can mean discipline, work, or skill. Therefore, Qigong has been defined roughly as "energy work," and "breath work." It also has been called "air energy" because, through, breathing exercises, energy is absorbed from the atmosphere.

Once a hidden practice jealously guarded by the elite spheres of classical Chinese society and later forbidden during the Cultural Revolution, Qigong today enjoys vast popularity among the Chinese people, official support by the Chinese Ministry of Health, and intensive scrutiny by the Chinese scientific community.

Qigong is one of Traditional Chinese Medicine's (TCM) principal methods of treatment. Though there are many schools, concurrent theories are these:

- The mind, body, and spirit energies can be regulated and cultivated through the relaxation and concentration of mental and physical exercises
- Control of respiration plays a central role
- Bringing the body into a state of maximum repose and self-regulation can help realize full physical potential, resist illness, recover damage caused by diseases, and balance the body's relation with the mind.
- "Balancing the human with the sky". In traditional Chinese thought, the sky is a general term for nature. Qigong researchers maintain that the human body and nature exist as an inter-related and inseparable unity. Imbalances in this unity are a key cause of illness. Therefore, humankind should strive for the conscious awareness of our inherent coordination with nature.
- Recent scientific research has begun to produce physiological evidence backing Qigong theory. For example, it has been shown that :
- Disordered or overstimulated cells in the cerebral cortex can be returned to a relaxed state through Qigong practice
- Positive physical changes can be traced to more efficient respiration and metabolism which in turn greatly reduces energy consumption
- The body's strength is fostered and more prepared to fight off illness by Qigong because of an improved immune system
- Qigong aids the generation of saliva and gastric juices thus improving digestion and absorption.

The Potential of Qigong

Qigong is a discipline anyone can learn. Many people practice Qigong simply because it makes them feel good, perform better, experience higher levels of energy and stamina, and reach their level of optimal health. Qigong can improve sports performance, prevent jet lag, and supercharge the immune system. Qigong practice has been shown to super-oxygenate the cells of the body. It can reduce stress, improve bowel function, and relieve the symptoms of insomnia and other sleep disorders. In the area of pain control, Qigong practice can relieve acute and chronic pain, reduce the pain of childbirth, and speed recovery from sports or other injuries. In addition, Qigong can increase the effectiveness of Western medications, may reduce the side effects, and even allow the use of smaller doses.

Many scientific studies have documented that Qigong has value in the treatment of more serious problems. It can reduce healing time after surgery by 50%, normalize the blood pressure, and heal tuberculosis. It can heal gastric and duodenal ulcers chronic atrophic gastritis (stomach inflammation), and liver disease. It can relieve nearsightedness (myopia) and improve mental performance. It also has been effective in the treatment of substance abuse, obesity, respiratory conditions, asthma, and allergies.

Benefits have also been seen in a long list of serious neuromuscular conditions, such as post-stroke syndrome, paralysis from brain and spinal cord injuries, multiple sclerosis, aphasia (loss of the power of expression of speech), Parkinson's disease, and cerebral palsy.

In more than thirty research studies, Qigong has been found to reverse the effects of aging. Qigong has improved or reversed the results of many medical tests that usually become abnormal with age. In addition, it has cured many of the diseases that are common to senior citizens.

Qigong has been shown to reduce deaths related to high blood pressure, reduce the frequency of strokes, reduce the incidence of retinopathy (deterioration of the back of the eye), improve the efficiency of the pumping action of the heart, and decrease blood viscosity ("thin" the blood). It has also improved EKG (heart) and EEG (brain) readings, normalized the level of sex hormones, and improved blood sugar levels in diabetics.

A slowing of the aging process is consistent with personal observations. We have met many Qigong masters in China and elderly masters routinely look about twenty years younger than their chronological ages. Their cheeks are smooth and shiny. They emit a healthy glow and they have few wrinkles in their skin.

The enhancements of sexual power and treatment of sexual dysfunction with Qigong has a long history. Chinese emperors allegedly learned Qigong techniques that delayed an orgasm, enabling them to have sex with a string of concubines, one after another. Entire books have been written about the application of Qigong in impotency, frigidity, and the improvement of a normal sex life. Some are available in English. We have treated many people successfully for impotency, other sexual dysfunctions, and for enhancing normal sexual qi.

Cancer patients usually benefit from Qigong practice. According to representatives of the Guo Lin Research Society, over one million cancer victims now practice Qigong every day. Their cancers have either stopped growing, shrunk, or disappeared completely.

As mentioned previously, Qigong can reduce or eliminate the side effects from chemotherapy. It also can reduce the need for pain medication, and improve the appetite and sense of well-being in patients with advanced cancer. Terminal cancer patients who practice Qigong usually die with dignity, with little or no pain, have a better quality of life, and feel comfortable right up to the end. Thus they avoid being medicated into a narcotic stupor, a sad and common fate in the West.

Though research shows that Qigong can improve health and miraculous cures have been verified, experienced Qigong masters caution it is not a "cure-all." There is one major characteristics of Qigong that sets it apart from other tales of miraculous recoveries. Healing benefits from Qigong are the result of the practice of a discipline that involves time, patience, and commitment. If people who benefit from Qigong don't continue to practice the measures that help them, their progress may disappear and they may slip back into their previous problem. They need to practice and/or have treatment until they have built up their internal Qi sufficiently to maintain that good health status.

Scientific Research

Qigong first gained scientific validity in 1953, with the establishment of the Shanghai Qigong Research Institute. Since 1982, Qigong research has spread throughout the world. Many Traditional Chinese Medicine hospitals incorporate Qigong in their core curriculum. The National Center of Complementary and Alternative Medicine at the National Institutes of Health has conducted and encourages research in Qigong. However, there is still a paucity of randomized controlled scientific data available.

Current data indicates that Qigong has healing properties and can be integrated and incorporated into the maintenance of health and the management of various medical conditions. Qigong is considered as part of mind-body techniques, which have been found to be efficacious as complementary treatments for musculoskeletal disease and related disorders.10 Many consider Qigong to be valuable in the care of both ambulatory and non-ambulatory patients in physical medicine.

The Qigong Institute, a nonprofit organization, developed the Qigong Bibliographic Database in 1994. An extensive review from the Database of approximately 1,300 references dating back to 1986 revealed clinical reports and scientific studies from China, Asia, the United States, and Europe that demonstrate and support the efficacy of Qigong, although many studies do not conform to the strict scientific protocol of randomized, controlled clinical trials. Controlled studies revealed that Qigong has a definite therapeutic role for hypertension, respiratory diseases, and cancer.

In studies where patients on medication were divided into two groups; one group that practiced Qigong and another group that did not, the results strongly suggested that practicing Qigong exercises favorably affects the physiologic functions of the body, consequently permitting the reduction of the dosage of drugs. In hypertensive patients, combining Qigong practice with drug therapy not only resulted in reducing the required drug dosage, but also reduced the incidence of stroke and mortality. In asthmatics, the combination of Qigong with medication resulted in reduction in the dosage of medication, the need for sick leave, the duration of hospitalization, and costs of therapy. In cancer patients, those who practiced Qigong manifested fewer side effects of potent cancer therapy. One study revealed that Qigong helps to rehabilitate drug addicts.

EWAHA and Dr. Chow have sponsored, along with many co-sponsors, the five World Congresses on Qigong and The Qigong Summit, formed the American Qigong Association (AQA), the American Medical Qigong Association (AMQA), and the World Qigong Federation (WQP) to bring about a solid Qigong community for both the professionals and the public-a clearinghouse-and to promote scientific research into Qigong so that it may be better understood by the Western medical and scientific population and to better serve the people.

The overall consensus of the investigators and reviewers of current data is the dire need for more sound research in all areas related to Qigong: to decipher the mechanism of Qigong for the scientific community, to demonstrate the efficacy of Qigong, to determine the appropriate type and amount of Qigong needed for health and for various medical conditions, and to assess cost effectiveness of Qigong. Supported by the rich background of thousands of years of history and a myriad of anecdotal evidence, it will only be a matter of time before Qigong is fully integrated into the conventional regimen of health maintenance and healing.

(We closed the program with everyone holding hands to the reading of the poem on <u>Love</u> by Emmett Fox......because without love there is no life or beauty, even though there may be Qi (the life force).

LOVE

There is no difficulty that enough love will not conquer;
No disease that enough love will not heal;
No door that enough love will not open;
No gulf that enough love will not bridge;
No wall that enough love will not throw down;
No sin that enough love will not redeem.

It makes no difference how deeply seated may be the trouble;
How hopeless the outlook;
How muddled the tangle;
How great the mistake;
A sufficient realization of love will dissolve it all...

If only you could love enough, you would be the happiest and
most powerful being in this world.

By Emmett Fox

Bibliography

• Effie Poy Yew Chow "Chinese Medicine: Contributions to Wholistic Healing," <u>Dimensions in Wholistic Healing, New Frontiers in the Treatment of the Whole Person</u>. Chicago, Ill: Nelson-Hall, 1979.

• Effie Poy Yew Chow <u>The Chow Model Integrated Healing System.</u> (A Non-Invasive Health Care Intervention) Pilot Research Project at the Columbia Lutheran Home, Seattle, WA. San Francisco: 1985.

• Effie Poy Yew Chow "Traditional Chinese medicine: a holistic system". <u>Alternative Medicines (Popular and policy perspectives), Tavistock Publisher, New York, N.Y. 1985.</u>

• Effie Poy Yew Chow, PhD, and May Loo, MD "Qigong" <u>Complementary and Alternative Medicine in REHABILITATION.</u> Eric Leskowitz. Churchill Livingstone Publisher, ST. Louis, Missouri, 2003

• Sancier, Kenneth M., and Effie Poy Yew Chow. "Healing with Qigong and Quantitative Effects of Qigong." The Journal of the American College of Traditional Chinese Medicine vol 7 no. 3, 1989.

• Sancier, Kenneth M., Effie Poy Yew Chow, & William Lee. "Effects of Mental Attitude and Qigong on Body Energy as Measured by a Muscle Test". Annual Meeting of the American association for the Advancement of Science, San Francisco, CA. January 14-19, 1989.

• Sancier, Kenneth M., and Effie Poy Yew Chow. "Effect of Qigong, Used in Healing\, on Body Energy as Measured by a Muscle Test", Annual meeting of the Pacific Division of the Aerican Association for the Advancement of Science. Chico, CA. June 11-15, 1989.

• Effie Poy Yew Chow, C. McGee, and K.M. Sancier. "Qigong", <u>Complementary Medicine.</u> Churchill Livingston, London, England. 1990's

• Bill Moyers. <u>Healing and the Mind.</u> Doubleday, New York, 1993. ISBN 0-385-46870-9.

• Charles T. McGee, M.D., and Effie Poy Yew Chow, Ph.D. <u>Miracle Healing from China...Qigong.</u> MEDIPRESS, Coeur d'Alene, Idaho, 1994. ISBN 0-9636979-5-1.

• David Eisenberg, M.D. <u>Encounters with Qi.</u> 1985, Penguin Books.

• Wong Kiew Kit. <u>The Art of Chi Kung: Making the most of your vital energy.</u> Published by Element Books, Inc, Rockport, MA, 1993. ISBN 1-5230-403-0.

• By Ted J. Kaptchuk, O.M.D.. <u>The Web That Has No Weaver: Understanding Chinese Medicine.</u> Published by Congdon and Weed, Inc. Chicago, 1983. ISBN 0-8092-2933-1.

• Harriet Beinfield and Efrem Korngold. <u>Between Heaven and Earth: A Guide to Chinese Medicine.</u> Ballantine Books, Random House, Inc., New York 1991. ISBN 0-345-37974-8.

• <u>Tao Te Ching</u>. Translated by Stephen Mitchell. Harper Perennial, 1991. ISBN 0-060091608-7.

• Frijof Capra: <u>The Tao of Physics. Shambhala Publications, Bounder, 1975.</u>

• Maciocia G: <u>The foundations of Chinese medicine: a comprehensive text for acupuncturists and herbalists</u>, London,1989, Churchill Livingstone.

• Omura Y: Simple method for evaluating qigong state: reversible changes in qigong master and subject; effect of qigong on bacteria, viruses, and acupressure points, 1st
Int ConfofQigong, 129,1990.

• Wan S et al: The study of traumatic paraplegia in canine model treated by Bagua Xun Dao Gong, ChinJSomatSci 1:115,1991.

• Wang C, Xu D, Qian Y, et al: Effects of qigong on preventing stroke and alleviating the multiple cerebro-cardiovascular risk factors: a followup report on 242 hypertensive cases over 30 years, 2nd World Conf Acad Exch Med Qigong, 123,1993.

• Xia H, Xu F, Cui C, et al: Effect of qigong exercise on electromyogram of poliomyelitis paralysis, 3rd Nat Academy on Qigong Science, 90, 1990.

• Yu H, Yan X, Xu L: Systematic investigation of the qigong state, 1st World Conf Acad Exch Med Qigong, 8, 1988.

Effie Poy Yew Chow, (PhD, RN, DiplAc(NCCAOM), Qigong Grandmaster) is the founder and President of the San Francisco, CA based international organization, East West Academy of Healing Arts (EWAHA) in 1973 and, more recently, the EWAHA Qigong Institute, the American Qigong Association, American Medical Qigong Association, and the World Qigong Federation. In July 2000 she was one of the original 15 appointees by President Bill Clinton for the White House Commission on Complementary and Alternative Medicine Policy. In June 2003, Dr. Chow was appointed to a 15 member national Task Force for the Chicago Museum for Science and Industry in their 21st Century Initiative for Life and Health. She is the recipient of over twenty awards including the "Humanitarian of the Year 1999" and the "Visionary of the Decade 2000" awards. The City and County of San Francisco made a proclamation of "Dr. Effie Poy Yew Chow Day" for November 22, 1997. She has been the only Qigong Grandmaster and acupuncturist involved in the development of national health policies within DHHS. She was also appointed to the first Ad Hoc Advisory Panel for the Congress-mandated Office of Alternative Medicine (now NCCAM) at NIH. She has made over three hundred media appearances and interviews in the area of complementary and alternative medicine. Dr. Chow received her training in Traditional Chinese Medicine, Acupuncture, and Qigong in China, Hong Kong, Taiwan, Canada, and the United States. She is a registered public health and psychiatric nurse and has received a Master's degree in Behavioral Sciences and Communications, and a Ph.D. in (Higher) Education. She co-authored with Dr. Charles McGee, "Miracle Healing from China…Qigong" and has two videos and an audiotape on Chow Qigong and meditation.

Her clinical practice and teaching covers the general spectrum of health and illnesses. She travels world-wide to see clients and lecture as she is internationally renowned for her exceptional success with difficult rehabilitative cases of chronic and debilitating conditions such as pain, paralysis, cancer, asthma, arthritis, Cerebral Palsy, and many other "hopeless" cases. As well, she helps world-class athletes reach higher performance levels and works integrally with the medical team who cares for the referred client. She believes in an integrated creative approach to health and life and prescribes at least 8 hugs and 3 belly-aching laughs a day to everyone!

East West Academy of Healing Arts (EWAHA)

A 501(c)3 nonprofit organization since 1973 dedicated to integrating holistic Complementary and Alternative Medicine (CAM) and Modern Western Medicine (MWM) with a special focus on Traditional Chinese Medicine (TCM) and Qigong. We foster the practice of excellence in promoting optimum health through educational, clinical, and research activities utilizing holistic subtle energy healing concepts of body, mind, and spirit, bringing the best of health care for all people: giving hope and results for our clients with serious and minor conditions where all else may have previously failed. We celebrate the miracle of life. Our new project, "The Children and Youth Project for Healing and Peace" will emanate this miracle.

MATERIAL DEFORMATION BY INTENTION

Jack Houck
JackHouck@aol.com

Abstract

This paper was presented at the Science of Whole Person Healing Conference on March 28, 2003. The purpose was to show that humans do have interaction with and effects on matter. This report captures the results of 22 years of research with experiments in psychokinesis (PK). The author began the PK Party workshops as an experiment to test his hypothesis that significant paranormal effects would be produced if a large peak emotional event could be orchestrated. It worked so well in the first PK Party (January 1981) that he has continued to conduct theses workshops. There have been 361 PK Parties (17,000 attendees) conducted by the author, and many more by others all over the world. Often controlled experiments have been conducted within the PK Party environment, some that are reported in this paper.

Introduction

In the following table are a few examples of paranormal phenomena divided into Extrasensory Perception (ESP) and Psychokinesis (PK) activities:

Extrasensory Perception (ESP)	Psychokinesis (PK)
• Remote Viewing (RV) • Body Scanning • Telepathy • Mind-Reading • Out-of-Body Experiences	• Material Deformation • Mental Healing • Telekinesis • Affecting Random Processes • Remote Effects

ESP activities are passive and PK activities are active. The first 10 years of my research were in applications of the mind concentrated on remote viewing.

The last 20 years have been concentrated on material deformation through PK. I continue collecting data while giving workshops teaching people how to do both RV and PK.

Remote Viewing Research

In the early 1970's, I became interested in how people could do remote viewing (RV). The term remote viewing was coined by Hal Puthoff and Russell Targ who were with Stanford Research Institute (SRI) International developing the technology to understand and apply RV. (Reference 1) The RV phenomenon is that a person in one place can somehow send their "mind" out to another place and "see" what is happening at that location. Later SRI and other research laboratories realized that the data came to the viewer in all the body senses, not just visual. The other laboratories began calling this remote perception.

Although I am an aerospace engineer, most of my spare time has been spent reading about phenomena that related to seeing-at-a-distance (e.g., out-of-body experiences, astral travel, near-death experiences). In my professional career at McDonnell Douglas, I managed an advanced research group with some Government contracts that provided some access to background data during 1970 through 1990. Mr. James McDonnell was very interested in similar phenomena and was providing some funding to parapsychology laboratories. He heard about my interests in 1980 and funded a coordinate remote viewing experiment (i.e., an experiment where the viewer is asked to see what is located at a target given by latitude and longitude coordinates in degrees, minutes, and seconds that is about 100-foot resolution). While documenting that experiment, I wrote a chapter on a conceptual model in an attempt to explain how remote viewing might work (Reference 2).

The conceptual model for thinking about how an individual can send their mind out to do remote viewing and PK is illustrated in Figure 1 and described in more detail in Reference 2. The area labeled STU is a representation of the mind passing into another dimension where all information is stored, similar to Jung's collective unconscious and the metaphysics term "akashic records." The acronym STU stands for Space Time Unit.

In remote viewing experiments, it is observed that the data a viewer produces often was correct about the target location, but not how that target location looked at the time the

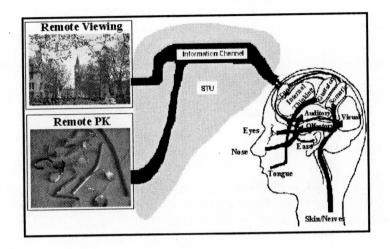

Conceptual Model of the brain and mind interacting with remote objects and scenes.

viewing took place. I call this a "time-shift." It appears as if the mind of the viewer goes to the correct target and locks onto a time when there was a peak emotional event occurring at that target. Thus the data that the viewer reports may be years before the time of the viewing, or even sometime in the future. Of course this makes evaluating the success of an experiment difficult. Figure 4 in Reference 2 attempts to show this time-shift effect. In talks presenting my Conceptual Model, I suggested that in order to minimize this time-shift effect, create a peak emotional event at the current time and some major paranormal event (e.g., psychokinesis) might occur. Parapsychologist Charles Honorton challenged me to test my model.

Psychokinesis Research

In January 1981, in response to this challenge, I conducted an experiment that I called a PK Party. PK stands for Psychokinesis, (which, as noted previously, is defined as mind-over-matter) and the idea of a party was to make it a wild emotional event (allowed in California). There were 21 people at the first PK Party in my home in Huntington Beach, California. Half of these people were participants in my RV experiments and the other half were members of the same tennis club I belonged to. Everyone was told that we were going to bend metal with our minds. The tennis players thought this was a big joke and the RVers thought they had God-given powers to perform perception type activities, but not PK activities. Fortunately, I had met a metallurgist named Severin Dahlen at work who was teaching children to perform PK at the University of California, Irvine. I invited Severin to come to the party and give the instructions. In preparation for this event, I had stopped at the Sears store and purchased a large zinc coated steel rod thinking that if it was bent, I would be impressed. I also provided my grandparents' sterling silverware for bending material.

At the party, the participants were sitting in chairs arranged in a circle around my living room, joking and laughing. Severin stood up in the center of the circle and proceeded to gave the following instructions:

First Step: Make a mental connection with what you want to affect
"Get a point of concentration above your head. Grab it and bring it down through your head, your neck, your shoulder, down your arm, into your hand and put it into the fork or spoon."
Second Step: Command (intention) what you want to happen
"Command the silverware to bend by shouting BEND, three times."
Third Step: Let go!
"Let go."

After these instructions, a minute or two went by and a 14-year-old boy began screaming that his fork was bending. Everyone could clearly see that the head of his fork was bending over slowly. I noticed that everyone's eyes were huge and I now call that "an instant belief system change." Shortly after that, almost everyone began bending his or her silverware very easily. They were jumping up and down, shouting, and screaming. This was a peak emotional event! They described the silverware getting warm or sticky, with the metal becoming very soft, like rubber, for five to 30 seconds. 19 of the 21 attendees at the first PK Party were able to do what I now refer to as "Kindergarten bending." One of the participants was a woman who had told a friend of hers before the party that she didn't see any sense bending silverware. Unfortunately, she created a mental block for herself. She came to subsequent PK Parties and finally was able to bend metal at the fourth party. I was the other person who did not bend at the first PK Party. I was busy looking around at what people were doing and was trying to analyze what was happening. It also took me four PK Parties to get the PK experience. Later on in the evening at the first PK Party, the same 14-year-old boy bent the large steel rod very easily. The next day I bought the rest of the steel rods the same size from Sears. The head metallurgist at McDonnell Douglas in Huntington Beach, California attempted to bend one of the rods and finally did by straining and using his knee. He was more than twice the size of the young boy.

The next month, I gave another PK Party. This time we used stainless steel flatware forks and spoons. (Knives sometimes break and could cut people.) I also added a number of experiments, including metal and plastic of various types. We put strips of thin metal in soda pop bottles and stuck them in corks securing the metal strips to the top of the bottles so people would not handle the strips. The strips continued to bend for three days after the party. A lot was learned using the PK Parties to create the PK environment while conducting experiments within the parties.

It was discovered that people could buckle the bowls of silver plated spoons. They could not do that using their brute strength, but they often could using PK. So we started "High School bending," where people bent things that were beyond what could be done by physical strength alone. Steel and aluminum rods were cut to lengths that could not be bent physically. The rods and silver plated spoons are used in High School bending.

"Graduate School bending" is when people are given two forks that have been checked and any bends removed. They hold a fork at the bottom of the handle in each hand. They simply command the fork to bend spontaneously. Sometimes one or both forks bend spontaneously. Any amount of spontaneous bending is significant and evidence of macro PK.

At the time this paper was presented on March 28, 2003, I had given 361 PK Parties that were attended by approximately 17,000 people since January 1981. All of these parties have been documented. The date, location, number of attendees, and the number of people who had success in each of the phases of the PK Parties are kept in a computerized database. Similarly, from PK Party #44 through #343 attendees filled out questionnaires, recording their perception of what they did and that data has been recorded in another computerized database. 59% of the 14,315 people attending those PK Parties turned in completed questionnaires. Pictures of individuals, couples or families were taken at each PK Party and a copy given to the people in the pictures when possible. Occasionally it was not possible to correlate the face in the picture with the name and address of the individual. Figure 2 shows typical results during these phases of a PK Party.

Kindergarten Bender   Telekinesis Achiever

High School Bender   Graduate School Bender

People's experiences at PK Parties

A typical happy Kindergarten bender is the woman shown in the top-left corner of Figure 2. People do use two hands in Kindergarten bending and are encouraged to feel for when the spoon or fork loses its structure (the grain boundaries of the stainless steel seem to melt allowing the grain boundaries to slip and the metal feels like rubber). Stainless flatware is used for Kindergarten bending because stainless steel has a very low thermal conductivity that translates to allowing the bender to have more time to find the window in time when the metal becomes soft. It stays soft between 5 and 30 seconds before it refreezes and returns to its solid state. When stainless flatware is stamped out at the time it is manufactured, dislocations are created along the grain boundaries in the flatware. These dislocations seem to act as transducers for the PK energy that turns to heat and melts the grain boundaries. Most stainless steel has a melting temperature of over 2000 degrees F. The actual grains in the stainless steel are not being melted, just the edges of the grains called grain boundaries. Thus the flatware is not hot to touch, but often people feel the warmth coming from within the metal. The overall success rate for people who try Kindergarten bending is 85%.

A man who was able to buckle the bowls of two silver plated spoons is shown in the lower-left corner of Figure 2. Buckling the bowl of a silver plated spoon is considered High School level bending because the shell structure of a spoon bowl makes it very strong. Very few people have been able to buckle the bowl of a stainless spoon because stainless steel is so strong. However, most silver plated spoons are made from pot metal and then plated with silver. The pot metal is not as strong and buckling those bowls seems to be possible when using PK and some strength with both hands. Often people describe the bowl buckling as if the metal felt like paper and very easily was buckled, when they are distracted. Aluminum rods (one foot in length and 3/8" in diameter) are often available for bending in PK Parties. Also, zinc plated steel rods with diameters up to ½" are often available. When people bend these they have done something spectacular. The overall success rate for people who try High School bending is approximately 32%.

A man who had both of the forks he was holding during Graduate School bend over spontaneously is shown in the lower-right corner of Figure 2. He was holding the bottom of the stainless flatware fork handles, one in each hand. He was concentrating on the fork in his right hand when I noticed that the fork in his left hand was bending over spontaneously (not using the other hand). I asked him if he saw the one in his left hand and then he looked at it and said "How did that happen?" At that moment, the fork in his right hand bent over spontaneously. This was another example of the PK working when he was distracted or let go. Young children seem to do spontaneous bending very well. The head of the fork may twist or the tines separate in different directions. Any amount of fork movement is considered very special and occurs for approximately 11% of the people who participate in the Graduate School phase of PK Parties.

Occasionally, I notice something especially interesting at a PK Party. Onetime, I saw that the small girl shown in the upper-right hand corner of Figure 2 had bent a large steel rod. I went over to where she and her mother were sitting and patted her on her head telling her how great I thought she had done. Her mother then said, "Oh, she can do more than that." I asked "Like what?" The little girl turned and pointed to the tennis stick figure with a counter weight for balance on the mantle above the fireplace and said "Move." The figure then spun around on the point of the stand it was on. This is referred to telekinesis, or moving objects without touching them. I have not conducted experiments within the PK Party environment on telekinesis, but that would certainly be an interesting area for additional experimentation.

One experiment that provides some insight into the PK effects was done with four old type hacksaw blades. Each blade was tested for its hardness with a Rockwell C hardness (Superficial 15N Scale) testing machine. All four measured very hard, although two of the blades were slightly softer than the other two. One of the blades was isolated from the other three by placing it in a separate home. From then on in the experiment, the separated blade was always tested at a different time than the other three blades so that they would never be together. The other three blades were placed in a brown paper bag and exposed at four PK Parties over a three month period. The bag was placed in the center of the circle of people involved in the PK Parties. Only my metallurgist and I knew the experiment was in progress. All the blades were tested the day before the next PK Party. This was done to allow any time effects to occur in the blades after they were exposed at a PK Party. The hardness of the three exposed blades all reduced from the original very hard steel of the hacksaw blades to near that of annealed steel, which is very soft. The control blade maintained its hardness throughout the experiment. The measured hardness of these hacksaw blades is shown in Figure 5 of Reference 3.

In another experiment, a Hall Effect sensor was constructed with two Hall Effect chips placed back to back (in order to cancel any temperature effects) and the output run through a bridge circuit to the chart recorder which was located about 20 feet from the sensor. The sensor was also enclosed in a thermos bottle for temperature isolation. The sensor was on a stand, placing it about four feet off the floor. The sensor was aligned perpendicular to the earth's magnetic field lines in order to minimize the effect of the earth's magnetic field.

A two minute cyclical signal occurred at the time the fork of a young girl, sitting within six feet of the Hall Effect sensor, had the top fall over resulting in a 90° spontaneous bend during the Graduate School phase of a PK Party. The data recorded on a pen chart recorder is shown in Figure 7 of Reference 3.

The reason Hall Effect chips were chosen in the first place was not to measure the magnetic field, as is their normal application, but to see if the current through them is affected by PK modifying the dislocations in them by changing the mobility of electrons moving through the crystal. However, subsequent use of the same sensor produced no results. The internal dislocations in any metal exposed to PK are changed, making this an unreliable sensor for feedback and training.

During PK Parties, it was often noticed that when a zinc-coated steel rod is bent using PK, its shiny surface would turn black. Reference 4 is an analysis of this surface effect using optical and scanning electron microscopes.

Reference 5 is a report on PK effects on clear plastic spoons and forks. It was noticed that children were able to bend clear plastic forks and spoons. Normally this material is very brittle and breaks when people try to bend it. The PKed area of the plastic looks cloudy to the naked eye. Under optical magnification, the cloudy area appears to have micro cracks emanating from a small bubble. It looks as if the spot of the bubble was heated causing that area to expand, creating the micro cracks. This effect seems to have some correlation to the heat being created along the grain boundaries in metal. The nice part about using clear plastic is that another feedback is provided to the person doing the PK in that they can observe the cloudiness as a signal for when the plastic is ready to bend.

One of the most unusual examples of bending at a PK Party was caught on video tape in May 1986. A video clip of a man pulling apart a spoon is available in Reference 6. The event occurred at PK Party #140 held in Santa Fe, New Mexico. The party was being videotaped and the photographer happened to catch this man pulling apart the spoon handle he was holding. The next day at lunch, I sat down across the table from this man and asked if he would do it again. When he agreed, I went to the kitchen and bought a dozen stainless flatware forks. Returning to the table, I handed him one of the forks. He held it for awhile, concentrating on it. Then he pulled it apart! I took the other 11 forks back to the structures laboratory at work and pulled the 11 forks apart mechanically using a tensile testing machine. The average force to break the forks was 850 lbs.

Over the years, I have collected data in formal and informal ways described here, and I have also gathered information through observation and anecdotal evidence. Typically there are 20 to 50 people at a PK Party. The success rate falls off when the PK Parties have fewer than 15 people. The largest party had over 400 people. Over 100 other people have given PK Parties all over the world.

Some additional observations are:

Everyone seems to be able to do PK.

Metal often continues to bend for up to 3 days.

The more dislocations in metal, the easier it is to PK.

Cast metals are very hard to PK.

Children bend clear plastic picnic spoons and forks easily.

Graduate forks must be replaced after three PK Parties or they stop bending spontaneously.

Approximately 50% of people who do PK at the parties are able to do it later by themselves.

On occasion "critics" have written about PK Parties with a negative connotation suggesting the chaos with lots of people, commotion, and noise is covering up fraudulent behavior. The noise does have purpose, however. The first two steps for doing PK seems to be easy for most people. However, the third step (letting go) is something many people talk about, but few know how to do. The noise and the people shouting with joy help distract people causing them to let go and then they have PK success. It is true that magicians have tricks where they can with slight of hand or diversion appear to bend objects like those in PK Parties. The 17,000 people who have attended PK Parties cannot all be magicians. Seeing a six-year-old bend a ½" diameter steel rod (18" long) about 20 degrees is very impressive.

Healing

Over these 22 years of giving PK Parties, I have noticed a number of events that would be considered spontaneous healing. For example, in the middle of a PK Party, a man would stand up and say that his back had just been healed. The PK "energy" seems to be magnified at PK Parties and is strongest at the center of the circle of benders. This seems to correlate well with the "chi energy" discussed in various martial arts disciplines. There are many alternative healing modalities that work with moving energy. Even though many of these techniques have complex process, viewing them simplistically, they generally can be boiled down to the same simple three steps used for PK. After all, if humans can affect material with intention, why not healing other humans? Researchers such as Dr. Larry Dossey, Dr. Yoshiaki Omura, and Dr. Daniel Benor presented scientifically collected data at the March Science of Whole Person Healing Conference.

In conclusion, there is powerful evidence that mind matters and there is interaction between the Mind and the material world. Many questions remain, however, and much additional experimentation is required.

References

1. Puthoff H, Targ R (1976) Proceedings of IEEE Vol. 64 A Perceptual Channel for Information Transfer over Kilometer Distances: Historical Perspective and Recent Research
2. Houck J (Winter 1983) ARCHAEUS 1, 1 Conceptual Model of Paranormal Phenomena, Now located on www.jackhouck.com
3. Houck J (1986) Journal of the United States Psychotronics Association, Number 5, pp 21-25. Remote Viewing and Psychokinesis Research, Now located on www.jackhouck.com
4. Houck J (Fall 1984) ARCHAEUS, Vol. 2, No. 1, p27. Surface Change During Warm-Forming, Now located on www.jackhouck.com
5. Metallurgical Report on Plastic Spoon Deformation, Now located on www.jackhouck.com
6. Houck J Unpublished PK Parties, Now located on www.jackhouck.com

MATERIAL DEFORMATION

David Robertson
Birbeck College,
London
davidrobertson@ic24.net

Material deformation has been performed by thousands of people from age four to over sixty. The majority are children. It has been studied by eminent scientists all over Europe including people such as :

David Bohm, co-author and colleague of Einstein
John Hasted, Head of Physics at Birkbeck College, London University
Charles Crussard, leading French metallurgist

Here are the primary references which every seriously interested reader will want to look at for the details.

1. J.B. Hasted, D.J. Bohm, E.W. Bastin and B. O'Regan, *Nature*, 254, 1975, 470

2. J.B. Hasted, *J. Soc. Psych. Res.*, 48, 1976, 365.

3. J.B. Hasted, *J. Soc. Psych. Res.*, 49, 1977, 583

4. Crussard and J. Bouvaist, *Mémoires scientifiques Revue Metallurgie*, February 1978, p. 117

5. Hasted,J.B.and Robertson,D.S.(1979) *The Detail of Paranormal Metal Bending.* Journal of the Society for Psychical Research. Vol. 50, No. 799, p.9-20.

6. Hasted, J.B. and Robertson, D.S.(1980) *Paranormal Action on Metal and its Surroundings.* Journal of the Society for Psychical Research. Vol. 50. p.379-398.

7. Hasted, J.B. and Robertson, D.R.(1981) Paranormal Electrical Effects Journal of the Society for Psychical Research. Vol. 51. No. 788. p. 75-78.

8. Hasted, J.B. and Robertson, D.S.(1981) Paranormal Elecrical Effects. Psychoenergetic Systems. Vol.4 p. 159-187.

9. J.B. Hasted, D. Robertson and P. Arathoon, *SPR/PA Jubilee Convention.*, *1982*, Paranormal Metal Bending Researches with Piezoelectric Sensors. Research in Parapsychology, Scarecrow press. p.39-42.

10. "The Metal Benders" John Hasted; ISBN 0710005970; Routledge and Kegan Paul.

11. PARANORMAL ELECTRICAL CONDUCTANCE PHENOMENA by COLIN BROOKES-SMITH JOURNAL of the Society for Psychical Research VOLUME 48 No. 764 June 1975

12. W.J. Crawford; The Psychic Structures at the Goligher Circle, Watkins London & Dutton, New York; 1921.

13. Observations on selected Italian mini—Gellers F.BERSANI Psychoenergetics, 1983, Vol. 5, pp. 99-128

The following observations are particularly striking:

1. Deformation is a mixture of softening and physical forces, possibly related to gravitation. Some substances like glass usually tend to shatter but exceptional subjects can bend them. There may be an activation energy for each substance, below which softening does not occur.

2. Experiments with arrays of sensors indicate the existence of a planar surface associated with metal bending events. This may have a very complicated microstructure. The surface movement is obstructed by glass but less by other substances.

3. Levitation events are often accompanied by vortex motion or arrays of vortices, sometimes the boundaries are very well defined. These are reminiscent of the structure of the surface associated with a magnetic fluid; they may indicate the onset of symmetry breaking.

4. Metal bending is associated with atmospheric conduction paths where there seems to be no evidence of ionisation. This may be a simpler system to observe and account for some mental effects on electronic equipment.

5. Physical deformation events can include rapid seed growth and extensive changes in genetic structure, usually restricted to the genetic range found on Earth. This may be related to the finding that effects on random event generators seem to be re-shuffling of the total event pool of the experiment. Seed experiments are relatively easy to perform and can be well controlled.

Another group of careful observers who have examined the processes of metal deformation in great detail are the leading magicians of the world (upon whom some scientists place great reliance). These magicians have especially studied one person who is particularly good at material deformation—Uri Geller with whom this author has also worked for many years. The comments listed on his website speak for themselves, and while Geller is obviously one of hundreds it is important to add these opinions to the data base, particularly for those who trust magicians more than Physics professors.

See part four of Uri Geller's Biography on www.urigeller.com for the details.

Here are a few of the magicians who have witnessed the phenomena:

Drew McAdam

Lee Earle

Barrie Richardson

Werry (Werner Geissler, 1925-2000)

Clifford Davis, Daily Mirror c1974

Peter Warlock

David Ben

Eugene Burger

Eddie Burke

Alan Slaight

Charles Lee

Abb Dickson

David Blain

Arthur Zorka

Ben Harris

Ben Robinson

Dandi

David Berglas

David Gilchrist

Denham Holmes

Dr. Penguin

Dr. Lawrence Ratna

Geoff Maltby

Harry Meier

Leo Leslie

Raimondi

Rev. Roger Crosthwaite

William. E. Cox

James Cottis

EFFECTS OF COLLECTIVE ATTENTION ON RANDOM DATA:

Patterns Where There Should Be None

Roger D. Nelson, Director
Global Consciousness Project
Princeton NJ
rdnelson@Princeton.edu

Abstract

The Global Consciousness Project (GCP) collects random data continuously in a network of over 50 locations around the world. We ask what happens to the statistical ensemble when there are globally shared events like New Years celebrations or September 11 2001. The results suggest that there may be a direct participation of consciousness as an agent in the physical world. The GCP is an international collaboration of researchers studying interactions of consciousness with the environment. We maintain a network of random event generators (REGs) that generate random data continuously and send it for archiving to a dedicated server in Princeton, New Jersey. The data are analyzed to determine whether the fundamentally unpredictable array of values contains periods of detectable non-random structure that may be correlated with global events. We do formal analyses testing hypotheses based on standardized procedures as well as *post hoc* and exploratory studies. Independent analysts looking at major events find evidence of substantial increases in structure correlated with the most intense and widely shared periods of emotional reactions to the events. Control assessments indicate that the non-random behavior cannot be attributed to ordinary sources such electromagnetic fields. The evidence suggests that the anomalous structure is somehow related to the unusually coherent focus of human attention on extraordinary events. Coherence of thought and emotion apparently creates a negentropic field that can change a random process; what we envision and intend has subtle but detectable effects. The implication is that creative intent to heal the whole person can be broadened to healing families, groups, and ultimately world civilization. This is the promise of global consciousness.

Introduction

The GCP builds on experiments conducted over the past 40 years at a number of laboratories, demonstrating that human consciousness can interact with true random event generators, to somehow induce non-random patterns that are correlated with intentional, mental efforts (Radin and Nelson, 1989). For example, small changes in the proportion of 1s and 0s are associated with participants' attempts to change the distribution of numbers produced by a physical random event generator in controlled experiments. The results show a tiny but significant correlation with the participants' assigned intentions (Jahn et al., 1997). The replicated demonstrations of anomalous mind/machine interactions clearly show that a broader examination of this phenomenon is warranted, and such research continues in a number of laboratories.

Variations on the theme include "FieldREG" studies that take the REG device into the field to see whether group interactions might affect the random data (Nelson et al., 1996, 1998a). The technology has recently been applied in studies of distant healing (Radin and Yount, 2003; Jonas et al.,2003). In related work, prior to the GCP, an array of REG devices in Europe and the U.S.A. showed non-random activity during widely shared experiences of deeply engaging events. For example, the funeral ceremonies for Princess Diana created shared emotions and a coherence of consciousness that appeared to be correlated with structure in the otherwise random data (Nelson et al., 1998b). Instead of the expected, unpredictable sequence of random numbers, small changes in the mean value indicated that something had introduced a non-random element that structured the sequence, making it slightly more predictable. In graphical terms, instead of a random walk (a "drunkard's" walk), the data sequence showed a steady trend.

These experiments were prototypes for the GCP. In the fully developed project, a world-spanning network of more than 50 devices collects data continuously and sends it to a central server in Princeton, New Jersey, via the Internet. The system is designed to create a continuous record of nominally random data over months and years, gathered from a wide distribution of locations. Its purpose is to document and display any subtle effects of humanity's collective consciousness as we react simultaneously to global events. Our research hypothesis predicts the appearance of increasing coherence and structure, or non-random trends, in data collected during major events in the world that share a common feature, namely, that they powerfully engage human attention all around the world, and draw us in large numbers into a common focus.

Method

The research methodology requires a brief introduction. The GCP Web site and prior publications present greater depth of description and discussion (Nelson, 1998c; 2001a). In a nutshell, the method is to collect continuous, concurrent streams of data from electronic devices designed to produce completely unpredictable and unstructured sequences of numbers. We identify events that powerfully stimulate shared human reactions, make *a priori* predictions that specify the analysis parameters, and then look at the temporally corresponding data to determine whether they show significant changes from the expected random quality.

At each of the host sites around the world, a well-qualified source of random bits (REG or RNG) is attached to a computer running custom software to collect data continuously at the rate of one 200-bit trial per second. This local system is referred to as an "egg" and the whole network has been dubbed the "EGG," standing for "electrogaiagram," because its design is reminiscent of an EEG for the Earth. (Of course this is just an evocative name; we are recording statistical parameters, not electrical measures.) The egg software regularly sends time-stamped, checksum-qualified data packets (each containing five minutes of data) to a server in Princeton. We access official timeservers to synchronize the eggs to the second, to optimize the detection of inter-egg correlations. The server runs a program called the "basket" to manage the archival storage of the data. Other programs on the server monitor the status of the network and do automatic analytical processing of the data. Scripts are used to create up-to-date pages on the GCP Web site, providing public access to the complete history of the project's results. The raw data are also available for download by those interested in checking our analyses or conducting their own assessments of the data.

The database is a continuously growing array, with over four million new 200-bit trials per day. Each trial has an expected mean (μ) of 100 and expected standard deviation (σ) of 7.071. Deviations from the expected mean can be converted to approximately normally-distributed Z-scores ($Z_i = (m_i - \mu)/\sigma$). For N eggs in the network, the Z-scores can be combined across eggs using the Stouffer method ($Z_s = \Sigma Z_i / \sqrt{N}$) to form a new Z-score representing the composite deviation of the mean at any given moment. This is an algebraic sum that becomes large when the eggs show correlated deviations. An alternative analysis addresses the variability among the eggs using either a direct calculation of the variance (s^2) across eggs or a sum of the Z_i^2, that is, the squared deviations.

For most of our analyses, we look at deviations of the squared composite Z-scores (Stouffer Z's), which are χ^2 distributed with one degree of freedom (df), assuming a null hypothesis. We predict that the eggs' output will tend to show increased deviations from expectation during the pre-specified period of time and we test this using a one-tailed χ^2 accumulation ($\Sigma Z_s^2 >>$ df, where df is the number of seconds or Stouffer Z-scores). The analysis represents the basic idea that the eggs will exhibit a degree of correlated behavior if they somehow respond to events in the world.

Results

One of the most obvious test cases for the hypothesis that widespread communal engagement will somehow produce an effect on our egg network is New Years Eve. We now have had an opportunity to look for patterns in the data around midnight during five New Year celebrations, including the unusually intense preoccupations for the much anticipated Y2K transition. We make the same two predictions, one that says the mean across all the eggs will diverge during the 10 minutes surrounding midnight, and a second that says the variance will decrease around midnight. To give an example, Figure 1 shows the average across all time zones of the amount of variation among the eggs around midnight on New Years Eve, 1999-2000 (Y2K). In order to test the statistical likelihood of the apparently focused decrease in variability we take the combined probability for the depth of the minimum and its distance from midnight, using an iterated permutation analysis. In this case the likelihood of having so deep a minimum as close as it is to midnight is about 1 in 100. In all five New Year celebrations we have examined, there is a substantial change in the variability among the eggs at midnight, apparently correlated with our focused attention.

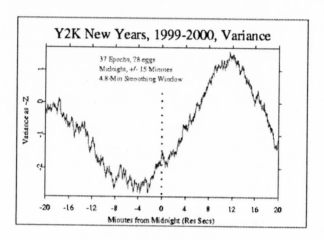

An example of the pattern of reduced variability among the eggs around midnight on New Years Eve. The curve shows the smoothed value of the signal-averaged variance across all time zones around the world.

The tragedies of September 11, 2001, are another obvious test case, a global event that should, according to the general hypothesis, affect the EGG network. The primary formal prediction for September 11 specified a period beginning 10 minutes before the first crash and continuing to four hours after, thus including the actual attacks plus an aftermath period of a little more than two hours following the last of the major cataclysmic events. The data show a fluctuating deviation during the moments of the five major events, as increasing numbers of people around the world were watching and hearing the news in stunned disbelief. This continued for almost half an hour after the fall of the second WTC tower. Then, a little before 11:00, the cumulative deviation took on a trend that continued during the aftermath period, with a final probability of 0.028. If we examine the larger context by looking at the behavior of the eggs over a longer period before and after September 11 we find that, while there is nothing unusual in the data from preceding days, the opposite is true following the attacks. During most of September 11, 12, and 13 there is a trend indicating correlated behavior among the eggs. The persistence and strength of the trend is unique in the four-year GCP database.

The second formal prediction addressed the variability of scores (the sample variance, s^2) for each second among the 37 eggs generating data on September 11. We predicted large fluctuations, and found increased variance among the individual eggs at the beginning followed by low variance after the intensely disturbing events. The idea was that we would see a degree of variability in the data that might correspond to the reactions of people engaged by this uniquely powerful emotional imposition. As Figure 2 shows, the variance exhibits normal random fluctuation around the horizontal line on the days before and after the attacks, but early on September 11, it takes on a steep and persistent rise, representing a consistent excess of variance. This continues until about 11:00, and shortly thereafter, a long period begins during which the data show an equally strong and persistent decrease of variance. A comparison can be made with algorithmic pseudo-random data plotted in the same format. In contrast to the real data, there are no long-sustained periods of strong deviation in the pseudo data. A permutation analysis provides an estimate for the probability of the extreme excursion in the actual data of $p = 0.0009$, based on 10,000 iterations. The corresponding permutation p-value for the control data is 0.756.

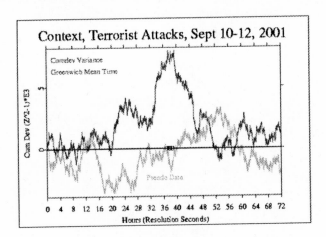

Cumulative deviation of variance across eggs for each second September 10-12, 2001. Events in the terrorist attack are marked with rectangles on the zero line. The curve labeled "Pseudo Data" shows controls from a pseudo-random clone data set.

The formal hypothesis testing is augmented by exploratory analyses that add breadth and depth to the picture. Interpreted carefully, they help understand the data, and they are a primary source for future analytical questions. Several people have contributed independent assessments of the GCP data. For example, Dean Radin produced a variety of analyses of the September 11 events, including an examination of the effect of location, and a completely general correlation with a measure of news intensity (Radin, 2001, 2002).

Peter Bancel focused on the correlation of the eggs' output over time. He computed the autocorrelation function of the second-by-second inter-egg variance using Fourier techniques. This represents the degree of predictability within the composite data sequence over a range of time intervals. The results indicated that the data were strongly autocorrelated during a substantial portion of the day. This is evidence that a common external source was partially defining the output of the REG devices on September 11 (Nelson, et al., 2002).

These examples give an idea of the kinds of events we have looked at, and the results of the focused analyses, but they should be considered in a larger context. In a sense, each individual prediction is another replication of the basic experiment, and the full database is a concatenation of many separate pieces of evidence for the general hypothesis. We have made 130 formal predictions over a four-year period, and the individual results need to be cumulated over time to provide a summary of the GCP experiment as a whole. Figure 3 shows the progressively growing excess of the χ^2s over their corresponding degrees of freedom for 130 analyses. It culminates in a composite probability for the whole array of events that is on the order of a few parts in a million. The dotted lines show various probability envelopes for the cumulative deviation from chance expectation, which is a horizontal trend at zero. The data curve would tend to fall inside these envelopes if only chance were operating.

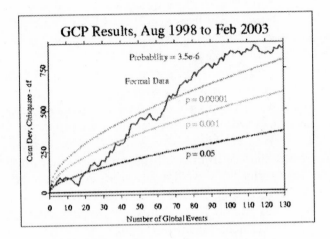

Overall results for 130 formal experiments over the past four years. The data curve shows the cumulative deviation from chance expectation of the individual "bottom line" χ^2s for the separate events. Expectation is shown as the horizontal line at zero. Dotted curves show the chance probability envelopes.

A variety of tables and graphical displays on the GCP Web site give up-to-date summaries of the formal results (Nelson, 1998c). Most of the table entries contain a link to a complete description of the detailed analysis for the event, and in many cases, further explorations and investigations that provide illuminating context for the formal prediction.

Discussion

The accumulating evidence for an anomalous effect on the GCP's network of REG devices placed around the world is strong. Multiple, independent analyses show structure in data that should be genuinely random. There is a small but highly significant statistical deviation from theoretical expectation for the REG outputs, integrated across all the active devices, and it is correlated with global events identified by experimenters without knowledge of the data or results. We do not have a theoretical understanding or a robust interpretation, but several potential explanations for the results may be considered.

Perhaps the first proposals that come to mind are spurious physical effects. For example on a day like September 11, we could speculate that some combination of extraordinary stresses on the power grid, or unusual electromagnetic fields, or huge increases in mobile phone usage might have altered the REG outputs. Such influences would center on New York and Washington, of course, but the eggs' average distance from New York is more than 4000 miles (~6400 km), and the anomalous effects are broadly distributed across the network. In addition, the design of the research-grade instruments includes both physical shielding and a logic stage that literally excludes first-order biasing from electromagnetic or other physical causes. Finally, empirical studies show no diurnal variation of inter-egg correlation to correspond with the strong diurnal fluctuations of natural and manmade electromagnetic fields (Radin, 2002). Thus, we are forced to look elsewhere for the source of the induced structure.

One way to think of these unexpected correlations is to consider the possibility that the instruments actually have captured the reaction of an inchoate global consciousness. The network was built to do just that: to see whether we could gather evidence for effects of a communal, shared mind in which we are participants even if we don't know it. Groups of people, including the group that is the whole world, have a place in consciousness space, and under special circumstances they—or we—become a stronger presence. Based on experimental evidence that both individuals and groups manifest something suggestive of a consciousness field, the GCP grew out of the hypothesis that there could be a global consciousness capable of the same thing. Pursuing this speculation, we could envision an integrated global mind that pays attention to events that inspire strong coherence of attention and feeling among its constituents. Perhaps a useful image is an infant just beginning to develop an integrated awareness, but already manifesting recognizable emotions in response to the enveloping comfort of cuddling or the intense discomfort of pain.

The hypothesis we set out to test is that the REG devices we use may respond to the concerted effect of large numbers of people turning their attention in one direction, becoming deeply absorbed in one focus. There are alternatives to such an explanation of the deviations as an effect of communal consciousness, including that the experimenters themselves might be the source of anomalous effects. This is a viable hypothesis according to professional parapsychologists (White, 1976), and we can accept the possibility that such an "experimenter effect" may contribute to the overall result. The characteristics of the individual events and their correlated outcomes, however, suggest that a broader and more comprehensive source is a major contributor. Either of these models—communal consciousness or experimenter effect—begs for an interaction mechanism. One suggestion is to co-opt the essential qualities of field theory for a "consciousness field" that carries information (Nelson, 1999). This is not completely out of touch with models in physics, and might be formalized in terms of David Bohm's concept of "active information" (Bohm, 1980). Other efforts to describe a mechanism that could produce the anomalous results in these experiments draw on the "observer" requirements of quantum theory. The idea is that future observation collapses a superposition of possibilities into a state that may represent reality (Schmidt, 1982; Walker, 2000). A recent formalization of this approach argues that no major changes to physical theory are required to address anomalous effects of consciousness (Shoup, 2001).

While there are viable alternative explanations for the GCP effects, the anomalous correlation is not a mistake or a misreading. It can be interpreted as a confirmation of the hypothesis that the eggs' behavior is affected by global events and our reactions to them. This is startling in scientific terms because we do not have widely accepted models that accommodate such an interpretation of the data. More important than the scientific interpretation, however, may be the question of meaning. What shall we learn, and what should we do in the face of evidence that we may be part of a global consciousness? Of course, this is not a new idea or a novel question. The results from this scientific study are an apparent manifestation of the ancient idea that we are all interconnected, and that what we think and feel has effects everywhere in the world. The discovery of patterns in the GCP data that appear to reflect our shared state of mind during great celebrations, or our shock and dismay when the social fabric is torn, implies that these insensate but labile electronic random generators can "see" the effect of massive, shared emotion and attention. The challenges posed by this unexplained effect are great, but it may be an unexpected source of incisive questions about the span of human consciousness.

Acknowledgments

The Global Consciousness Project would not exist except for the immense contributions of Greg Nelson and John Walker, who created the architecture and the sophisticated software. Paul Bethke ported the egg software to Windows, thus broadening the network. Dean Radin, Dick Bierman, Jiri Wackermann, and others in the planning group contributed ideas and experience. Rick Berger helped to create a comprehensive Web site to make the project available to the public. The project also would not exist but for the commitment of time, resources, and good will from all the egg hosts. Our financial support comes from individuals including Charles Overby, Tony Cohen, Reinhilde Nelson, Michael Heany, Alexander Imich, Richard Adams, Richard Wallace, Anna Capasso, Michael Breland, Joseph Giove, and an anonymous donor. The Institute of Noetic Sciences provides logistical support as a non-profit home for the project, and the Lifebridge Foundation has provided generous support for documentation of the GCP. Finally, there are very many friends of the EGG project whose good will, interest, and empathy open a necessary niche in consciousness space.

References

1.   Bohm, D. (1980). Wholeness and the Implicate Order. Boston: Routledge & Kegan Paul.
2.   Crawford, C. C., Jonas, W. B., Nelson, R., & Wirkus, M. (2003). Alterations in Random Event Measures Associated with a Healing Practice, *Journal of Alternative and Complementary Medicine*, 9(3): 345—333.
3.   Jahn, R. G., Dunne, B. J., Nelson, R. D., Dobyns, Y. H., & Bradish, G. J. (1997). Correlations of random binary sequences with pre-stated operator intention: a review of a 12-year program. *Journal of Scientific Exploration, 11,* 345-367
4.   Nelson, R., Boesch, H., Boller, E., Dobyns, Y., Houtkooper, J., Lettieri, A., Radin, D., Russek, L., Schwartz, G., & Wesch, J. (1998b). Global resonance of consciousness: Princess Diana and Mother Teresa. *Electronic Journal for Anomalous Phenomena, eJAP.* Retrieved October 28, 2001, from the World Wide Web: http://www.psy.uva.nl/eJAP.

5. Nelson, R. D. (1998c). *The Global Consciousness Project.* Retrieved June 9, 2003, from the World Wide Web: http://noosphere.princeton.edu.

6. Nelson, R. D. (1999). *The Physical Basis of Intentional Healing Systems.* Technical Report PEAR 99001. Princeton Engineering Anomalies Research, Princeton University, Princeton, NJ.

7. Nelson, R. D. (2001a). Correlation of global events with REG data: an internet-based, nonlocal anomalies experiment. *The Journal of Parapsychology, 65,* 247-271.

8. Nelson, R. D. (2001b). *Exploratory Studies: The Global Consciousness Project.* Retrieved June 9, 2003, from the World Wide Web: http://noosphere.princeton.edu/res.informal.html.

9. Nelson, R. D., Bradish, G. J., Dobyns, Y. H., Dunne, B. J., & Jahn, R. G. (1996). FieldREG anomalies in group situations. *Journal of Scientific Exploration, 10,* 111-141.

10. Nelson, R. D., Jahn, R. G., Dunne, B. J., Dobyns, Y. H., & Bradish, G. J. (1998a). FieldREG II: consciousness field effects: replications and explorations. *Journal of Scientific Exploration, 12,* 425-454.

11. Nelson, R. D., Radin, D. I., Shoup, R., & Bancel, P. A. (2002). Correlations of continuous random data with major world events. *Foundations of Physics Letters, 15(6) 537-550.*

12. Radin, D. I. (2001). *Global Consciousness Project: Analysis for September 11, 2001.* Retrieved June 9, 2003, from the World Wide Web: http://noosphere.princeton.edu/dean/wtc0921.html.

13. Radin, D. I. (2002). Evidence for relationships between random physical events and world news. *Journal of Scientific Exploration,* in press.

14. Radin, D. I., & Nelson, R. D. (1989). Evidence for consciousness-related anomalies in random physical systems. *Foundations of Physics, 19,* 1414-1499.

15. Radin D. I. & Yount, G.. Healing Intent by Johrei Practicioners, Personal communication, 2003.

16. Schmidt, H. (1982). Collapse of the state vector and psychokinetic effects. *Foundations of Physics, 12,* 565-581.

17. Shoup, R. (2001b). Anomalies and constraints: can clairvoyance, precognition, and psychokinesis be accommodated within known physics? *Journal of Scientific Exploration, 16,* 3-18.

18. Walker, E. H. (2000). *The Physics of Consciousness.* Boulder: Perseus Publishing.

19. White, R. (1976). The limits of experimenter influence on psi tests. Can any be set? *Journal of the American Society for Psychical Research, 70,* 333-370.

SUFI RAPID WOUND HEALING: A CASE REPORT

Howard Hall, Ph.D., Psy.D.
Case Western Reserve University and
Rainbow Babies and Children's Hospital
Cleveland, Ohio
Howard.Hall@uhhs.com

Introduction

Very little scientific attention has been paid to spiritual healing approaches from the Middle East. Rapid healing of "Deliberately Caused Bodily Damage" (DCBD) has been reported by a Middle Eastern Sufi (Islamic mysticism) school known as Tariqa, Casnazaniyyah, an Arabic-Kurdish name meaning "the way of the secret that is known to no one". [1-5] Followers (dervishes) of this school have been observed demonstrating instantaneous healing of deliberately caused bodily damage. For example, dervishes have inserted a variety of sharp instruments such as spikes and skewers into their bodies, hammered daggers into the skull bone and clavicle; and chewed and swallowed glass and sharp razor blades without harm to the body and with complete control over pain, bleeding, infection, as well as rapid wound healing within 4-10 seconds. [1-3] These unusual healing phenomena have also been noted to be reproduced under controlled laboratory conditions and do not appear to be similar to hypnosis. [1-3] An interesting aspect of this phenomenon is that such extraordinary abilities are allegedly accessible to anyone and not restricted to only a few talented individuals who have spent years in special training. [1-3] The ability to have rapid healing from deliberately caused injury, according to the Casnazaniyyah School, is allegedly based on a spiritual link between the practitioner and the Shaikh, who gives permission for such a demonstration. [4]

Similar observations of Deliberately Caused Bodily Damage phenomena have been observed in various parts of the world in a variety of religious and non-religious contexts. [4, 6] For example, trance surgeons in Brazil have employed sharp instruments to cut, pierce, or inject substances into a patient's body for therapeutic purposes. Laboratory EEG investigation of trance surgeons have observed that this "state of spirit possession" for the healers was associated with a hyper-aroused brain state (waves in the 30-50 Hz band).[6] Unfortunately, there has been very little scientific attention given to the investigation of these rapid healing claims in the United States. Even worse, such claims for extraordinary healing abilities have been met with scorn and have even been challenged by so-called skeptic groups (Committee for the Scientific Investigation of Claims of the Paranormal (CSCIOP)) who offer monetary incentives to discredit such claims in unscientific and dangerous settings.[7,8] (See Dossey, 1999 and Fatoohi, 1999 for a response).[9,10] Clearly what is needed in this area is a demonstration of such rapid wound healing within a Western medical setting. The scientific study of such spiritually based healing approaches, holds much promise for addressing some of today's most serious medical issues as well as providing some empirical bases for spiritual claims.

The investigation of such unusual healing phenomena raises the questions of what should be measured within a scientific context? Would standard measures of brain and immune activity be associated with changes in rapid wound healing? On the other hand, should standard measures, such as EEG activity, be used in less standard ways? Would high frequency EEG activity need to be examined for hyper aroused brain states? Would new approaches, such as the examination of changes in the output of random event generators (REG), be needed to detect "fields of consciousness"?

Case Report

With the support of the Kairos Foundation of Wilmette, Illinois, a Sufi practitioner (J.H) was invited from the Middle East, to a local radiology facility in Cleveland, Ohio July 1, 1999. This person had permission from the Shaikh of his Sufi school to perform a demonstration of rapid wound healing following the insertion of an unsterilized metal skewer, 0.38 centimeters thick and approximately 13 centimeters long, while being videotaped by a film crew, and in the presence of a number of scientists and healthcare professionals. This was apparently the first demonstration from this Sufi School in the United States. The practitioner consented to sign a release of liability for the medical facility and personnel against claims from possible injuries that might occur. Emergency medical technicians were present. The major goal of this demonstration was to document the authenticity of rapid wound healing following a deliberately caused injury in a medical setting.

Method

The demonstration was also conducted with radiological, immunological, EEG evaluations, and a zener noise diode random event generator (similar to the one employed at Princeton University by Dr. Robert Jahn and colleagues). Based on previous studies in Brazil with healer-mediums engaged in quasi-surgical practices, it was hypothesized that DCBD would be accompanied by alterations in brain waves and effects on random event generators. The alterations in brain waves found with the Brazilian healer-mediums showed statistically significant enhancement of broadband 40 Hz brain rhythms. [6] A statistically significant deviations from random behavior in random event generators was found, run covertly while the Brazilian healer-mediums were in trance. This methodology was developed by Robert Jahn and Associates at the Princeton Engineering Anomalies Research Laboratory (PEAR). [11, 12] Such energy fields have been considered as theoretically associated with the rapid wound healing. [6]

EEG

Nineteen-channel EEGs (International 10-20 System) were recorded during baseline resting conditions, while the dervish inserted the skewer through his cheek, and immediately after removing the instrument. A Neurosearch—24 topographic brain mapping system was employed (Lexicor Medical Technology, Boulder, CO). Electrode application was accomplished with an elasticized electrode cap; electrode impedances were 5,000 ohms or less. Data were visually edited, and all epochs containing artifacts such as those due to eye blinks, scalp muscle activity, and bodily movements of the subject were excluded from further analysis.

Random Event Generator

Without informing the dervish, an electronic random event generator employing Zener noise diodes, was run plugged into the serial port of a computer. The distribution of binary digits was tested for possible significant deviations from random behavior. Data were acquired before and after the self-insertion, as well as during the experimental condition.

Immunology

Prior to the insertion of the skewer, and about one hour after the piercing, blood was collected from the practitioner and three controls for an immunological analysis of the percent change in CD4, CD8 and total T cell counts. Flow Cytometry: Four-color direct immunofluorescent staining with monoclonal antibodies was performed on aliquots of heparinized peripheral blood collected from each participant group. Blood was processed within twelve hours of collection. All monoclonal antibodies (mAbs) used in this study were purchased from Becton Dickinson Immunocytometry Systems (BDIS), San Jose, California. Antibody staining was performed on 200 microliters of whole blood as described by the manufacturers. In all assays four-color analysis was performed. In general, 10,000 lymphocyte-gated cells were analyzed in a FACScalibur (BDIS) flow cytometer using CELLQUEST (BDIS) and PAINT-A-GATE software. Non-specific staining was assessed by the use of fluorochrome-conjugated monoclonal mouse immunoglobulins (BDIS).

Results

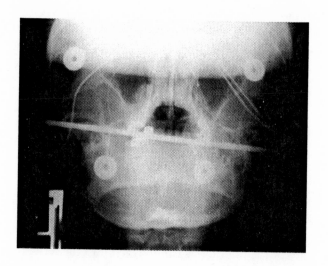

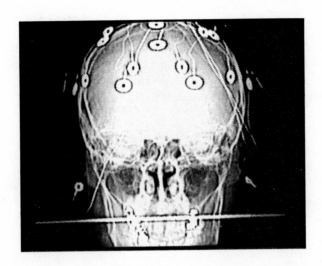

Radiological images were done while the skewer was inserted (Figure 1). Axial CT images through the lower mandibular region showed artifact from dental metal (Figure 2). In addition, there was a horizontally oriented metallic bar which elevated the left lateral soft tissues just anterior to the muscles of mastication. There was no associated underlying mass. A single frontal fluoroscopic image showed a presence of EEG leads over the maxilla and mandibular regions (Figure 3). There was a transverse metal superimposed extending from the soft tissues on the right through to the left without interval break.

Because of movement and scalp muscle artifacts throughout the experimental, self-insertion condition, it was impossible to assess the EEG for the hypothesized 40 Hz brain rhythms. The frequency spectrum of scalp muscle discharge overlaps the 40 Hz EEG frequency band of interest. However, during the post-insertion period compared to initial baseline measurements, there was more power in the theta band (4.0-8.0Hz) at all electrode sites. The average power was 23.32 micro volts squared compared to 19.79 micro volts squared, an increase of 17.84%. Statistical significance was not assessed.

The random event generator during baseline periods did not differ significantly from random behavior. However, during the self-insertion condition, there was a trend toward significant non-randomness. The chi-square equaled 3.052, d f = 1, p = approximately .07.

Discussion

The behavior of the random event generator was in the predicted direction of non-randomness. This has been interpreted by our and the PEAR laboratories as being associated with states of heightened attention and emotion. Further, PEAR has proposed that a "field of consciousness" is associated with such non-randomness.

Unfortunately, the 40 Hz brain wave hypothesis was not testable because of the excessive amount of scalp artifact and so awaits further exploration. The presence of increased theta rhythms after the insertion condition (and a slight decrease in average alpha power) suggests a mild hypo-aroused altered state of consciousness.

The Sufi performing this feat was doing so for the first time. It would seem possible that with further practice or by testing more experienced subjects, it may be feasible to obtain EEG data without large amounts of scalp artifact. Because the subject reported no perceived pain during the self-insertion, preliminary relaxation exercises might eliminate all or most of the artifact. This would enable us to test the 40 Hz hypothesis definitively. Clearly, further work is indicated.

The immunology did not reveal any major difference between the Sufi practitioner and the controls. In the practitioner the increase in CD4 and decrease in CD8 resulted in no actual change in the T cell compartment. In control 2 no change was observed either in CD4, CD8 or total T cell counts. In control 3 there was a mild increase in CD4 percentage, greater than the decrease in CD8's resulting in a net increase in the total T cell compartment. In control 4, both CD4 and CD8 populations increased also resulting in a net increase of total T cell populations. These data suggest that the variation found in the practitioner was not different from normal controls.

The radiological film documented that the skewer had actually penetrated both cheeks, thus addressing skeptic groups that such practices are the result of fakery. Following the removal of the skewer there was a slight trickle of blood which stopped with compression of clean gauze to the cheek. The physicians and scientists present documented that the wound healed rapidly within a few moments. The practitioner also reported that there was no pain associated with the insertion or removal of the metal skewer.

This demonstration was conducted outside of the traditional religious context, where chanting, drumming, and head movements are generally part of the ceremony when done in the Middle East. Thus, our case study argues against the necessity of a religious context with its accompanying state of consciousness being important for the successful out come of such a demonstration. According to the records of the Major School of Tariqa, the Cleveland case study demonstrated for the first time that DCBD could be done at such a large distance separating the dervish from the Master. Never before had such a demonstration taken place where the dervish was thousands of miles away from the energy source and yet still able to exhibit the paranormal features characteristic of DCBD phenomena. Before this project, the farthest distance separating the Master from the dervish performing DCBD was only a few hundred miles. This would suggest that this is a very robust phenomenon independent of the distance separating its source and the scene where the DCBD phenomena occurs.

It should also be pointed out that the skewer stayed in the dervish's cheeks for more than thirty-five minutes. There is no such record at the Major School of Tariqa of implements remaining in the body for that length of time. Field observations have shown that the maximum time for such implements to stay in the human body has been about a half minute. Thus, this case study argues against the necessity of a very brief piercing period for a successful outcome of DCBD. Furthermore, the dervish of this demonstration reported that there was no pain associated with this piercing, there was minimal bleeding and no post procedure infection. It should not be overlooked that about a half hour after the completion of the demonstration, the dervish, along with seven other people who witnessed the DCBD event, had dinner together.

Such a demonstration has implications for healing and pain control for a variety of medical conditions. From an evidence-based perspective, this Sufi paradigm has the benefit of allowing for the scientific investigation of "paranormal" or spiritually based healing phenomena of rapid wound healing. This research can be conducted within a western setting with scientific measurements. Replicated of such investigations is needed.

References

1. Hussein, J.N., Fatoohi, L., Al-Dargazelli, S., Almuchtar, N. (1994a). The deliberately caused bodily damage phenomena: Mind, body, energy or what? <u>International Journal of Alternative and Complementary Medicine</u>, <u>12</u> (9), 9-11.
2. Hussein, J.N., Fatoohi, L., Al-Dargazelli, S., Almuchtar, N. (1994b). The deliberately caused bodily damage phenomena: Mind, body, energy or

what? International Journal of Alternative and Complementary Medicine, 12 (10), 21-24.

3. Hussein, J.N., Fatoohi, L., Al-Dargazelli, S., Almuchtar, N. (1994c). The deliberately caused bodily damage phenomena: Mind, body, energy or what? International Journal of Alternative and Complementary Medicine, 12 (11), 25-28.

4. Hussein, J.N., Fatoohi, L.J., Hall, H.R. & Al-Dargazelli, S. (1997). Deliberately caused bodily damage phenomena. Journal of the Society for Psychical Research, 62, (849), 97-113.

5. Dossey, L. (1998). Deliberately caused bodily damage. Alternative Therapies, 4 (5), 11-111.

6. Don, N.S. & Moura, G. (2000). Trance surgery in Brazil. Alternative Therapies in Health and Medicine, 6 (4): 39-48.

7. Mulacz, W.P. (1998). Deliberately caused bodily damage (DCBD) phenomena: A different perspective. Journal of the Society for Psychical Research, 62 (852), 434-444.

8. Posner, G. (accessed April 20, 1998) Taking a stab at a paranormal claim. Available at: <http://www.csicop.org/sb/9509/posner.html>

9. Dossey, L. (1999). Response to Peter Mulacz (Letter to the editor). Journal of the Society for Psychical Research, 63 (856), 246-250.

10. Fatoohi, L. (1999). Response to Peter Mulacz (Letter to the editor). Journal of the Society for Psychical Research, 63 (855), 179-181.

11. Nelson, R.D., Bradish, G.J., Dobyns, Y.H., Dunne, B.J., Jahn, R.G. (1996). FieldREG anomolies in group situations. Journal of Scientific Exploration, 10 (1), 111-141.

12. Nelson, R.D., Bradish, G.J., Dobyns, Y.H., Dunne, B.J., Jahn, R.G. (1998). FieldREG II: Consciousness field effects: Replications and explorations. Journal of Scientific Exploration, 12 (3), 425-454.

THE SCIENCE OF WHOLE PERSON HEALING

Research Data Summary on Qigong and the Differentiation of Qi into Body Pathways, the Physiology and Properties of Mind/Body Wholeness and its Clinical Application to Disease and Athletics

Phillip Shinnick. Ph.D., M.P.A., L.Ac.
Director
The Research Institute of Global Physiology, Behavior and Treatment, Inc.
1070 Park Ave
NY, NY 10128
212 426 3744
Phillip@pbtinstitute.org

Abstract

Research on Qigong, a term used for a variety of traditional Chinese energy exercises, cultivation and therapies (Chen 2003), has occurred primarily in China. A summary of scientific approaches and measurements to Qigong is provided and a reference to the Qigong Institutes' data base of scientific studies. A clinical study of 400 subjects is provided to show that the propagation of Qi from internal organs is also informational by deviating from common understandings of normal pathways under aberrant conditions. The physiology and properties of meditation by a Master is provided. A study of Chronic Heart Disease tests the physiologic previously measured state of the brain, blood lactate and oxygen consumption in a synchronized state of meditation in a single case study of self help in an acute condition. Self help practices of Qigong helped heat regulation while Zen meditation helped mind disturbances and breathe regulation dyspnea. With conscious intention to heal, the emission of Qi is possible for a number of therapies and practices. Studies of Qigong Masters have shown this. In athletics, conscious intention has lead to extraordinary performances while Qigong practices are important for training and injury prevention. These same practices are helpful in disease and enrich the culture.

A Brief History: Unifying all the Sciences of Man for Healing

The organization of this paper does not reflect the chronology of its development. For example, what is known about Qi from signal detectors was not available when this study started. At first, in 1985, I conducted a series of experiments resulting in a protocol for 400 cases examining the theory that organs had energy or Qi pathways on the outside of the body applying the Bi-Digital O-Ring Imaging Test.[1] The purpose was to see if there was a Qi system apart from a Western science understanding of a dermatome. Concomitant to this Simon Freed, Ph.D. and I tried to measure the global physiologic characteristics of Wholeness/synchronization during meditation and translate these into general properties associated with the deepest state of meditation. This became much easier for us by looking at parallel analogous inorganic matter when subjected to low temperature. Science has already examined state changes in molecules at low temperature for seventy years and the macro-molecule occupying a macro-cell of lowest energy in Bose Einstein statistics and the theoretical "condensate' quantum liquid, possessing superfluity have been confirmed and authenticated experimentally.[2]

Late in this period Dr. Freed (at 95) suffered an acute attack of his underlying condition of Chronic Heart Disease. We decided to use his case as a way to

---

1. Shinnick P (2003) Med Acu: J Phy Phy. May
2. Shinnick P Freed S Possible "Qi", the Life Energy, in Organic Physiologic State of Ch'an (or Zen) Buddism and Inorganic State of Superfluid Helium. (Under Review)

measure and treat with these techniques of meditation and qigong in his immediate fragmented diseased state. We were researchers at the Heart Disease Research Foundation. In other words we now knew something about the physiology of Wholeness but what about attempting to change a fragmented or diseased state into a whole state with self help. Midway through the study Dr. Freed experienced some remarkable results from the meditation and Qigong. We decided to set up a research institute to study global physiologic characteristics and behavior combining Occidental and Oriental treatment. He died three months later of cancer of the esophagus.

Ken Sancier, Ph.D had been a student of Dr. Freed at Brookhaven National Lab (later, Dr. Sancier became a research scientist at Stanford University) and he joined our effort to establish a research institute. We set up two research institutes and supported another. Dr. Sancier founded the Qigong Institute and helped us incorporate the Research Institute of Global Physiology, Behavior and Treatment, Inc. (PBT) which gave funds to the Qigong Institute in its inception. The Qigong Institute Database now has thousands of references. Dr. Sancier recommended that the PBT work with Kevin Chen Ph.D., M.P.H. Initially, the PBT financially supported Dr. Chen's proposed pilot study on the inhibitory effects of external Qi emission on transplanted hepatocarcinaoma in mice. Then Dr. Chen and Qigong Master Behui He founded the World Institute of Self Help and I joined as a trustee. The PBT supported financially WISH's conference, The First World Symposium on Self-Healing and Consciousness Power in 2001. http;//www.wishus.org WISH was established in response to the fact that many chronic disease are not curable with modern medicine, and that many drugs used to treat these disease have long lasting side effects. WISH provides training in self-help internal Qigong, particularly for cancer patients.

William Tiller, Ph.D., our scientific advisor, pointed out what was needed was not duplication of what had already been done (that Qigong can be measured or even that it works on biological materials) but a summary of all the research already finished in China on Qigong. Dr. Chen finished his first effort the fall of 2002 and I summarize here.

Athletics and Energy

Rustum Roy, Ph.D. and Effie Chow, Ph.D., RN. have urged me to incorporate my own athletic background within the framework of what has been learned about qi and energy in the last few decades. My understanding of athletics came from recording into a daily journal with as many variables as possible; diet, intensity level, technique, heart rate, emotional state, breath, sickness, competitive record, and particulars about the workout itself. I started yoga and meditation 35 years ago and combined this with more traditional techniques of training in my sport. I added a new sport, swimming (15 years ago), and new energy exercises, Gung Fu (15 years ago), and Tai Chi Chuan (28 years ago.) aother The forms of meditation besides Zen which I have practised since 1964 are Siddha (19 years ago), and Tibetan meditation (22 years ago.)

At various times I have been on the U.S. Olympic team, a U.S. team captain in track and field, a coach, a college athletic director, a founder of Sports Science at Rutgers University and a sports medicine doctor. I worked at the Center for Dance and Sports Medicine in New York for fifteen years. I serve on an International Olympic Committee on peace and sport.

The ancient tradition of Olympic competition included Ekkiheria (a sacred truce during the Games establishing a strong peace initiative during the Games) combined with the development of literature, poetry, art and music. This was the ancient tradition of the Olympics; many of us Olympians went to Mt. Olympus and gathering around the altar of Zeus to pledge and hear the ancient Greek recitation for athletics, peace and culture.

Science has developed all sorts of performance enhancing and restorative drugs which have undermined the necessity to master mind/body unity. Modern science wants to find a way to create a modern superman through drugs, without culture, without soul, stamped on the forehead with a manufacturing logo.

The best promise against what modern science has to offer athletes is to understand culture always has to be renewed with each new generation and offer a science which has real value to the individual; to help liberate from ill-health, disease, suffering, pain and emotional turmoil and create an athletics, through training and performing, which attempts to synchronized the mind and body and calm the mind for Wholeness. Voluntary and involuntary meditation can assist athletics in this higher endeavor as will be shown.

Many of my understandings of energy have come from training and competition which require the integration of all aspects of the personality—-the mind, body and spirit.

Overview

Scientist in the U.S. are attempting to prove to other scientists that Qi exists and devising ways to convince other scientists to study this phenomenon. Other cultures, like China, have studied Qigong since the late 70's resulting in a proliferation of studies after early pilot studies showed qi can be measured. The summary of Qigong research from 1977 to the present was made available through the Qigong Institutes' Database compiled by Dr. Sancier and available for researcher at the Qigong Institute website http://www.qigonginstitute.org. Dr. Chen used this database and many of the studies he presents he translated from Chinese.[3]

Definition of Qigong and Methodological Restrictions

First, we must come to an understanding of a definition of Qigong. Qigong is a term used for a variety of traditional Chinese energy exercises, cultivation and therapies, as suggested by Dr. Chen.

The Lin definition of Qigong is a good start for as a way for a template of common understanding.

> Qigong is the self—training method or process through which cultivation of qi (vital energy) and yi (intention and consciousness) achieves optimal state of both mind and body (Lin1977a)

Furthermore the Chinese Society of Qigong Science definition:

> The distant and directional effects produced by well trained Qigong practitioner under the Qigong state.

Internal qi is for self help and health and external qi is for healing others. This external qi implies three characteristics, qi exists only when a practitioner enters into the qigong state of mind, the qi can travel a distance (affecting heat, light, electricity, magnetic waves, radiation and other signals), and qi is directional depending upon the intention and focus of the practitioner.

---

3. Kevin C An Analytic Review of Studies on Measuring Effects of External Qi in China. (Under review)

Certain methodological restrictions result from research experience. Not all qigong practitioners can emit qi and ones that can may not at certain times. Qigong practitioners can affect the instruments of measurement so a certain understanding of the research design may be important for the practitioner but not necessarily where or how the measurement instrument works. Repeated trails are important because of inconsistencies.

The major methods of measuring external qi effects according to Chen's research are the following detectors, 1) physical signal detectors (light, electricity, heat, sound, magnetism) 2) Chemical dynamics methods (reactions) 3) biological materials detectors (in vitro cells, DNA synthesis, Vitamins, cancer cells, organic matter such as a leaf, etc.) 4), animal studies (because of psychological factors) in diseased states (i.e. changes in cancer cell growth rate) and healthy states (life span), 5) human studies in diseased states and detectors for repair of tissue, bones, etc. and the qi affect.

Major Methods of Measuring EQ (emitted qi) and Results

Physical Signal Detectors
Far-infrared detector.

Utilized a far-infrared detector (8-14 mµ). A modified far-infrared radiation was detected at a distance of 50 cm from the palm of a Qigong practitioner; with modification as high as 80% at the frequency of 0.3 Hz. This contrasted with the control group (non-qigong subject), which showed almost no difference for the infrared radiation itself in wavelength or intensity. The specificity is in the modification of frequency. The results of similar tests to another Qigong healer showed that there was no difference in the amplitude modification, but a difference in frequency modification, reflecting the different characteristics of EQ frequencies emitted by practitioners trained in different qigong methods.

AGA thermo gram.

An AGA thermogram can display the entire procedure of qi emission by reading the thermal flow moving from his arm to his palm and finally to his finger tips. Then, the surface temperature of the patient's afflicted area, although one meter away from the healer was raised by 3°C. Meanwhile, when a control subject was introduced in this study, they found that correlated changes could be induced on the corresponding parts of a non-Qigong practitioner when standing next to the qigong healer, but not without the qigong healer present.

GE micro-pressure detector (Placed from 0.5m to 2m)

Ge micro-pressure detectors were placed at the distance of 0.5, 1.0, 1.5, and 2.0 meters from the qigong practitioner. The qigong practitioner emitted *qi* toward the target (Ge germanium detector) through two of his fingers. At first, there was no recorded signal and the qigong healer reported some mental difficulty in pinpointing the target for *qi* emission. However, after some practice, he could pinpoint the target and repeatedly produced some signals on the micro-pressure detectors. They recorded many micro-pressure signals from the Ge detector at all four distances with a little time lag, which they explained as the reflection of the unspecified particle flow from EQ. Maybe the qigong healer might tire after a number of *qi* emissions and the signals might then become weaker and weaker in this situation. Supporting this idea was the fact that after the qigong healer ate something substantial, the signal would again be strong.

8 mm microwave radiation meter.

With an 8 mm microwave radiation meter, they used the near field (20-40 cm to antenna) to test the EQ and the far field (4 to 5 meters to antenna) as the point of reference. They conducted 50 trials, 28 of which have formal records of radiation curve. Twenty-two of these trials have significant increases in the wavelength to above 10 mm during the period of *qi* emission.

Infrasonic Sound Detector (Denmark B-K Corp's Infrasonic Sound detector 1,3,5,6,10 or 40 cm distance)

The subjects included 10 qigong healers (aged 28-61) and 10 controls (non-qigong practitioners, aged 17-41). The test was performed in a soundproof lab with baseline noise less than 40 dB. The testing equipment was Denmark B-K Corp's Infrasonic Sound Detector. During the test, each subject was required to sit in a comfortable position, relax lightly close his eyes. The distance between the sound sensor and the testing point was at 1, 3, 5, 6, 10, and 40 cm. The tested acupoints included "Laogong" (on the palm), "Baihui" (on the top of the head), and "Mingmen" (at center of the back near the waist). The subject was instructed to focus his attention on the tested acupoints during the examination. The test results were derived from testing each point at all of the specific distances. The qigong group had recorded significantly higher infrasonic sound pressure than the control group (p < .001). The range of infrasonic sound pressure detected for the control group were between 40.6 and 43.6 dB decreasing as the distance increased, while the range of infrasonic sound pressure detected for qigong group were between 48.8 and 54.7 dB, and was not effected by the distance to sensor. This study provided some support to the qigong theory of "Where the intention goes, the *qi* goes".

Chemical Dynamic Methods Using Qigong with Yi or intention and directionality

Glucose Oxidase luminal
Glucose +O2————>Glucose Acid + H2O2[→Fluorescence→Photoelectron Current]

Glucose is made of a 5 hydroxyl group and 1 aldehyde group, after oxidizing reaction, aldehyde group becomes carboxyl group (organic acid). The reaction speed is accelerated after Qigong by 400%. The photoelectron current can be measured and reaction speed measured when luminal is mixed with hydrogen peroxide.

H2O2————→H2O + O2

Hydrogen peroxide is an oxidizer and under the influence of EQ decomposes, just measure the oxygen.

Strong Light
C6H14 +Br2———————--→ C6H13Br + HBr

Under a strong light Hexane and Bromine will produce bromohexane and hydrogen bromide. Bromine has a deep blood color with similar properties as Chlorine. The acceleration of reaction happens faster after Qigong, with no strong light, with the normal brown (fading from deep bloods red) left after the reaction fades even more.

Detector Using Biological Materials

Biological material, such as individual cells (in vitro) and biological tissues, are assumed to possess vital energy themselves, and are especially sensitive to the EQ emitted by qigong practitioners; the concept of a biological detector has existed for a long time.

Liver cancer cell and lung cancer cell cultures, DNA synthesis and DPPC liposomes

Chinese researcher reported a strong effect from EQ on liver cancer cell (BEL-7402) and lung cancer cell cultures (SPC-A), on the cells of living organisms, on the blood plasma eAMP, on the structure and pharmaceutical characteristics of Vitamin C, on the DNA synthesis and living cycles of liver cancer cells and that EQ, on structural changes in water and aqueous solutions, on the phase behavior of dipalmitoyl phosphatidyl choline (DPPC) liposomes and enables the growth of Fab protein crystals. As well, on the inhibition growth of the microstructure of E-coli bacteria and tumor cells in mice, on the inhibitory growth of hepatitis B virus and of human liver cancer cells.

Using tree leaves to detect the effect of EQ is one of the classic, well-known and simple studies. It uses a fresh tree leaf as the sensor, with two extra-fine probes inserted into different veins of the selected leaf, and then connects them to an electronic signal amplifier to adjust the amplification. During these experiments, they were able to detect field potentials from the tree leaves before any external intervention. When the qigong healer emitted qi to the leaves at the distance of 50 cm, the observable field potential was several times stronger. When the qi emission was stopped, the signal strength returned to its baseline. In the control group, where a 35°C heating device was used at the same distance, the leaves showed no response (to exclude the possibility that the detected change was due to the body temperature of the qigong healer). When a non-qigong person treated the leaves, there was no effect. These "tree leaf sensors" can be used continuously for eight hours, and then they need to be replaced with new leaves. From the viewpoint of traditional science, these "tree leaf sensors" do not truly meet the conventional standard of a detector, nor do they have perfect reliability of performance; however, they became a classic biological detector in the study of EQ.

Detectors Using Living Sensors

There has long been skepticism about the therapeutic effects of qigong, and the effects of qigong are often attributed to psychological suggestion (e.g., Lin et al. 2000). Researchers shifted their focus of qigong studies to living organisms that closely resemble the bio-characteristics of humans. It seems that almost all conventional animal or biological models used for research could become suitable biological sensors for detecting EQ

Effect of EQ on cancer growth

In the studies examining the effect of EQ on cancer growth, metastasis and survival time of the host, tumor models were formed in 114 mice by transplantation of U27 or MO_4 cells into their subcutaneous tissues. The tumor-infected mice were randomly divided into two treatment groups for three separate studies—qigong group (exposed to EQ 10 to 30 minutes daily for a period of time) and control group (no treatment). In study 1, mice in both groups were sacrificed on day 20 after the transplantation. The average tumor volume in the qigong group was significantly lower than that in control (2.2 vs. 6.3 cm^3; $p < .001$). In study 2, the mice were sacrificed on day 23 and all axillary lymph nodes and the lungs were taken out individually to be examined histo-pathologically for metastasis. The metastasis rate in the EQ group was significantly lower than the control group (1/16 vs. 6/15; $p < .05$). In study 3, the mice were not sacrificed but were allowed to live out their lives and the time of death was recorded for each. The average survival time in qigong groups (n=10) was significantly longer than that of the control group (35.4 vs. 30.5 days; $p < .01$). The same authors performed similar studies in different settings and they each reached the same conclusion.

Effect of Qigong anti-cancer and Anti-tumor effect of EQ on the immunologic functions of Tumor Bearing Mice (TBM)

Investigated the anti-tumor efficacy of EQ emission on transplanted hepatic cancer in mice. In this study, 30 nude mice that had been injected with transplanted hepatic cancer cells were randomly assigned into one of three groups: (1) the control group (no-treatment); (2) the imitation group (sham healer imitated qigong healer's movement); and (3) the qigong group (treated by a qigong healer). The qigong or sham treatment included emission of EQ towards the mouse cage at a distance of 8-10cm for 10 minutes every other day for a total of four sessions or 40 minutes. The results from three repeated experiments were similar: compared with the control group, the tumor growth-inhibitory rates of the qigong treated group were 70.3%, 79.7%, and 78.7%, respectively ($p < 0.0001$). The inhibitory rates of the imitation treated group were 9.5%, 2.6%, and 2.5%, respectively ($p > 0.05$). An electron microscope showed that the morphological alterations in the qigong-treated mice included decreased cell volume of most cancer cells; nuclear condensation, nuclear fragmentation; decreased ratio of nucleus and cytoplasm; swollen mitochondria with poorly organized mitochondrial cristae, some vacuolated; many apoptotic bodies in extra-cellular space. These results indicated that EQ of a well-trained qigong healer could inhibit the growth of transplanted hepatocarcinoma in mice.

The Effects of EQ on Human Bodies

Reported benefit of qigong therapy include degenerated disc disease, rheumatoid arthritis, myoma of the uterus, shoulder peripheral neuritis, fractures, cataracts, cardiovascular disease, irregular pulse, hemi-paralysis, and asthma.

No longer do we have to conjecture about the existence of Qi, since now it is measurable in a variety of ways——for light, electricity, heat, sound and magnetism (magnetism needs more study) and is shown to effect chemical molecular changes, biological materials, and living organisms. The inhibition of cancer cells, speeding up or slowly down of biological processes and chemical processes require directionality with intention. This has been shown and is the yi part of Qigong.

What about the physiological state under the Qigong state measured from a global aspect? In 1990 there had been studies of Master meditators and some physiological data of what a meditative state's physiology was.

Wholeness: Synchronization in Human Physiology and Involuntary use of the will

If one looks at the physiology of meditative states one can see that there is a synchronization that occurs. We looked at the brain in a meditative state and also blood lactate and oxygen consumption during this 1990 study period. (Figure 1) Data is starting to appear to differentiate between a meditative state and the Qigong state, but for now, the global physiology of meditation elucidates. Qigong is a term which has meditation as one of the practices but the qigong state can be for internal Qigong or external Qigong. This exposition fits under the internal Qigong state.

Dr. Freed and I tried to put this physiological understanding within the framework of signal theory (noise level), conditioning (physiologic habits), learning and emotions with an assumption of a coherency of structure of this basic physiologic state of a Master meditation. Also we identified this coherent state as Enlightenment, historically this term has been associated with Wholeness and mind/body unity. In this article, for clarity purposes, the discussion will be within the framework of Japanese Buddhism because of the long historical development within the West. It is very apparent that there are many meditation practices, I myself besides practicing Zen mediation for many years as did Dr. Freed; also practice Siddha yoga meditation, several schools of Tibetan mediation, all quite extensively as well as Shao Lin Gung Fu, Qigong and Five Element Tai Chi Chuan meditation. Literature is evolving to show certain physiologic differences between these types of meditations, but for our purposes here Zen Meditation is a meditation involving the involuntary use of the will.

The Science of Zen Meditation: Signal Theory, Conditioning, Habits, Learning and Emotion

The physiology of this type of mediation is involuntary use of the will According to Hui-neng (China, 637-713 A.D.) associated eminently with Ch'an Buddhism, Enlightenment is authentic only when initiated (awakened) spontaneously in a sudden unforeseeable experience. It is preceded by long practice in Meditation entered from ordinary life also abruptly. Fig. 1A (Benson, 1975) indicates roughly the Mediator's consumption of oxygen. [4] It is characterized by

---

4. Benson H (1975) The Relaxation response, William Morrow & Co. New York

an abrupt drop. The low level of consumption remains flat, felt by the Meditator as a sustained Quiet. The unchanging consumption of oxygen suggests a prevailing single physiologic state. The low noise-level (Freed. 1965) of the physiologic activities during this Quiet is viewed as of primary significance in the discussion that follows.[5] It is taken to express exceptional coherence in structure and activity through-out the body-mind. We shall return to this in the discussion of the electro-encephalograms of Meditators.

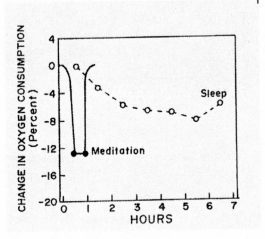

Figure 1A is a rapid drop in oxygen consumption during meditation which is not seen in normal sleep. (Benson. 1965)

5. Freed S (1965) Science, 150 576-584

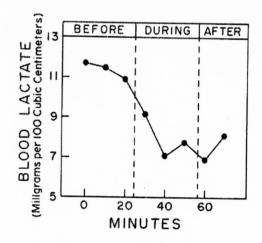

Figure 1B shows a drop in blood lactate during meditation.

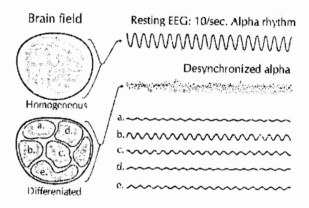

Figure 1C. Idealization: alpha rhythm of EEG in state of "relaxed wakefulness" and its desynchronization. (After Lindsley. 1961 and Pribram, 1971).

The goal of Meditation is Enlightenment. Its nature is intimated by Herrigel (1960) in the following quotation: "For the Zen Buddhist, everything that exists apart from man animals and plants, stones, earth, air, fire, water lives undemanding from the center of being without having left it. For a Zen, he must not become as a little child but like forest and rock, like flower and fruit, like wind and storm. In the East this reversal (to the center) and homecoming is not left to chance, the way can be prepared and methodically followed, above all, in Japan."[6] The center becomes accessible spontaneously upon removal of the classically recognized obstacles: ignorance, delusions, and fears. They have fragmented man's perceptions, behavior, and correspondingly, his physiology. Obstacles surface in his Meditations. There, in the processes of the Quiet they are changed to less threatening form and finally are let go. The resulting void finally permits the spontaneous unification of the fragments.

Meditation is subject to many variations, personal and cultural. Most Meditations have one feature in common, total mindfulness of actualities of the present moment. Mindfulness was regarded by the Buddha as essential for effective Meditation. It consists in total absorbing attention to the actualities while the Meditator remains completely relaxed physically. A form of Meditation, the Buddha is believed to have favored, mindfulness-of-breathing is somewhat as follows: with eyes unclosed, one starts by giving total attention to regular breathing as the air enters and leaves the nostrils and impinges above the upper lip. What is attended to can be greatly enlarged. Beginners are helped in maintaining unswerving attention against spontaneous distractions by mentally counting the breaths. Mindfulness must become so completely absorbing that the Meditator is unaware of the breather. The spontaneous distractions surfacing from the unconscious were named "obstructing devils" by the Buddha, translated by the Japanese as "makyo"—not always an overstatement. The breathing, after an interval, which becomes shorter with practice (longer at first), experiences a sudden spontaneous reduction in volume and also in rate. A distinct Quiet possesses the Meditator, A new state of consciousness is entered. Following the termination of the session, some characteristics of the quiet persist. See Figure 1C. Further-on, we shall touch upon examples of Meditation free of methodology.

We take as postulate that the makyo-like obstructions, even when apparently trivial in content, occupy central importance as obstacles in the development required for reaching Enlightenment. Briefly, a major reflex of the makyo is "the I" and a major expression of the 'I' is devastating emotion, noise

---

6.   Herrigel E (1960) The method of Zen, Routledge and Kegan Paul. London

throughout the body-mind. Makyo have been identified by Buddhists with visions, nightmares, hallucination, as distorted forms in dreams of events in childhood. Of course, these occupy central roles in Western psychiatry. The attitude toward them differs fundamentally in the Orient. During Meditation these phantasms are not to be dwelled upon, "interpreted". Instead they are, if possible, a struggle between forces of light and darkness (Yasutani, in Kapleau, 1989). This attitude leads in the course of Meditation to a reduction in the intensity and number of the makyo and conversely progress in unification.

What proves to have particular physiologic significance in the transition to the Quiet is the spontaneous appearance of prominent alpha rhythm in the electro-encephalogram (EEG) of the Meditators. For controls, we first observe the EEG of ordinary man depicted schematically in Fig. 1C, lower (Lindsley, 1961, Pribram, 1971).[7,8] The upper picture is the resting EEG of these subjects with eyes closed, giving the alpha rhythm (about ten cycles per second) which disappears when eyes are opened. A very weak sensory stimulus, a faint noise, quickly (within 0.3 second) fragments the singly rhythm into superposition of many having low amplitudes. The "homogeneous brain field", at left of 'quiet wakefulness' is fragmented by the noise into components, a b, c, d, e (below), independent rhythms, ascribed by Lindsley, (1961) to separate neural aggregates. He suggested that at de synchronization, neural elements in aggregates function independently as information-processing channels (Pribram p. 207, 1971.) The swift de synchronization of the alpha rhythm by very weak stimuli has been named, the 'alarm reaction'. This simple representation is not, of course, intended to cover the complex neoronic activities of alarm. This emotional surge of widespread nerve excitation jams information-channels, distorts communication into incoherent snatches, and renders neuronic messages indecipherable by the brain. In consequence responses that follow may be grossly inappropriate.

On the other hand, the alpha rhythm of the Meditators with eyes unclosed, under even stronger sensory stimulation, suffers no fragmentation and remains unresponsive to what ordinarily excites alarm. The homogeneous brain field is stabilized by the Oneness holding in Meditation. In contrast to ordinary man, Meditators despite stress, arrive at the "unification and tran-

7. Lindsley DB (1961) in Sheer D, (ed) Electrical stimulation of the brain, University of Texas Press, Austin

8. Pribram KH (1971) Languages of the brain, Englewood Cliffs, Prentice-Hall, New Jersey

quility of mind" (Kapleau, 1989), rather of the body-mind according to the unifying conception of Buddhists.[9] This tranquil state shows little disturbance in its alpha rhythm with its low level of background noise.

Bases for these observations are amply provided by studies of EEG of Zen Meditators (Katsamatsu & Hirai, 1966).[10] Strong metallic clicks merely interrupted but did not shatter their alpha rhythms. Responses to the last click of a succession was as fresh as to the first in contrast to that of ordinary control subjects who became habituated, unresponsive to further clicks. Among Meditators no indications were evident of any residual influence of earlier clicks. Only the present click, the Buddhist Now, was perceptible to the Meditators.

After several years in the practice of Meditation, a further sudden transition occurs spontaneously, the awakening of Enlightenment (Samadhi, Satori); in Chinese, Giu Xing, awakening of clarity-liberation from noise, confusion. Meditators are agreed, they have experienced unification into a coherent Oneness. Similarly, experience through totally different modes of Meditation by mystics of the Middle Ages was perceived as profound unitization (Underhill, 1961). The level of background noise of this supreme Quiet makes possible super-vivid perception of faint signals and finer distinction between closely similar ones. (Freed, 1965) This maximal sensitivity in the reception of information may reflect increased coherence through molecular relocation and reorientation within the former fragments. Thus would be created globally a virtually homogeneous field of Quiet permitting a super-flow of clear information.

Electro-encephalograms of the Zen maters are consistent with this approach. Particularly revealing and appropriate are simple statements of their experience: "The Zen masters more clearly perceived each stimulus than in their ordinary waking state. In this (quiet) state they cannot be affected by either external or internal stimulus, nevertheless he is able to respond to it and yet is never disturbed by it. Each stimulus is accepted as stimulus itself and is treated as such. One Zen master described such a state of mind as that of noticing each person one sees on the street but not looking back with emotional curiosity," (Kasamatsu & Hirai, 1966).

---

9. Kapleau RP (1989) The three pillars of Zen, Anchor Books Doubleday, New York

10. Kasamatsu A Hirai (1966) Folia Psychiatria et Neurologica Japanica 20, 315-336

The Zen masters "more clearly perceived each stimulus than in their ordinary waking state" since it was not blurred by the lower level of background noise during the state of Enlightenment or during the Quiet of Meditation. In their ordinary waking state the noise-level of background is especially high when the original neutral (such as visual) signal had been conditioned to represent an emotionally charged conditioned stimulus. A Zen master cannot be emotionally disturbed or "affected by either external or internal stimulus" since it had been conditioned in the past. This, an unconditioned component of the conditioned stimulus, would not be responded to in the ever present Now of Enlightenment. Thus the conditioned stimulus had been deconditioned through the unresponsiveness. The master is therefore never disturbed by coupling of a chance neutral stimulus with a noisy emotional stimulus.

This feature is confirmed by the last remark. The master "notices each person on the street but he does not look back with emotional curiosity". The visual signal he noticed was no longer conditioned as ordinarily to evoke the emotions and noise of unconditioned stimuli of the past.

Attention to the Present: Learning and Emotion

We have then empirical evidence that long practice in Meditation (when total attention is given to actualities of the present moment) had created awareness exclusively of the present, the Now. This state of awareness is made possible through the concurrently created unresponsiveness to conditioned stimuli.

Perceiving and responding only in the Now, how does the ideal Meditator learn or acquire information? The usual answer is, by observation in the momentary present free of specific earlier stimulation, without time—requiring processes of association. Let me quote a wish frequently expressed, "Perhaps we can break the power of thought and become free once again as we were at one time in our childhood before thought began to exercise its tyranny over us." (Fowler, 1975)

How does the infant, the neonate, perceive and learn? According to contemporary studies (Fantz, 1967), it is precisely by momentary observation uninfluenced by pedagogic preparation or effort. Rather, the neonate acquires information by assimilation into the totality of his development. [11] Similarly the eighteen month old learns to speak single words, pairs of words etc.

---

11. Fantz RL (1967) in Stevenson HW, Hess EH, Reingold HL, (Ed) Early behavior development approaches, John Wiley & Sons. New York

Consequently learning as well as responses with what he has learned involves a measure of Oneness and may be regard as *spontaneous and creative*. Because of similarities in behavior, we infer that ideal Meditation and Enlightenment provide conditions for "becoming free again as we were before thought began to exercise its tyranny over us."

Let us consider the destructive emotions: hate, fear, anger, envy, etc. They cannot be removed by opposing them with their opposites.[12] They can be removed only by being brought to zero intensity. Krishnamurti, 1984 appeals not to distance oneself from them but to come ever closer. Observe one self unrelentingly for the smallest sign of hate (for example) in all one's activities, no matter how irrelevant they may appear. "Pay total attention to uncover component of hate. In a sense you are possessed by hate, you are hate." Mindfulness in all aspects of the hate may lead if one is fortunately determined enough, to an equivalent of Meditation. Finally a Quiet descends. Unresponsiveness to the conditioned stimuli involved take over. The habitual reminding-stimuli, near-replicas of those that had surrounded the formation of the hate cease fueling the obsession. They are brought to zero. The door is actually open to love and instances are known for the complete reversal to occur.

The courageous all-out encounter with the hateful self is the creativity of Jiddu Krishnamurti (1984). The spontaneous direct action of his total attention makes unnecessary the classically prescribed methodologies of Buddhist Meditation.

Assimilated in the Now of Enlightenment are transcended duality between opposites or between contradictions as ordinarily accepted. Each member of the duality such as good-bad, subject-object, inside-outside, common sense-nonsense, expresses conclusions reached through habit or conditioning. What is left of the time-bound duality in consciousness is a generalization that the members have in common. The noise-level of the background generated by the generalization now free of conflict is lower than what ordinarily accompanies the separate members. Through its unresponsiveness, Oneness and Enlightenment have been maintained. Having negated potential resistance (noise) from conflicting duality, Enlightenment with its swiftness and precision of responses and its virtual "functional contact" of molecular structure may well be uniquely effective in a super-flow of clear information.

---

12. Krishnamurti J (1984) The flame of attention, Harper & Row, San Francisco

Factors erasing destructive emotions are liberating also in other circumstance. In the following they are expressed as spontaneous super-flow of information: Factors erasing destructive emotions are liberating also in other circumstance. In the following they are expressed as spontaneous super-flow of information:

Dangerous Sport: Free of Fear, Heightened Perception and a Quick Strike

Swordsmanship of Zen masters several centuries ago (Suzuki, 1959) surpassed what was displayed by the most skilled professionals in this dangerous sport.[13] The professional had learned his art and critical techniques from famous teachers. On the other hand, the Zen master as always gave "all absorbing attention to the actualities of the present moment" and thereby had attained all-important mindfulness. He acted from a Quiet in total body-mind creatively, effortlessly, without awareness of self. The professional's activity was essentially a performance of the habitual self, disturbed by the lightening, unprecedented strokes of the master's blade. Fearful of being cut to pieces, uneasily he faces the master who with undisturbed perception had instant, clear information of the initiation of his opponent's next move. This information without distortion in the prevailing low noise-level of background was transmitted swiftly and effectively to the unitized decision-making and responding physiology.

Unifying the Opposite in Mind/Body Athletics

One can see how meditation within this framework would improve an athlete's performance and create the condition for precision, quick response times, overcoming fear and emotions, ease of effort, and clarity of mind and body. Most sport requires coordinated synchronized movement of the body and aspects of one's personality (fear, anxiety) can make one drop the ball uncontrollably or stumble and fall. The inner doubts are the real demons in

13. Susuki ST (1959) Zen and Japanese culture, Princeton University press, Princeton.

sport and physical training is just the start. I used a meditation based upon the unity of opposites in a major competition to qualify for the Olympics Games and US Olympic Trails after a two year lay off with no jumping while in graduate school. I arrived at the competition one day after my written exams for a Ph.D. with a headache and my mind full of words and body crunched from writing and studying. I found a dark room 100 yards from the competition area in a building and laid flat on my back and started to take my breath cycle down slower and slower over one half hour till it went to once every two minutes for a cycle. At the same time I thought motion while not in motion. I went through each step of the long jump step by step looking at my body position. When I reached the deepest state with little breathing I started to move into various jumping positions, stretching in these positions and thinking less of the form but getting physically into the form. At first these posses were stationary then slowly I started to move faster and went outside. I ran several sprints moving faster while thinking little. Minutes later on my jump I sprinted all out but felt in slow motion. I made several mistakes, one during a stride and one on the take off, which is remarkable since I took 20 strides and it takes about 5 seconds for the whole jump. I jumped the number two jump in the world and made the qualification standards and US Olympic Trails scheduled three weeks later. Not in motion think motion and when in motion don't think.

Properties of Wholeness

Dr. Freed was a scientist who, when examining a system liked to change the system to see what properties emerged, usually by taking the system to low temperatures. In meditation at its highest state a quiet appears much like a low temperature state. We projected a parallelism between super fluid helium at near absolute temperature and the physiologic state of meditation and found many shared properties which are listed below. This parallelism although of limited scientific value was helpful to come up with properties which could be useful as attributes for discussion application to other systems or situations.

1. State of Oneness of high stability and coherence
2. Extremely low noise-level.
3. Result from abrupt transition between states.
4. Active solely in the present, the NOW free of reactivation from the past, free of memory
5. Transcend duality between opposites.
6. Respond as Oneness and appropriately to stimuli and pressures.
7. Transmit information of exceptional clarity
8. Display behavior to 'ordinary' man as "strange", generally expressing liberation from ordinary constraints.
9. Basic states (at 'zero' noise levels) consist inherently of both stationary and moving aspects.

At virtually zero noise-level holding at lowest temperatures, oneness is uniquely expressed by the superfluid in ^{4}He II. It consists of macro-quantity of identical helium atoms occupying the single macro-cell of lowest energy in Bose-Einstein statistics. This the theoretical 'condensate' quantum liquid, possessing superfluity coherent and homogeneous, made so by collision and diffusion because of zero-point energy or operation of the Heisenberg uncertainty principle. Identification of the superfluid with the condensate has been amply authenticated experimentally (references and discussion e.g. Tilley and Tilley, 1990).[14] The superfluid has no viscosity and its motion is intrinsic, requiring no difference in pressure. The motion constitutes a characteristic of the 'stationary quantum state' of the macro-wave function.

Therefore, superfluity transcend the duality: stationary/mobile. Spontaneous, abrupt transition at 2.17 ° A (the lambda TΥ point) initiates (awakens) appearance of the superfluid component of 4Helium II. The fraction of superfluid component in ^{4}He II grows with decrease in thermal agitation becoming approximately 100% below 1.2 °A (Tilley and Tilley, 1990).

The superfluid because of its zero viscosity, its inner super-mobility retains no structural impress from the past. Time is ever the present, the NOW. Any disturbance instantly permeates the entire superfluid. It's Oneness and restoration to homogeneity is also instantaneous. Homeostasis extends quickly over total system. Compared with the flow of information

14. Tilley DR, Tilley J (1990) Superfluidity and super-conductivity, (3rd Edition) Adam Hilger, New York

above 1.2°A, superflow of information occurs below 1.2 °A in the super-fluid. It would arise from a reduction in resistance to its transmission because of freedom from conflict of dualities, freedom from constraints such as narrow channels leading to receptors of the information.

Unitization of fragments, here of helium atoms into a single quantum fluid and unification of dualities are also expressed in the behavior of the superfluid. An example is "siphoning-in reverse" which is spontaneously performed when an empty vessel is partially lowered into a superfluid with its rim markedly above the superfluid level. The outer wall becomes covered with a thick film of superfluid that moves over the rim to fill the vessel up to the same level that holds on the outside. Here the duality, inside/outside is transcended (ignored) likewise the duality, up/down.

Another example where ordinary barriers to unification of spaces are overcome is the superflow of ^{4}He II through micro-channels of a vessel's walls so narrow as to block the flow of ordinary liquid helium above the lambda point, 2.17 °A. They strongly impede the flow of gaseous helium below 2.17 °A. The content of some "strange" behavior in superfluity may have behavioral correspondence in Enlightenment. The following quotation comes from Tilley and Tilley, 1990. "Observation of the liquid helium at the instant that its temperature is reduced below 2.17°A, reveals a remarkable alteration in its appearance. Liquid helium, He, is maintained below 4.2°A by lowering the vapor pressure so that boiling occurs under reduced pres-sure. Above 2.17°A bubbles of vapor form within the bulk of the liquid in the customary way and the whole liquid is evidently agitated as these rise to the free surface and escape. On the other hand, as soon as the transition point, TY is reached the liquid becomes quite still and no more bubble are formed

---

15. Shanghai College of Traditional Medicine (1987) O'Connor and Bensky D (Ed) Acupuncture a Comprehensive Text. Eastland Press, Seattle, Washington.

Differentiation of Qi: The Application of the Bi-digital O-Ring Imaging Test to Toxic Organ Pathways and Clinical Medicine

The properties of fragmented states are the opposite of the above properties and one can see this with disease, which I will present after some more explorations into the nature of qi. Before the reservoir of knowledge on Qigong became known, in 1985, I tried to see if there was such a thing as organ qi energy as explained in Traditional Chinese Medicine with pathways on the skin on the outside of the body.

In Traditional Chinese Medicine (TCM) qi has many forms.[15] One differentiation of qi (something can be differentiated by going from one level to another level) is the pathways on the surface of the body called meridians, originating with organs which have internal and external pathways, according to TCM. Omura in 1985 showed how meridian like pathway could be imaged on the surface of the body using tissue of an organ as a control reference.[16] Using a triple blind technique where the subject, tester and assistant did not view each other, we imaged the lung pathway using the lung as a control reference but with more information, tobacco was held in the subject's hand. (Figure 2) This pathway deviated from the classical meridian with this new information, a differentiation that became fragmented. This was later confirmed by subsequent cases of patients with lung disease. Pathways change according to variables in the body such as a micro-organism or toxin to the organs. Pathways are informational.

Briefly, from 1985-1989 we looked at 400 cases and from that 30 cases could be matched to organs from clinical patients who complained of pain. The others related to a dermatome field from the spinal chord. The protocol was simple, each organ representation point or alarm point was tested for abnormality and each spinal vertebra was tested for abnormality. Acupuncture was given to these points; if patient did not get pain relief then we tested the abnormal points on the spine with organ tissues randomly selected for comparison. Several interesting results came from this study. The first was the four phases

---

16. Omura Y (1987) Acu & elec-Ther.Res, Int.J. Part I. pp. 53-70. Vol. 12:1

of the diaphragm. A women complained of neck pain and this neck point was randomly matched to organs tissues and other non organ tissue selected at random. A diaphragm tissue resonated to this point. (Figure 3) After imaging the diaphragm pathway at random, acupuncture was administered to this point and the pathway changed. This was done three times until it stabilized. Subsequent clinical tests showed that people with asthma, allergies or respiratory problems got stuck in one of these phases. This particular patient had cervical neck problems. A patient who had chest pains randomly matched to heart tissue manifest in three phases. (Figure 4) No laboratory test confirmed any abnormality. He suffered from emotional stress. This showed that stress and emotional can affect the qi pathways as well as micro organism or toxins.

Aberrations were noted in the following organ pathways not reflected in TCM, the gall bladder, ovary, bladder, prostate, colon, heart and lung. The hip gall bladder aberration pathway symptoms were associated with scoliosis, infection, colitis, constipation, hip spurs, food allergies, parasites, gallstones, osteoporosis, and mechanical problems with the vertebrae, emotional stress and spinal diseases of asymmetry. (Figure 5) In women, this same configuration was associated with the ovary rather than the gall bladder and went to a point directly over the ovary anatomically. (Figure 6) The ovary aberrant pathway was associated with hip or sacral pain, medial calf pain, scoliosis, pronation of the feet, weakness of the calf muscles, cysts, herpes, infection to the ovary, lumbar radiculopathy, psoas insufficiency, obesity, depression, scoliosis, short leg, arthritis of the hip and postural imbalance. The bladder prostate aberrant configuration crosses around the leg. (Figure 7) Other bladder symptoms include scoliosis, weak abdominals, psoas insufficiency, and chronic immune deficiency. The colon hip pathway was associated with hip pain, constipation, herniation and bulging, scoliosis, pain to bottom of feet, and subtalar joint dysfunction. (Figure 8)

The heart pathway around the thoracic was associated with chronic costochrondritis and hypertension and showed three phases, one before acupuncture and two after. (See Figure 4) A diaphragm pathway was found in four phases. (See Figure 3) Asthma patients tended to get struck in one phase as did smokers and individuals with pain along the pathway. Mechanical problems with the cervical vertebrae were associated with abnormal phases of the diaphragm as were pain in the neck, posterior deltoid or scapula. Constriction of the throat, chronic rhinitis, deviated nasal septum and stress were also associated with certain diaphragm phases. Pathways imaged with tissue after acupuncture usually resulted in the abnormal pathway disappearing or shifting more medial. Asymmetry to the spine creates organ pathway aberrations.

In sum, organ pathways deviate from the normal pathways under conditions of pain and injury to the body, disturbances of internal organs, or mental stress. The variable that connects various cases is asymmetry—scoliosis, short leg, rotated rib cage and the assortment of deviations from assumed symmetry. Also, scars on the pathway or plastic surgery causes deviations. The heart and diaphragm show phases, three for the heart and four for the diaphragm, depending upon the degree and kind of disturbance. Multiple starting positions in the hand for the lung and colon were found and account for more variations due to either condition of the lung or colon, or dominant position of the hand throughout the day due to the reversible forearm.

From this study one can see organ qi pathways deviating under diseased conditions and go back to "normal" patterns after treatment with acupuncture or meditation. Qi can be differentiated according to internal organs and fragmented due to disease or a variety of structural or skin abnormalities. If the organ is synchronized, then its pathway will be normal, if de-synchronized then it will be fragmented and deviate from that normal pathway.

Differentiation; The Fragmentation of Disease: The Application of Qigong and Meditation to an Acute Condition of Chronic Heart Disease.

Exertion, overstrain or cold wind and temperature can create symptoms of Chronic Heart Disease—tiredness, fluid in the lung, cold symptoms, sputum production, cough, rapid breathing, nausea and abdominal spasm, no appetite, mental disturbances, insomnia and restless sleep, and fear. These transcendent states of Qigong and meditation could help theoretically in the terminal phases of life; i.e., escaping from conditioned thinking associated with fear. We wanted to test this general understanding with a particular case.[17]

This single case study is based upon observation between the dependent variable (breath, rate, anxiety, frequent urination, bad dreams, and abdominal spasms and sputum production) and the independent variables (acupuncture,

17. Shinnick. P and Freed S "A Case Study of the Synchronization of Human Energy in an Acute Condition of Chronic Heart Disease through Complementary Treatment." (Under Review)

meditation, qigong and medication). In order to create a time line a daily diary or log was kept which attempted to quantify the signs and symptom. (Appendix I) The breath was observed in the ratio of seconds of inhalation to seconds of exhalation, breaths per minute, and smoothness of the process—were their hesitations or jerkiness in the inhalation, exhalation and conversions? Sputum production came from observation of number of expectorations per day and volume of each expectoration (10 cc per day at peak). Dr. Freed wrote down nightly dreams and sleep quality as well as any other observations. Blood pressure measurements were taken the same time each day and later in the day if required. The initial fluid in the lung measurement came from an X-ray and subsequent decrease or increase measurement came from daily listening to voice quality and fullness from back palpitations. Amount of swelling was determined by observing the malleous and degree bone oblivation plus over the bridge. Urination volume first came from an average normal volume per day 900cc and variations from that determined by frequency per day and volume of each urination recorded as large, medium, below and poor average volume.

Symptoms: Phlegm, cough, fluid in the lungs, dyspnea, dream disturbed sleep, abdominal spasms, blood pressure drops, edema, coldness, esophagus restriction

Treatment: Calm the cough, expel phlegm, extend the breath, harmonized fragmented breath (choppy breath), relax abdominal muscles, open esophagus

Given this variety of symptoms, an attempt was made to categorize methods of meditation into physiologic terms and apply them to Chronic Heart Disease.

Meditation: Voluntary and Involuntary

Voluntary Meditation Technique.

These techniques use volition to move or hold voluntary muscles, as in breath control (coordination of abdominal muscles with the breath) or as in Qigong by assuming certain physical position while coordinating breathing.

Breath control

These breathing techniques are to calm a cough, expel phlegm, break the short breath cycle, harmonize the fragmented breath, and relax abdominal spasms. During the time of fluid in the lung; it creates a more efficient breath and calms panic.

The principle for rapid breathing and fluid in the lungs is to extend exhalation and inhalation, and after a large inhalation relax the exhalation and let the air out slowly. In this regard the exhalation should be twice as long as the inhalation until the breath is brought under control. For cough and phlegm with an uncoordinated breath (which may have good volume) and abdominal spasms, the breath is to be harmonized. This means watching the cycle to see hesitations, contractions, and the sequence of the abdomen to the breath. Ideally the abdomen extends out upon inhalation. During a crisis it is important to first extend the length of time of the inhalation and exhalation and then coordinate and harmonize the cycle with the abdomen.

For rapid breathing, attempt to extend and slow the exhalation by relaxing after inhalation. *For spastic breath*, focus each breath on the obstacle or hitches in the exhalation or inhalation cycle, and try to create smoothness. *For an abdominal spasm*, use the internal force of the breath to extend the abdomen on inhalation and lower the abdomen on exhalation. This method stabilized the subject's emotional state and left him in comfort although he was slowly becoming weaker.

Dr. Freed was in a deficient state and small disturbances such as the start of a bath or shower, or overdoing something would ignite a rapid breath episode. This out-of-control physiology seemed all consuming; it felt like an invasion from somewhere else, totally unfamiliar, consuming, and frightening. This can be an episode of rapid breathing or dreams not in themselves frightening, just vividly seen past events. An event of seemingly no meaning except that there was a past event, then another, and another, in no sequence or order. The emotional reaction is fear; this fear compounds any condition resulting in a rigidity of the body, and an uncoordinated state of the breath and stomach. A crisis can occur spontaneously if this state persists.

Qigong

Generally speaking there are two types of Qigong, internal and external. Internal strengthens ones own Qi or warmth and external can benefit others. Before his winter crisis the subject regularly did five to ten minute of daily internal Qigong meditation as follows. Generally, volition is used to recruit the voluntary muscles. The subject would stand with knees slightly bent and arms in a circle as if holding a ball. His fingers were about an inch apart and he would gaze at the ground through fingers, focusing on the floor about one meter ahead. When his fingers started to tingle then his mind would focus on a particular part of the body, and the sensation of warmth to that part would follow. Sometimes after assuming the correct position he would swing his arms to each side. The arm in the direction of movement would swing further out to the side as if holding a bow and the other hand would remain as if there were an arrow in the other hand.

With daily practice this resulted in the subject being able to bring warmth to any part of the body on which he focused his mind. Enlisting his will to activate the voluntary system occupied part of his mind and therefore avoided distraction and created a unification of thought, mind and body.

The subject had been doing inner Qigong for about five years. He had had a rash on his back from swimming in a river in Central America about fifty years earlier, which he wanted to treat with this method. After doing the meditation for about five to ten minutes each day over a period of five years; the area receded to10% and returned by 30% during his illness.

One morning after the six-week research had ended; Dr. Freed was still in bed when I arrived. He said, jokingly, "I've got one foot in the grave. It's time for Qigong." PS examined SF's cold forehead and entire body. With great effort he slowly sat up and then stood. He did the usual standing Qigong meditation but nothing happened. He then made upward arm motions, and within a half dozen movements he said he felt some warmth. After lying down a small area of warmth in his abdomen was noted. Six hours later he was working in his study after full warmth had returned to his body.

Involuntary: Meditation

Involuntary means not using volition or will to move voluntary muscles.[18] The technique is simple—sit or lie still, not moving any muscle, and watch the breath but don't try to do anything. One can focus one's consciousness on the upper lip and feel the breath coming in and out. With experience, eventually the breath quiets, thinking becomes minimal, and a quience or equipoise (harmonious balance) appears. With an active mind this also creates a time when dualism and contradictions can flourish with

18. Hirai T (1989) Zen meditation and psychotherapy. Japan Pub, NY.

no harmful effects to the body. In Heart disease, with this capability, one can experience a disordered physiology and still maintain the meditation and improve. This sitting state was SF's daily meditation for years. For a beginner, against heart disease, in a fearful state, this is difficult to impossible. Zen meditation is not possible in a crisis situation such as panting or dreams disturbed sleep or intense fear. After Dr. Freed's near death crisis when he was able to us this meditative technique, a calm physiology resulted. Dr. Freed felt a profound thankfulness for this quiet and ability to meditate in the Zen state

Conscious intention and performance in athletics

Unlike disease, athletes voluntarily put themselves into training and competitive situations which are anxiety ridden, stressful, fearful, intimidating and sometimes create injuries. Like disease, depending upon the situation, either voluntary or involuntary meditation should be used. In disease, relief from pain is what one looks for; in athletics pain sometimes advances your conditioning. For athletics the reward is getting mind and body together and experiencing a synchronization that is not possible in daily life. Many athletes use the game as the only time there mind and body work together, to hit the ball harder or more accurate or beat their opponent. Exceptional performances can make you a hero for a lifetime and beyond, and for some this is what one motivates all the hard work. In a larger context Wholeness in athletics means the integration of the personality using athletics to liberate oneself from habits harmful to health, to create clarity in all aspects of ones life by creating a synchronized state, and, to learn to stay in the moment. Also that one can perform under stress, emotional upset and confusion if one learns how to change states of consciousness when necessary.

Great athletes know one thing, that at the moment they have to perform, they have to be present, not distracted, and not emotionally upset or thinking of something in the past or future. From training and competitive diaries I kept I found that it doesn't matter what state one is in before the competition only at the moment the event takes place. One day in Flagstaff Arizona in 1968 while competing against the German Olympic team in a pre-Olympic meet, fifteen minutes before the event I did not have my shoes or competitive uniform (lost in flight), I had a headache from the altitude, the runway was lousy, the pit lumpy and the wind shifted all the time. I jumped 26' 9 1/2/" for the third longest jump in the world that year and the fourth longest in US history; a jump that would medal in any Olympics up to that point. After two average jumps and a foul I had two jumps at 26'91/2", I felt as if I was dropped down a slid and I just had to just stay balanced.

Money and the motivation to become a hero can lead toward shortcuts; using an amphetamine to keep awake in baseball or sprint faster, taking anabolic steroids to build muscle mass for weight lifters or football players to get stronger or blood doping (taking blood out of the body then putting it back in later) for cross country skiing or distance running. Tom Waddell, a 1968 Olympic team member in the decathlon and team physician during the training camp at South Lake Tahoe told me before he died of cancer of the liver from AIDS that he gave out anabolic steroids to the athletes at the training camp.[19] He felt it was scientific thing to do. Now we know these "scientific training" regimes included anabolic steroids in Socialist systems as well as our Capitalist system. Maybe I wasn't realistic and should have thought of giving my country a victory by taking advantage of this synthetic boost. Knowing that your competitors are taking anabolic steroids is the hardest of all mind sets to overcome and it has taken thirty years for the Olympic movement and particularly the US Olympic Committee to test for these illegal drugs.[20] An example is the first time I attempted the decathlon while in graduate school in 1966 I scored the highest ever in some events for the decathlon and my total scored more than the 1956 Olympic Champion Bob Mathis scored to win. Normally without improving much I could be on the 1968 Olympic team in the decathlon but average athletes started taking steroids and the event changed. The decathlon doesn't require a single world class mark but only average to good marks in all events. I know this because I trained with these athletes who are now world famous and broke the world record in the decathlon. I decided to go back to the long jump and not use drugs.

My training has been an intensely private matter with me but at the urging of Dr. Roy and my position on an International Olympic Committee

---

19. Shinnick P (1994)"Waddell: World Class as Person and Athlete in The New York Times, June 26,
20. Shinnick P (1973) "Competition and Drug Usage," in Proper and Improper Use of Drugs by Athletes. Hearings before the Sub-Committee of the Judiciary. US. Senate. US. Government Printing, July 12th, 13th,

and UNESCO committee on building a cultural of peace has made me discuss drugs and sport to create a cultural that is more humane and peace oriented. There is a need to develop an alternative to the present madness in sport.

I know from experience that great performances are effortless, intensely in the present and synchronized in mind and body. Many coaches try to get their athletes to be more motivated and thereby have more will power but the important thing is to be able to get into a competitive state and out again at the right moment. Most athletes have a motivation to do well but their fears, anxiety, outside stress and own internal distractions are their demons.

Modern athletics has the same distractions as they did hundreds and thousands of years ago, money, fame, and access to the opposite sex. These can be corrupting influences which take one out of the moment. Getting ready for the competition requires another state of consciousness and this state could be measured the same way that Qigong Masters measured by signal detectors have been discussed. This could be done now with the same detectors. Besides the signal detectors, global physiologic measurement should be made. Ways to get in and out of this state would be very helpful for athletes.

Athletics at its highest level requires techniques much like internal Qigong however a lot of athletics is equivalent to external qi with intention or yi. Take the javelin, one has to throw the javelin with your body and use the arm at the last minute like a whip but the mind has to be focused on the eventual direction of the javelin and where to throw it on the release. I was taught by an Olympic thrower to pick a point in the sky or clouds and bury the tail and tip of the javelin into that point. My first throw ever in competition was near 200 feet, with no practice. I buried the tail and the point in a hole in a cloud and when this all lined up the javelin took off and sailed and floated as if suspended. One thing is clear, one can not think of the outcome only the process and one must keep the mind engaged until the act is over— it is like shooting a basketball then relying upon hope rather than follow through.

Direction is very important in all ball games especially when an athlete releases the ball but doesn't follow through with their mind. When catching a ball, if you take your concentration off the ball you can drop it. Intention and directionality are what makes sport exciting. Athletes project themselves into space or project physical objects into space much like external qi and this happens best when their physiology is not differentiated or fragmented. If differentiated then movement and breath should be used together much like what was talked about in Chronic Heart Disease. Fear can cause the abdomen to spasm or one's breathe to be shortened and the techniques outlined above in disease would be appropriate in training, before and during competition and afterwards for recovery. One time I called my fellow Olympian friend Kenny Moore about a time I was running a marathon and all of a sudden a pallor came over me, I couldn't run another step, the thought of running 14 more miles after I'd done 11 seemed to me overwhelming, I couldn't breath, I turned my head to tell my friend I had to give up and he didn't hear me. On my second attempt my lips froze and I caught his eyes, all of a sudden I felt good, he asked, "What did you say?" I said "Forget it." Moore told me as you get more experienced you find you have these little bumps along the way and that you just have to wait them out and they pass. He just laughed at me and said, just hang in there and like a black cloud it passes, you just learn to move out of it. Non athletes don't understand this, if you are afraid of something in training it will haunt you until you make peace with it and it goes away or doesn't become a problem.

I swim on a tri-athlete swim team three mornings a week, starting at 6:00 AM. Sometimes I awake at 3:00AM and go back to sleep then wake up rested ready to go and look at the clock, 3:05AM. This goes on every five minutes till 5:15AM. It is fear. At practice the antidote is letting go in the water, let the water hold you up, synchronize your breath, don't panic for air, stay calm, stay in your form, stay long in the water and take fewer strokes. The fewer strokes I take the faster I go. If I get it I swim life time bests laughing at the end and not tired. Most of the time I panic in the middle of a work out, especially doing the butterfly stroke and loss my breath and pant. The antidote is the same as in Chronic Heart Disease. Lactic acid builds up and your body constricts in on your lungs like you can't breath and you feel weak but you are swimming fast. The normal reaction is to speed up and breathe more often just to keep pace. In this case you have to let go in the water, when this happens rather than sink you raise higher in the water and start to plane and it is less effort. Then you have to extend the stroke and the breath and slow them both down to go faster. This way you glide more and rest in the glide.

Doing yoga and stretching your spine diminishes the anxiety about the swim work out. Qigong principles are very similar to what is necessary in a training workout, stay inside not outside, stay in the body not the mind, relax. In Zen meditation one must just relax the muscles. This is difficult if the swimming pool is at 78°F and the temperature outside, walking to practice, is 5°F. For one year my hands went numb after a one hour hard workout from the cold. I had to wear a top shirt to keep warm for that first year, now I am cold for three warm up laps. It is the breath that can warm you up if you get it right without tensing in the water. Qigong is similar, moving and breathing in synch.

The body in motion works best around a centered stable energy. We saw this in the properties of Wholeness. The story about the unity of opposite in jumping illustrates that point, in motion one feels stable with the mind in quiescence. I roomed with a world class sprinter (silver medalist) who told me how to sprint; concentrate on your solar plexus and move your thighs quickly up to the solar plexus and try not to push off the ground as normally done. I tried it and beat a person who tied the world record in the 100 meters. You also sprint increments at a time, don't look too far ahead. If you get the high jump right on the take off it feels like someone is pushing you from behind and you have to struggle not to fall off the direction it takes you. It is very easy if you don't interfere.

A Case Study in Athletic Intention: the 1968 US Men's Olympic Trails in the Long jump.

Justice itself can be a distraction. In the 1968 Olympic Trails, I jumped past the Olympic record and appeared to have made the US Olympic team, again, when I saw the Olympic coach take my competitor aside and coach him, against me. This was against the Olympic rules, to do this on the field during Olympic competition. Next jump of my competitor, because the coach had settled him down, jumped 8" past his life time best and 3" beyond me. The coach permitted this athlete is run along side of me just off the runway to distract me. This distraction caused me to foul a world record jump and be displaced off the team. At that time athletes had no rights of appeal. (The coach felt I was too outspoken against racism.) This distraction jolted me out of my stable inner self and affected not my ability to jump but to stay within the boundaries of the rules of competition; I went over the take off board and fouled the jump. I let my anger out and lost control. I let the injustice distract me from staying within my jumping form. Weather can do this as well. My sense of justice was my achilles heel. Remember the discussion between the Master meditator and a good meditator? A small signal (injustice) triggered an alarm response from the good meditator but not the Master. A bad official's call can change an athlete's game and destroy it if the athlete doesn't get back to the present and stay in it and not be affected by something that just happened, especially injustice. The real problem was my intention. I thought if I jumped past the Olympic record I would make the US Olympic team then break the world record at the Olympic Games. (I already had broken the record five years earlier but it is the Gold Medal that people recognize) The Olympic record was 26' 5", I jumped 4 times at 26' 6 ½", just as I intended. It seemed a sure bet; it wasn't, I had the longest fourth place jump recorded in history, which ranked me fifth in the world. I didn't make the team. A better intention would have been to place in the top two since three made the team, no matter what the distance. I lacked vision. Sometimes you get what you want but that is not enough. Intention can interfere with spontaneously reacting to a situation in an appropriate way.

Even the fact that I had a great jump that was not fair is a part of modern sport with the many officials with times and measurements. At one time sport was played at sunrise and sunset, harvest, birth, death, at important political moments, like William Penn wrestling a member of the Five Nations of the Iroquois after negotiating land sale, and at celestial events. The Northwest Indians played soccer, with a small ball, between opponents with boundaries over ten miles. Traditionally referees were not necessary, now they define something which doesn't match the reality of the situation and call it part of the game. A bad call defines reality when really it distorts it. It is the modern delusion of sport, the fiction of definite belief.

Long term participation in sport can be ruinous to the joints as many modern spare time sportspeople are finding out. In 1970 at an Olympic training camp I experience hip pain and had X-rays taken. The diagnosis was advanced arthritis of my hips; take 8 aspirins a day. There is no cure. I started yoga that year and every X-ray I have taken since then of my hips was negative. I did yoga everyday and it extended my career by years with no bad effect from the jumping and pounding. Now I do it three times a week, but do it in temperatures of up to 220°F for an hour. The body adapts to temperature changes quite easily. One day in Africa in 1968 on a Goodwill Tour I decided to take on the bear (confront the forces of nature.) I think it is necessary to extend the limits of training about once a month depending upon the situation. I did ten repeat 220 yards at high noon on the equator in Tanzania with only enough rest to recover from nausea at 22-23 second pace, a pace that would win a high school race. It was near 100 degree F. It took a week to recover and I felt strong for a year. It also helped that I stayed in Africa for six weeks and absorbed the heat. If one takes on the bear every once in awhile then one doesn't need to extend themselves that much in practice at any one time. Most of the sports injuries I see come from not stretching out. About a third of the total training in sport should be yoga, meditation and doing Qigong type of meditation. Many just see their body as an extension of a tennis racket to pound that ball and beat an opponent.

Coaches, Masters and Self help in Athletics

Most of my competitive career I had no coach and the coaching advice I got was usually wrong. I watched films of great athletes and with this vision actualized it through my body. I keep diaries, I made observations, I meditated and did yoga. Some need constant guidance and coaching and it is these athletes that fall apart after their coaches leave or they move on to another educational level. I did a study once of football players on college teams and found sadism, an authoritarian atmosphere, bad information flow through the team, degradation of players for being injured, harassment of players to quit to get their scholarship (salary) and a winning at all cost attitude. Professional sport is not much better. It is through this training that military attitudes get promoted, order, obedience, give your body up for a cause, and nationalistic and racist and sexist attitudes. The Master student relationships in traditional healing arts may have some of these characteristic. Athletics should be unencumbered by officials, coaches, and doctors so they can develop as human beings. Look at the number of people who fall apart after they quit their sport, it is an indication they didn't learn anything about athletics and   health. This is exactly the reason that the healing arts must be combined with sport at an early age, to heal injures, prevent injuries, recover from hard training sessions by meditating, develop an inner voice, learn how to actualize your athletic intention, and be liberate from ignorance, fear, delusion and suffering. This is the ancient tradition of Olympians and of the healing arts; they fit together, the best of the Occident and the Orient. The creative spirit comes from energy, intention and consciousness.

There are gifted Masters who share their knowledge, like Qigong Master Benhui He who trains cancer patients self help healing techniques and shares his understanding with scientists or Bill Bowerman from Oregon who could take average athletes and make them into Olympic Champions by teaching them rather than directing them.

Training for Strength, Endurance, Speed, Flexibility, and Competition

My basic strategy was always simple, become the fastest, strongest and in the best shape of any jumper or athlete in the world, and later I learned, be the most flexible. In 1971, after competing for almost ten years at the world class level I came up with a system of training which I thought would overcome some of the problems I had; not being able to hit my mark on the runway, nagging injuries, mental alertness when competing, consistent speed when necessary, adequate rest and recovery, declining strength and a top mark in the world in the last two years.

The system was simple, three days of working out and a day of rest. Each day was at top speed, strength and endurance depending upon the day with yoga everyday. If you practice one way you will compete that way. In other words if you get used to running at a certain speed that is how fast you will be. The three days of working out must include a day for endurance, a day for speed work and a day for strength training and a day of rest. On anyone day the work out could change, for example, if I sprinted on the third day and took a rest I can sprint on the first day of the three day cycle if I felt good. If after a day of rest I was stiff and sore then I would do endurance work. The endurance work was running uphill for four miles then racing downhill at a fast past for another four miles. The day of strength work out I would use the Olympic bar and do clean and jerks (forcefully jerking the bar off the floor to my chest and back down again.) at between 150 and 220 pounds, step up onto a bench with 350 lbs. held on my shoulders, one legged. Also it included bench presses and other exercises with heavy weights. Without concentration one can not lift the weights and will be injured. The day of speed work included one half hour of yoga and stretching, then ten easy wind sprints of 100 yards with easy strides. Then 6-10 run throughs on the runway pretending to jump each approach, then several 150's sprints going all out but relaxed. The sprint had to be at a world class sprinters speed or about 13.5 for 150 yards (2-3 times). During this period I ran 9.5 yards for 100 yards on a terrible track beating several athletes who had tied the world record. One big problem is that I would train at a certain pace but compete at another pace; this is a big problem with getting steps right in the jump. If you sprint faster in competition your approach is different and you will foul. But how do you train at a pace similar to competition? The answer is the yoga and the flexibility it brought me, I could train all out, all the time and not be sore. To do this one must be relaxed and mentally alert.

During the Olympic year, 18 months after I started this regime, I had one of the top three jumps in the world at my only competition. During the National Championships 18 days before the Olympic trails in 1972 on my first jump just 20 feet from the take off board, my shoe split down the side and flew off me like a piece of paper. I was in the best shape of my life. I had to borrow a pair of shoe. The shoe had longer spikes and when I hit the take off board my hamstring went into a spasm and I pulled a muscle. This was my third attempt to become Olympic Champion and all my competitors had retired and if I could have gotten to the Games the probability was very great that I would do well since I had never jumped below my best at any Olympic event. Eighteen days later I tried to compete in the Olympic Trails but only got 8th at 25' with a pulled hamstring muscle. This distraction came from staying with people the night before the competition who thought I was too old to still be competing. This distraction and lack of support lead me to be confused and pack the wrong back up shoes for competition. For eighteen months I had no mistakes in training except this one day using longer spikes then the ones I practiced and competed in. High performances training is very frail.

Injuries and Memory

During my early competitive years I suffered from migraines, allergies, acid reflux, two brain concussions, cracked bones in my feet, tendonitis, hypoglycemia, diaherra, pulled (groin, hamstring, abdominal, deltoid, and calf) muscles, arthritis of the hips, scoliosis, nerve impingement in my lower back and neck, multiple knee injuries, sprained ankles, jammed toes and mononucleosis. I played football, basketball and in track ran the hurdles, high jumped, long jumped and ran the sprints.

Injuries come from poor practice and competing conditions, lack of flexibility, doing something out of the ordinary, postural and muscle imbalance, asymmetry in the body, anxiety, distraction, lack of nourishment and accidents. Getting an injury means that one's approach to flexibility and strength is probably wrong. Accidents do happen so one has to see injury as part of the possibility of what will happen. It always happens. During the injury recovery one must completely reshape the body so that the injury is no longer in one's memory. How does one sprint all out when in the back of one's mind the possibility of another injury will happen to the injured part?

One has to practice overcoming the fear of injury and guarding and become more flexible and stronger. One has to learn how to compete while under control, be relaxed and tolerate the disappointment that comes from people's expectations (who are not aware of your injuries.) If I waited till all my injuries were healed completely then I wouldn't be able to compete. The Olympics come only once every four years. In the 1964 Olympic year, even though I made the team, first meet of the year, I pulled a hamstring on a bad runway. I hurt my back from running differently and I wore a back brace when not practicing or competing, my right foot dragged when I walked, I was in constant pain, and suffered from skin rashes and sinus infections. I ranked in the top ten in the world and the only time I didn't hurt was when I competed. No one likes to hear about injuries so most of the time I didn't discuss my injuries to anyone, it only led to people say I was injury prone and using it as an excuse not to do better. As I became older I injured myself less frequently, solved my health problems and adopted meditation, yoga, only natural foods, and alternative treatment for my injuries, which didn't include injections, anti-inflammatory pills, antihistamines, muscle relaxers, excessive vitamin pills and performance enhancing drugs.

Many athletes will run repeatedly on an injury without reshaping their body to get stronger in the injured area. It is best to work an injury but not to excess. These people will permanently do damage because they overcome their pain in a way that is harmful to them. One has to practice getting the injured part of their body in very flexible positions and also strengthen it through weight training. Without this they will get injured again. Most athletes suffer now from injuries they never took care of when they were young,

Practicing for Future Diseases

In a little study I did last year, I reviewed hundreds of my patient's cases and found those that were successful in muting deadly symptoms of disease in later life had previous experience in meditation or yoga and could quickly bring these skills to bear in a short time even though they had not done the techniques for years. Peace, culture, sport, health, enlightenment, and all the healing arts should go together to liberate people from both internal and external factors which lead to pain, suffering, delusion and ignorance.

All Figures missing can be found on pbtinstitute.topcities.com. Website for the Research Institute of Global Physiology Behavior and Treatment, Inc.

Acknowledgements

Xiao Yan for help in preparation of the manuscript.

Cellular Therapy: A Future Medicine

Ewa Carrier, M.D.
9500 Gilman Drive, MC: 0062
La Jolla, California 92093-0062
ecarrier@ucsd.edu
Tel: 858-657-6790
Fax: 858-657-822-0835

Abstract

Hematopoietic stem cells have been clinically used to treat cancers not responding to standard chemotherapy for three decades now. It was known that hematopoietic stem cells, which are obtained from the patient's or donor bone marrow, may restore patient's hematopoiesis (blood forming function) after high—dose chemotherapy. Recently, it was discovered that it is possible that hematopoietic stem cells can differentiate into other tissues as well, and repair conditions such as stroke, heart infarct and liver failure. These therapies are still investigational, but seem to have very few side effects. They possible may become a base for the future, non-toxic cellular and regenerative medicine. Hematopoietic stem cells are readily available and can easily be obtained from the bone marrow or blood. Adult stem cells reside in most of the tissues and potentially have the ability to differentiate and repair damaged tissues. It is unknown why under normal conditions they do not proliferate sufficiently in response to events such as Alzheimer's disease, stroke or heart infarct. One possible hypothesis is that our bodies became impure, and therefore unable to utilize the normally occurring healing mechanisms. Extensive research has been recently initiated to study the ability of different sources of stem cells to repair damaged tissues. While there are ethical issues associated with the use of embryonic stem cells, there are no ethical or moral issues with the use of mesenchymal, cord blood or hematopoietic stem cells. We have developed animal murine model for genetically diagnosed diseases and heart infarct. We are studying embryonic and hematopietic simultaneously to determine their migration and repair potential. Relevant data on these models, migration, chimerism, tolerance and functional improvement will be presented.

Introduction

Stem cells are cells that have self-renewal capacity and multi-differentiation potential. They reside in almost every part of the body, in their own "niches" ready to proliferate and repair. There are nervous stem cells, muscle stem cells, liver stem cells, hematopoietic (blood forming) stem cells, etc.

The hematopoietic stem cells can be obtained by direct aspiration from the iliac bone (under general anesthesia) or from the peripheral blood following the process called pheresis. They have been used for almost three decades for the treatment of cancers and most recently for autoimmune disease.

Recently, it has been shown in animal models that stem cells can "trans differentiate" into the cells of other tissues, although this has not been completely proven. Embryonic stem cells obtained from the blastocyst are pluripotent and can differentiate into all tissue types. There are, however, ethical issues associated with their use and they tend to form tumors *in vivo* teratocarcinomas.

Recently, cord blood obtained from the placenta of a newborn baby has been used for treatment of congenital and malignant diseases in children.

Mesenchymal stem cells, or stromal cells, are cells that form support for hematopoietic stem cells. They have been shown *in vivo* to trans-differentiate into bone, fat, muscle, cartilage, heart, nerves, etc. The *in vivo* experiments have not yet confirmed the functional capacity in these organs.

There are different kinds of stem cells living in the body that may have the capacity to migrate and repair damaged tissue. The resilience of adult stem cells in various tissues indicates that there is a regenerative/repair potential inherent to these tissues.

<u>Why is this mechanism not activated in events such as stroke, heart infarct, or diabetes?</u> There are two distinct possibilities:

1. These events are too overwhelming for the system to respond. Perhaps, we were designed to live long, quiet lives and not suffer from civilization-induced diseases.
2. Spiritual or bodily impurities accumulate in our bodies as a result of negative emotions and environmental contamination.

The present science on "regenerative medicine" focuses on methods to achieve or enhance this self-repair system. The uses of various sources of stem cells and cytokines (proteins with specific stimulating or modulating function) are presently being investigated.

The potential diseases or disorders that may be amenable by this approach are:

1. Degenerative diseases of the brain
   Alzheimer's
   Parkinson's

2. Heart disorders
   Heart infarct
   Congestive heart failure

3. Diabetes

4. Muscular disorders

5. Spinal cord injury

6. Others

The cell lines from embryos have been established and *in vivo* differentiation experiments are in progress.

Animal models for cellular therapy in stroke, heart infarct, Crohn's disease and liver failure have been established. Functional and proof-of-principle experiments are in progress.

The questions that need to be answered are:

1. What is the best source for cellular therapy?

2. What is the optimal route of injection?

3. Can enologenous adult stem cells be activated?

4. Can adult stem cells trans-differentiate?

5. How to enhance the naturally existing repair system?

The cellular therapy may become a mainstay of a future, non-toxic approach to treatment of many congenital and acquired disorders.

References:

1. Kurtzberg J, Kosarus B, Stephens C, Snyder EY. Umbilical cord blood cells engraft and differntiate in neural tissues after human transplantation. Biology of Blood and Marrow Transplantation, Volume 9, Number 2, Feb 2003.
2. Orlic D, Hill JM, Arai AE. Stem cells for myocardial regeneration. Circ Res. 2002 Dec 13;91(12):1092-102. Review.
3. La Barge MA, Blau HM. Biological progression from adult bone marrow to mononucleate muscle stem cell to multinucleate muscle fiber in response to injury. Cell. 2002 Nov 15;111(4):589-601.
4. Lagasse E, Conors H, Wary X, WeissmannIL, Grompe M. Purified hematopoietic stem cells can differentiate into hepatocytes in vivo Nat Med. 2000 Nov;6 (11):1229-34.
5. Wagers AJ, Sherwood RI, Christensen JL, Weissmann IL. Little evidence for developmental plasticity of adult hematopoietic stem cells. Science. 2002 Sep 27; 297(5590):2256-9.
6. Feraud O, Vittet D. Murine embryonic stem cell in vitro differentiation: applications to the study of vascular development. Histol Histopathol. 2003 Jan; 18(1):191-9.
7. Sachinidis A, Kolossov E, Fleischmann BK, Hescheler J. Generation of cardiomyocytes from embryonic stem cells experimental s tudies. Herz. 2002 Nov; 27(7):589-97.
8. Zhao X, Liu J, Ahmad I. Differentiation of embryonic stem cells into retinal neurons. Biochem Biophys Res Commun. 2002 Sep 20; 297(2):177-84.
    PMID: 12237099

WHOLISTIC INTEGRATIVE CARE

Combines:

- Complementary/ Alternative Medicine
- Integrative Care
- Wholistic Healing

Dan Benor, M.D.
DB@WholisticHealingResearch.com

Introduction

There is a heightened interest in integrative care—the blending of complementary/ alternative medicine (CAM) with conventional medical practice. On the one hand this is motivated by patients' demands for services that complement conventional medical care, and on the other hand by health care providers' awareness of economic opportunities and to a lesser extent by their awareness of the benefits of complementary therapies.

Wholistic approaches empower patients to participate in their own health care. They enhance the integrity and the spirit of dignity in the healing encounter between patients and caregivers—who are increasingly under pressures of time and monetary constraints that are eroding their roles as carers. Complementary therapies introduce philosophies and methods of health care that promote whole-person care and acknowledge the place and needs of the caregiver in this process.

While a growing number of medical and nursing schools have courses on CAM, many presentations lack important elements of these approaches. For example, very few courses focus on wholistic approaches that consider the person who has the illness rather than upon the illness the person has. In addition, the courses often focus on complementary therapy methodologies (e.g. inserting acupuncture needles at certain points to control pain) without the associated CAM philosophies of health care.

CAM introduces five broad themes.

1. CAM therapies are potent interventions that can enhance health and help to treat many illnesses that conventional medicine has limited means to treat. Illnesses that can be helped include allergies; arthritis; asthma; heart disease; backaches, headaches, and other pains; irritable bowel syndromes; menopausal problems, urinary tract dysfunctions; neurological disorders (including post-traumatic brain disorders, such as cerebral palsy and strokes); cancers; AIDS; chronic fatigue syndrome; and many more.

Members of the public are rapidly learning the benefits of complementary therapies and are voting for them with their dollars in a big way. Several surveys have shown that just about as many dollars are paid (out of pocket) for complementary therapies as are paid (mostly out of insurance) for conventional medical care. Public pressure has been a major driving force in accelerating the pace of development of integrative care.

2. Wholistic and CAM therapies offer ways to humanize medical care. Both health care professionals and the public often complain about the dehumanization of conventional medical care. In the name of efficiency, and under the combined intense pressures of information overload, departmentalization/ mechanization/ bureaucratization of medical care, and financial pressures, doctors and nurses are being limited in the types of treatments they can offer and in the units of time per patient allotted to provide them.

a. *Patients are dehumanized by conventional medical care.*

Patients are stripped of their responsibility for their own care when they come for examination and treatment. They are expected to follow the routines, orders and prescriptions of institutions, of doctors and of nurses and hospital orderlies without question. Under this system, you are described as "the chronic backache in bed 7" rather than "the person with the backache in bed 7."

Members of the public are also choosing complementary therapists because they feel that doctors focus too much on their diseases and too little on themselves as people. CAM therapists spend 30-120 minutes per session with their clients, compared to 10-30 minutes for visits to doctors. Conventional medicine focuses on your symptom and disease management of your medical or surgical problems, while CAM therapies focus on you as the person who has the problems.

Some nurses and doctors who are sensitive to this aspect of medical care take wholistic approaches—which they might identify as good bedside manner. However, very little of wholistic philosophy is taught in medical schools. Under financial pressures nursing staff have been eliminated and the work load of the remaining few nurses has been increased and has been shifted towards more administration and less direct patient care. Nursing schools are more sensitive to this, but many nurses find that they are unable to apply these principles because their jobs have been pared down to focus increasingly on mechanized ministrations to patients' physical needs, with little time permitted in their schedules for attention to psychological and spiritual needs.

b. *Health care professionals are dehumanized by conventional medical care.*
Medical and nursing students very frequently complain that their professional studies are stultifying and dehumanizing—discouraging and squelching their idealism and sensitivity to feelings in themselves and in their patients.

Excuses are given by medical educators that the enormous load of information that must be studied in medical and nursing school leaves no time for "inessentials" such as discussions of stresses and feelings. Nursing and medical students are expected to ignore their feelings about patients, such as anxieties about caring adequately for their patients, dealing with patients' grief, and dealing with fears about their own mortality—again with the excuse of time constraints.

The same applies to doctors and nurses after graduation. The pressures of heavy workloads and clinical responsibilities are taken as excuses for not budgeting time for self-care. This is certainly a major reason why medicine as a profession has one of the highest rates of burnout, depression, alcohol and drug abuse, and suicide.

Wholistic healing emphasizes self-care of the caregiver as prevention to such problems. Self-care that includes wholistic integrative care introduces health care practitioners experientially to these approaches.

3. *Wholistic, integrative care empowers you to assume greater responsibility for your self-care.* Conventional medical care disempowers people from taking responsibility for their own health. Health care professionals are the diagnosticians and prescribers of treatments for problems.

Wholistic approaches provide whole-person care—addressing people rather than diseases, caring rather than curing, using all possible therapeutic modalities rather than a limited few, and empowering respants wherever possible to use self-care approaches and to be active participants in decisions regarding their health.

The very word patient suggests a passive person who patiently waits for treatment. Bernie Siegel proposes that we use the word *respant*, designating people with problems as responsible participants in their own care.

4. *Wholistic integrative care awakens and nurtures intuitive and spiritual awarenesses.* The western medical model is mechanistic and reductionistic. It assumes that physical causes will eventually be identified for all illnesses, just as they have been with infectious diseases, hormonal, and genetic disorders. It is a linear, *either-or* model.

Wholistic and integrative approaches are *both-and* models. While they acknowledge the contributions of conventional western medicine, they also include contributions of emotions, mind, relationships (with people and the environment), and spirit as vital factors in health and illness.

Wholistic care introduces concepts and practices that include the *body-mind* and *person-spirit* aspects of health and illness.

The importance of intuitive and spiritual awarenesses extend far beyond the therapeutic encounters of individuals. These awarenesses are vitally needed to address the ills of society and of Gaia, our planet.

5. *The philosophies of wholistic integrative care enrich the lives of health caregivers and respants.* Wholistic care includes the cultural traditions and philosophies that accompany the complementary therapies. In many cases these suggest lifestyle changes—such as diet, meditation, yoga, and the like—that you may find pleasant and helpful.

Many clinics and hospitals now offer some CAM modalities. Growing numbers of medical schools are offering courses in complementary/ alternative therapies. For the most part, aspects of these therapies are transferred into the medical model and are presented as methodologies that address symptoms. For example, acupuncture, chiropractic, and osteopathy are used for pain; Chinese herbs for eczema; and so on. The rich theoretical and philosophical contributions of these therapies are largely ignored, as well as the understanding of disease that contributes to disease.

Knowing that there is an alternative to the Western medical model, particularly as it is practiced under managed care, may alert you to new, productive, more satisfying options through integrative care. There are many such models and practices.

Guiding philosophy for Wholistic Integrative Care

Terminology informs, guides, and shapes the actions of therapists and public. Particular attention to terminology will be given to clarifying new ways of conceptualizing and approaching health care.

Integrative Care: Allopathic Medicine combining with CAM Therapies.

Allopathic Medicine: Conventional, Western medical care as provided in the average hospital, medical clinic, and private doctors' offices.

Complementary Therapies: Term for therapies such as acupuncture, chiropractic, homeopathy, massage, osteopathy, yoga and many more approaches. I prefer this term over the more frequently used Alternative Therapies. Complementary promotes collaboration of colleagues using allopathic and complementary therapy approaches, working as equals for the benefit of people needing help. This term is the essence of a both/ and approach to health care.

Alternative Therapies: Term most commonly used for what we are calling Complementary Therapies. Alternative suggests that people have to choose between types of therapies on an either/ or basis. I feel this term is divisive and promotes competition rather than collaboration. The term is also used to denote methodologies transferred from the various complementary therapies and applied for symptom management within allopathic medical frameworks.

Complementary/ Alternative Medicine (CAM): Synonym for Complementary and Alternative Therapies.

Wholistic Healing Approaches and Therapies: Approaches that seek to bring people to a state of wholeness in body, emotions, mind, relationships (with other people and the environment), and spirit. The "w" is inserted to distinguish these approaches from another usage for holistic therapy—the application of methodologies taken out of context from their rich philosophical and cultural frameworks and applied piecemeal as techniques for symptom management, without acknowledging or applying the guiding theories and philosophies that properly should accompany them.

Body-mind Therapies: Approaches that assume that the mind, emotions, and body are an integral unit in health and illness.

Spirit: That part in each of us that is known (and can only be known) intuitively, with an inner knowing that is immanent and transcends logic, that connects with the vast worlds of material nature and of noetic (beyond words), transpersonal/ Divine realities. The spiritual is invariably distorted when it is translated into words.

Soul: Term used by some to indicate an enduring aspect of life that survives physical death and incorporates the lessons the spirit learned into an enduring consciousness. (Others may reverse the meanings of *spirit* and *soul* as defined here.)

Bodyspirit Therapies: Approaches which assume that the soul and spirit incarnate for lessons in the school of physical life, and that illnesses, emotional difficulties, and relational challenges are such lessons.

Wholistic care

- *Addressing the person rather than merely treating her or his problems.*
- *Including body, emotions, mind, relationships, and spirit.*
- *Disease is addressed along with disease.*
- *Health awareness and prevention of illness.*
- *Caring and curing are emphasized equally.*
- *The person who is the therapist is as important as the therapeutic modality used.*
- *The recipients of care are full participants in their own care and treatment.*

Wholistic care addresses the person who has the disease rather than the disease the person has.

Western medical practice has tended to specialize in treating various parts of people. Several factors have contributed to this trend:

First, the overload of medical information makes it impossible for any one practitioner to master all aspects of medical care. Specialists can master certain parts of medical knowledge and develop treatment skills to much greater degrees than generalists.

Second, greater technical skills and efficiency are developed when teams of health care professionals specialize in narrower aspects of medical and surgical care.

Third are the personal preferences of practitioners. Health carers may find greater interest in medical, surgical, psychotherapeutic, social, or spiritual aspects of their patients.

Fourth, medical training focuses heavily on physical causes of disease and often does not prepare health care professional to deal with psychological causes and concomitants of acute, chronic, and terminal illnesses.

While the sub-specialization of medical practice may suit the treatment preferences of practitioners and may promote efficiency in medical management, many patients complain, "There is no one who addresses me as a whole person. I am a person with an illness, not just an illness. And I have all sorts of problems around the illness that are a part of the illness and need addressing just as much as the physical part of the illness does."

This is one of the main reasons why people are paying billions of dollars annually out of their own pockets for complementary therapy treatments.

Wholistic medicine addresses the whole person—body, emotions, mind, relationships (with other people and with the environment), and spirit, assuming that each component may need attention individually but that each is intimately related with all of the others. Emotional or relational problems may bring about stress reactions in the body. Physical conditions may influence psychological states and alter relationships. Spiritual upliftment may make difficult emotional and physical problems more tolerable. We tacitly acknowledge this in our language, as the origins of the word heal are in the Germanic and Old English roots of haelen, "to make whole."

Many complementary therapists practice within wholistic frames of reference. For instance, acupuncture assumes that proper balances in subtle energies within the body and diet are vital to health. Homeopathic clinical histories may require two hours of explorations concerning a person's personality, stresses, lifestyle, family history, and relationships, in addition to very detailed explorations of symptoms, history of illnesses, immunizations, and more. A broad range of hands-on therapies views the body and psychological states as a unity, sometimes referring to this as the body-mind. These include many types of massage, reflexology, Applied Kinesiology, Healing Touch, Therapeutic Touch, Reiki healing, and more. Some practitioners of these therapies also focus upon spiritual awareness in their interventions.

Clients of many complementary therapists are often as pleased with the fact that someone has taken the time to listen to them as with any of the specific therapeutic interventions they receive.

However, not all complementary therapists have a wholistic approach. Some apply various methodologies in a mechanistic manner, focusing primarily upon symptoms and not on the whole person.

Self-care is strongly emphasized in wholistic treatment. Diet, abstention from harmful substances, exercise, relaxations, meditation and imagery exercises may be prescribed as essential aspects of treatment.

The role of the wholistic health care professional is often that of a model, a counselor and a companion in the journey of life—as much as that of a therapist and advisor.

When you bring a problem to a wholistic therapist, one of the first questions you may be asked is, "What do you think this symptom or illness is saying?" This often leads to a discussion of stress factors, dietary and lifestyle considerations, and support systems that you may be able to alter in order to improve your condition. "Who is the pain in your neck?" or "What do you think your stomach is grumbling about?" may bring into focus some of the ways in which people somatize their stresses or unhealthy lifestyles.

De-stressing is a major focus of wholistic care, both as a treatment and as a preventive health measure. Learning to deal with illness is another focus.

Caring is emphasized more than curing. Although complementary therapies may add many options for treating illnesses, the wholistic approach emphasizes caring for the person as the highest priority. The caring and counseling skills of the therapist are often as important as their knowledge and skills in their particular therapeutic modality.

Death is accepted as a natural part of the life process. People are helped to understand and anticipate the process of dying, to make living wills in which they specify the measures they wish to have applied to themselves when their physical and mental health may be severely impaired.

The physical and psychological wellbeing of health carers is of great importance in wholistic care because the carers are themselves instruments for enhancing the wellbeing of patients. Wholistic carers believe that one of the most important ways of introducing holistic approaches is to model for their patients that which they wish to teach.

Wholistic carers often follow many of the self-care practices that they advocate, such as diet, exercise, and various ways of de-stressing.

Wholistic care encourages carers to find peer support and supervision that enables them to de-stress from the burdens of clinical caring. De-stressing enables carers to be more available for their respants, to deal with the responsibilities and stresses of clinical care, to empathize with patients' emotional distress, and to model for respants how to deal with problems.

Wholistic care is much more a set of attitudes and ways of being than a set of methodologies. Those carers who have adopted wholistic approaches usually find that their lives are substantially enriched and their ways of coping with stress are markedly enhanced. However, this approach may not appeal to every health care professional.

Towards an Understanding That "Spirit First, Mind Next, Body Follows" Is the Most Important Universal Principle Affecting Health

Sidney E. Chang, PhD.
schang@yoko40.freeserve.co.uk
Sukyo Mahikari / Yoko Civilisation Research Institute

After graduating from the University of the West Indies in Jamaica, I took a PhD. in molecular biology at the Cambridge University. Then, for twenty-five years, I worked as cell and molecular biologist in the field of cancer research. Now, I work as a consultant for Sukyo Mahikari.

As a young man I was sceptical about the existence of God. Later, this scepticism was reinforced as I became more and more engrossed with my science. I believed that science would eventually give people a rational explanation about the nature of life.

Fifteen years ago, in June 1988, I was scheduled to go to Hood College, not far from Bethesda, to attend an international meeting on "oncogenes", a topic that at that time was fast becoming an important area in cancer research.

However, I did not reach Hood College for the oncogene meeting because I became seriously ill with flu a few days before the meeting began and I could not travel. I was devastated by this flu and it left me feeling exhausted, mentally and physically, for many months afterwards. Indeed, my condition was such that I could only continue my research work on a part time basis. A year after my initial illness I was diagnosed as having post-viral chronic fatigue syndrome. As a scientist, I was very disappointed that there was no medical treatment or remedy for my condition.

One consultant recommended homeopathy and massage to ease my condition, and another recommended meditation. Because these therapies helped me, I tried many other therapies including reflexology, shiatsu and macrobiotics. Despite some progress, by November 1990, it was evident that I was still not well. I was given extended sick leave from my research institution.

One therapist told me that, in his opinion, my illness was a manifestation of a deep-seated causation at the level of spirit, the realm of the source of life. He introduced me to Sukyo Mahikari, and recommended that I receive "True Light".

In the practice of the art of True Light, a purifying spiritual energy is transmitted from the hand of the giver, at a distance of about 30 centimetres, to different points on the receiver including the forehead, back of head and neck, and the kidney region, for up to 50 minutes. I was told that True Light is the spiritual energy of God and that the purpose of receiving Light was not for healing or solving misfortune, but to purify spirit, mind and body.

When I agreed to receive True Light in November 1990 I was extremely sceptical. However, after each session of Light, I generally felt more relaxed and my sleep improved. Sometimes, I had what I came to understand are "cleansings", the discharge of impurities and toxins from my body in the form of fever, runny nose, phlegm, skin eruptions and diarrhoea. On one occasion, for about 24 hours, I had the distinct taste in my mouth of a nasal spray that I had used for several years and which I had stopped using one year previously at the recommendation of my homeopath. I was quite surprised by this experience.

Mahikari members encouraged me to be positive and to offer prayer—gratitude for the many blessings that I received each day, and apology for the spiritual impurities that had been accumulated by my family, my ancestors and myself, over many lifetimes, and that might have been the primary cause of my illness.

One evening, I apologized to God for possibly contaminating my soul with spiritual impurities through my arrogant attitude with regards the use of animals in my laboratory experiments. When I did so I started to cry and suddenly I felt a heavy burden lift from my shoulders. Through this experience I was able to deepen my understanding of the importance of apology and I began to realise that apology is not only about humility but also about accepting one's spiritual responsibility as a human being.

Through receiving Light, my prayers and my efforts to be more grateful and positive, my health condition gradually improved. In other words, I discovered that, for the sake of my health and wellbeing, it was important for me to cultivate a more God-centred and holistic attitude. Eventually, I recovered fully from my illness and returned to work as a full-time scientist in December 1991.

I began to practice the art of True Light myself in November 1991, and through the practice I have had many wonderful experiences.

One day, I gave Light to an elderly lady who had a mini-stroke several months previously. She could not use one of her hands and so I gave Light to it, and to other points where toxins accumulate. The lady fell asleep. When she awoke she exclaimed: "It has gone". "What has gone?" I asked. Her daughter explained that ever since her mother had the mini-stroke she had a constant pain in her head. Now, the pain had disappeared. In addition, the lady could move her hand and feed herself.

On another occasion, I gave Light to an elderly gentleman who had difficulty walking. Afterwards, he had what his wife described as "volcanic diarrhoea", an experience that caused some alarm. Afterwards, however, the gentleman was able to walk unaided.

One can do experiments with True Light. For example, just before this presentation began, two identical bottles of red wine were opened, mixed and then divided into two portions. During the presentation, a colleague is giving Light to one half of the contents of the wine bottle, but not to the other half. Later, you can decide for yourself whether there is a difference in aroma and taste in the two wine samples. *[postscript: after the session, some members of the audience who tasted the wine said that they did notice a marked difference between the two wine samples]*

Whilst it may be relatively straightforward to do experiments with wine, food samples, or growing seedlings, experiments with people are not so straightforward. This is because the spiritual condition of people is not easy to evaluate, thus making it difficult, for example, to choose a group of controls. Nevertheless, clinical studies can be done, and have indeed been done.

It is also possible to evaluate well-documented case histories and to draw conclusions from them. In this respect, this conference is an excellent opportunity to discuss potential collaborative research projects to investigate the nature of True Light. However, in my opinion, the best way to study True Light is through one's personal practice of the art of True Light.

Within the framework of Mahikari teachings, spirit, mind and body are interlocking aspects that function in harmony according to the universal principle of "Spirit first, mind next, body follows".

If the relationship between spirit, mind and body is compared to a river, spirit is the upstream aspect, mind is the midstream and body is the downstream. If a river upstream is contaminated, the river midstream and downstream will inevitably also become contaminated. Similarly, if a person's spirit is contaminated, that person's mind and body will also become contaminated. Therefore, no matter how much attention people may give to keeping mind and body fit and healthy, if their spirit is contaminated with impurities accumulated in this and previous lifetimes, inevitably there will have impurities in their mind, manifesting as negative thoughts or feelings, or confusion, for example, and/or their body, manifesting as chronic illnesses, for example.

Through experience, one can appreciate that the principle of spirit first, mind next, body follows, is the most important of the many immutable universal principles that exist. Other principles that affect people's lives include the principle of cleansing that is closely related to the phenomena of reincarnation and karma.

By understanding how these principles and phenomena work together, one can perceive that many difficulties in life including illness, are natural mechanisms that allow people to eliminate impurities of spirit, mind and body. In other words, the universe has in-built mechanisms by which spiritual impurities, or negative karma, accumulated by people in this and past lives are erased, and balance restored. By cultivating a deep understanding of how universal principles work, people can gradually find purpose and meaning in their experiences, and recognise that the primary cause for most illnesses is not at the level of body or mind, but at the level of spirit.

It is my opinion that the practice of Sukyo Mahikari can support practitioners in the various disciplines comprising whole person medicine by offering a deep understanding of the immutable principles that govern the universe as well as a practice of purification that is effective at the deepest level of illness causation.

Finally, it is also my opinion that Mahikari teachings provide a plausible explanation for many unexplained phenomena including personality changes following organ transplantation, multiple personality disorders, birth defects, and so on. A description of these teachings and how I gradually accepted them could be the subject of a future paper.

HYPOTHESIS OF THE BIOFIELD

Savely Savva
MISAHA@aol.com
Monterey Institute for the Study of Alternative Healing Arts (MISAHA)

The current pragmatic development of biomedical science proved to be effective, though very expensive to the society. Since the most complex control system of the organism remains largely unknown, it is reasonable to trace associations of wrong or missing signals with particular physiological deviations and try to make up for failures. A typical example is the discovery and application of insulin in the treatment of diabetes that saved millions of lives. However, this kind of compensation increasingly incurs unforeseen damages to the organism. The deeper science penetrates into biochemical processes of life, the more complex picture it encounters: what, for example, controls processes such as splicing, methylation, glucosition, protein synthesis on ribosomes, etc. remains unknown. Similarly unknown and unpredictable are possible long-term reactions of the organism's general control system to invasions at such deep levels. It is the testing of new remedies developed in the absence of the big picture that constitutes the rapidly increasing cost of health care to the society.

The purpose of the International Symposium "Paradoxical Effects in Biophysics and Medicine" we are working on is to start a coordinated scientific effort aimed at understanding the physical basis of life, the function and the physical carrier of the general control system of the organism. This and only this approach will lead to the understanding and broader utilization of such medical practices as acupuncture and so-called energy or biofield therapies. This will provide a scientific basis for the utilization of mind-body phenomena including placebo effect.

As Craig Venter, CEO of Selera Genomics, remarked on national TV at the announcement of deciphering the human genome in 2001, we are facing a different, nonchemical level of organization. It seems that since nobody knows how to approach this different level of organization associated with life, the biochemical approach remains dominant: biochemists know how and want to deal with molecules only. Yet, there are many scientists throughout the world who inquire into this "mysterious" level of organization that we call the Biofield.

M. Bischof (1998) starts his review of biological holism and field theories with the 1890 work of German embryologist Hans Driesch (1891). The first to introduce the concept of the biofield as the morphogenic factor in embryogenesis was Alexander Girwitsch (1944)

> "...the place of the embryonal formative process is a field (in the usage of physicists) the boundaries of which, in general, do not coincide with those of the embryo but surpass them. Embryogenesis, in other words, comes to pass inside the fields.... Thus what is given to us as a living system would consist of the visible embryo (or egg, respectively) and a field."

In their Commentary to Beloussov's "Life of Alexander Gurwitsch..." biologists J. Opitz and S. Gilbert (1997) write:

> "...The concept of the morphogenetic (or embryonic) field was extremely robust in the 1930s, as is evidenced by the debates concerning the structure of the fields. Huxley and deBeer (1934) popularized the notion of the "gradient field," extending the work of Morgan and Child on regeneration, while Weiss' 1939 book put forth a more ecological and interactive notion of the field (see also Schmalhausen, 1938; Filatov, 1943). However, after World War II, the concept of fields went into dramatic decline. There were several reasons for the decline. First, biochemical methods (such as those employed by Needham) were not adequate to enable embryologists to analyze field properties such as limb polarity, neural patterning, and lens induction. Second, there was the decline of the scientific infrastructure in Germany and other European countries. The Spemann laboratory, for instance, had scattered around the world. Third, Morgan and other geneticists were in direct opposition to the morphogenetic field, which they saw as a rival to the explanation for heredity. They actively blocked the publication of materials by those investigators (especially C.M. Child and his students) who favored field explanations (see Haraway, 1976; Mitmann and Fausto-Sterling, 1992; Gilbert et al., 1996). Fourth, the field concept had been made extensively holistic and refractile to the scientific analyses of its time. Although Weiss and Spemann vehemently claimed that embryonic fields were real, physical entities, they could not be analyzed by the techniques of their day. Indeed, Weiss' fourth postulation in his characterization of morphogenetic fields made it doubtful that fields could ever be reduced to biochemical analysis. This was seen by many geneticists as evidence of poor science.
>
> The notion of the field persisted, especially in studies of limb generation and of Drosophila imaginal discs (see Hueftner, 1948; Gilbert et al, 1996).

The last theoretical exposition of the embryonic fields prior to the 1980s was probably that of Curt Stern (1954). In this remarkable article, he equated embryonic fields with the prepattern of the embryo. After analyzing the data concerning the ability of genes to regulate where and when they are expressed, he noted, "Yet this astonishing result fits perfectly well into existing concepts of the embryologist. He has discovered the existence of prepatterns, which he calls embryonic fields...Under normal circumstances, the differentiation takes place in only a limited part of the whole field, at a peak, figuratively speaking. Once differentiation has set in on the peak, no other differentiation occurs within the larger field...The prepatterns of the embryonic tissue in Drosophila, which call forth a response of genes involving the differentiation of bristles, are embryonic fields of larger dimensions than the limited points of normal location of bristles."

Stern also hypothesized that the fields were themselves the products of genes. From here on, the fields are considered (when considered at all) as epiphenomena of gene expression. As part of the genetic explanation of embryology, genes were considered primary. Fields, if they existed, were merely gene products.

During recent years, there has been a re-appreciation of morphogenetic fields as units of developmental and of evolution (see Goodwin, 1982,1995; De Robertis et al, 1991; Opitz, 1993; GilbertetaL, 1996). Interestingly, Stern (1954) hinted that changes in embryonic fields might allow for evolutionary novelties to arise."

The following hypothetic definition of the biofield comes from viewing the organism as a self-controlled cybernetic, thermodynamically open system (Savva, 1997, 1998).

The biofield is the general control system of the organism that evolves in ontogenic development being based on all the genetic material available at any stage of development and differentiates into subordinate biofields of organs, tissues and cells. At the organism's level it holds four fundamental programs of life: development, maintenance, reproduction and death with their physiological and behavioral aspects. The mind is an essential part of the biofield serving behavioral aspects of all fundamental programs and securing conservation of the species, the population and the organism (see the graph above).

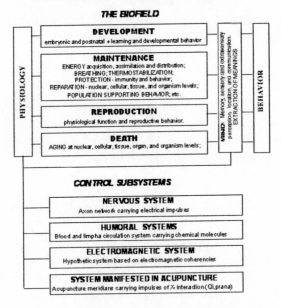

ORGANISM'S GENERAL CONTROL SYSTEM
SPECIES- AND INDIVIDUAL-SPECIFIC PROGRAMS

The word mind is used rather than consciousness in order to distinguish the general decision-making mechanism from awareness associated with the latter in higher species. The function of the mind includes memory, extraction of meanings out of perceived information and fundamental drives such as attraction to the food and opposite sex, avoidance of threats, etc. All the four above-mentioned fundamental programs are apparent in all living organisms and, although they are transferred through a single genome, i.e., chemically encoded, the attempts of reducing them to chemical interactions are obviously inadequate.

More complex organisms are operated by the biofield through four independent control subsystems using different agents and channels of communication: nervous, humoral (chemical), electromagnetic (hypothetical electromagnetic coherencies and biophotons in tissues and organs, for instance, Van Wijk, 2001) and one manifested in acupuncture (called Qi, prana, etc. in Oriental cultures).

What is the physical carrier of the biofield?

We suggest that it is one or more yet-unknown fundamental physical interactions, in addition to the strong, weak, electromagnetic and gravitational interactions currently recognized in physics, capable of communicating with all known fundamental physical interactions and with control subsystems of the organism. This or these interactions, that we will call "X-interaction, are manifested in parapsychological phenomena such as anomalous information transfer (location in space and time) and psychokinesis (interaction with other biofields including psi healing, with physical fields, material objects and man-made devices). Thus, observing effects of conscious intents of specially gifted individuals on physical and biological objects may shed light on the X-interaction—the physical carrier of the biofield.

The following are but a few examples of published scientific observations of human intent interference with other physical fields, material objects and living systems. These observations indicate that X-interaction cannot be reduced to any one of the known four fundamental interactions.

Interference with weak (internuclear) forces:

1. Speeding up and slowing down the rate of americium^{241}Am nuclear decay. The intentional changes of half-life were registered between + 9.5% and—12% with the probability of random effect less than 10^{-10} (Yan Xin et al., 1988c, 2002—the latest and most complete presentation),

2. Low temperature nuclear transmutation of lead into gold in concentrations up to 300 ppm only in presence of a psi operator was observed in Professor J. O'M Bockris' laboratory at Texas A&M University (Bockris, 1997, Savva, 1999)

Interference with electromagnetic fields:

1. Rotation of the plane of polarization of a polarized laser beam by 30 ang. min. (Dul'nev, 1995) and 7o ang. (Yan Xin et al., 1988a)

2. Induction of an intensive temporary peak in laser-induced Raman spectrum of tap water with maximum at 2100 1/cm (Xin Yan et al., 1988d, 2002) indicating changes at the intermolecular level.

3. Temporary various changes in the microstructure of water as observed through scattering of laser beam λ=632.8 nm at various angles by intent of several psi operators (Pyatnitsky and Fonkin, 1995)

4. Deviation of the electrical resistance of a thermo stabilized thermo resistor (Boldyrev and Sozhina, 1992)

5. Increase of adsorption and dispersion of a monochromatic laser radiation ($\lambda=10.6$ μm and 4 mm) by air, nitrogen and carbon dioxide (Volchenko et al., 1992)
6. Deviation of UV adsorption spectra of DNA water solution in the area of 220-280 nm—three independent observations (Yan, 1988b, Rein, 1995, Stepanov & Mozhaisky, 1997)
7. Induction of a periodic electrical signal from a piezoelectric sensor (Ye and Fan, 1983)
8. Induction of a pulse magnetic field 100nT and up to 27×10^6 nT (Dulnev et al., 1998), rotation of a compasses needle (Dulnev et al., 1998, Shen & Sun 1991)

Interference with the gravitation field:

1. Moving the plate of an encased precise analytical balance equivalent to 100 mg force (Dulnev et al., 1998)

Interference with performance of man-made devices:

1. Predetermined deviation from randomness of various random number generators (this study has been conducted in at least two highly credible scientific laboratories in the US showing the probability of randomness $p < 10\text{-}13$) (Schmidt, 1992, Jahn, 1997)
2. Increase of the concentration of dislocations (missing atoms in microcrystalline structure) in "metal bending" experiments with local increase of surface (Vickers) hardness (Hasten, 1979)

The above is by no means a comprehensive review of published scientific observations. We intentionally did not mention observations of phenomena such as remote viewing (mental location in space and time) studied by Hal Puthoff and Russell Targ (1979) at Stanford Research Institute, that were confirmed by at least four other laboratories; dematerialization and materialization of material objects, moving of material objects and transteleportation, and many others representing a very peculiar interference of the human mind with physical mass (see for instance Song, 1999).

Interference with living organisms:

A substantial body of information is available on effects of human intent on living organisms. Daniel Benor, MD (1998) reviewed more than 150 controlled studies on the subject conducted by 1994. Among objects of influence were **enzymes and cells** (including malignant cells) *in vitro* and *in vivo*, **fungi/yeasts, bacteria, single-cell organisms, animals** and **humans**. Many reviewed studies on humans were conducted in clinical conditions and included contemporary diagnostic procedures. (Benor's and Yount's abstracts are in *MISAHA Newsletter* #32-25, 2001). Among different names and slightly different techniques representing this phenomenon used for therapeutic purposes are Therapeutic touch, Reiki, Qigong, Energy healing (used in the NCCAM 5-year Plan) and Biofield therapies. Perhaps most widely known and used in the USA is Therapeutic Touch (TT), a technique developed by Dolores Krieger, professor of nursing at NYU, now widely used by holistic nurses (Krieger, 1973, 1979). For instance, Dan Wirth (1992) in a well-designed double-blind study involving 44 subjects that underwent punch biopsies on the skin and received either 5 minutes TT or infrared warming showed a significant acceleration in the rate of wound healing in treated individuals compared with controls, with $p < 0.001$.

Most gifted healers seem to be capable of communicating with the highest levels of the general control system, the biofield, reversing or replacing particular programs of death. Just as a picturesque example, a very convincing eighteen-minutes video record is available on full recovery of Mrs. Nelda Buss from ALS who was treated by a gifted psychic healer, Dean Kraft. Her husband, Mr. Buss, scientist, video recorded the recovery progress every three-four months from 1986 to 1992 covering the whole process.

The above-mentioned experiments and observations seem to have shown that the physical carrier of the biofield and bioinformation, **the X-interaction:**

1. Cannot be significantly blocked by any physical screening,
2. Produces effect independently of distance unlike the known isotropic physical fields such as centered gravitational or electromagnetic fields. The bioinformation field may be anisotropic, net-like, as suggested by A. Denisov (1975), which can explain the absence of attenuation in reverse proportion to the square of distance, (r^2), and
3. Acts along emotional (or intentional) bonds that must be established between the operator and the subject (or object).

A good illustration to the latter provide long-running and meticulously designed studies of the effect of operators on random event generators (REG) by H. Schmidt (1992) and R. Jahn et al. (1997) at Princeton University (PEAR): an operator affects only one REG on which he/she focuses attention while all other REG in the laboratory and in the world are not affected. Also, in many experiments conducted in Russia authors observed "selectivity" in psi operators' distant interference with measurement devices such as micro calorimeter (Parkhomov, 2002) or magnetic transducer (Dulnev, 2002). In the latter case a target device at 15 km distance reacted to operator's intent while at the same time a similar device in the next room did not.

All the above-mentioned observations suggest that current broadly accepted physical models are insufficient to describe phenomena and processes associated with life and mind. A detailed analysis of these and alternative physical models is presented in the following James Beichler's article.

The majority of previous studies were aimed at showing that the phenomenon of interaction or healing just exists and not at discovering detailed physiological and genetic responses to operator's intervention. The contemporary methodological arsenal of biochemistry and molecular biology permits to repeat some of the previously conducted studies at a new methodological level and by this deepen the understanding of life, the biofield and X-Interaction. Following are but a few examples of such studies where psi-gifted individuals seem to have interfered with biofields of organisms or cells.

E. Rauscher and B. Rubik (Rubik, 1966) observed the effect of *psi* healer O. Warrell on poisoned *Salmonella typhimurinum* bacteria. The motility and physiological activity were measured, the latter by IR absorption of metabolic products in IR absorption spectra. Bacteria in the *psi*-treated samples survived much longer than in the control. Attempts were made to relate the effect to different mechanisms of poisoning (two antibiotics, two added mutation-promoting substances, two stages of bacterial development) in order to get a clue of the mechanism of the *psi* intervention. Although the study confirmed the existence of the phenomenon, authors could only conclude that "...the simple explanation that the healer treatment accelerates the mutation rate seems insufficient." Even if the presumed mechanism of the antibiotic effect (inhibition of protein synthesis) is correct, the healer must have interacted with the bacterial control system which is apparently reactive to the human bioinformation field.

Garret Yount (1997) studied effect of the intent of Chinese Qigong masters on human brain tumor cells growing *in vitro*. The cultures served as the target for both control and test runs. In best-result runs the viability of the cancer cells decreased by 90% compared to control cultures as measured by trypan blue exclusion analysis.

Ge Rong-chao et al. (1998) found that cells of wheat sprouts grown in 45 minutes under the influence of Sun Chu-lin revealed a very high activity of ATPase compared to that in cells of normally grown sprouts of the same size. This indicates that other cytophysiological and possibly cytogenetic parameters may be altered by the intent of Sun Chu-lin.

Repeating these and similar experiments with observation of changes at cytogenetic, cytophysiological and biophysical levels may elucidate the structure and function of the biofield and it's physical carrier.

Further studies of the biofield and the X-Interaction should take into consideration some **methodological specificity** of experiments engaging human operators. One of the arguments against studying the biofield and the phenomena associated with it is that the obtained experimental results are not reproducible. It is understood that complex actions and reactions of the operator's organism depend on a broad variety of internal and external conditions that never will be precisely defined, controlled or reproduced. This can be called "biophysics uncertainty principle" that often, but not always, can be overcome by a probabilistic approach. However, it would be incorrect to say that none of the parapsychological experiments with gifted psi operators were reproduced. For instance, experiments on rotating the plane of polarization of a polarized laser beam were repeated with different operators, although with a different quantitative effect (Dulnev, 1995, Yan Xin et al., 1988). The same was with UV adsorption spectra by water solutions of DNA (Yan, 1988, Rein 1995, Stepanov & Mozhaisky, 1997), and with measuring magnetic field emanated from operator's hands (Dulnev et al., 1998b, Shen & Sun, 1991, Kokubo, 1999), and with destroying cancer cells *in vitro* (Rein 1992, Kmetz 1981, Yont and Qian, 1997). It is not the results that are not repeatable but the conditions of the experiment. It should be recognized that

1.   Very few people have exceptionally strong psi abilities,
2.   Those who have may perform variably depending on their psychological and physiological conditions as well as on time, geographical location, and psychological factors of the environment,
3.   The effect may be directly correlated with the quality and intensity of the information-emotional bond between the operator and the object, and the perception of the task by the operator,
4   The emanation of the message by the operator in many cases may be in a form of relatively short impulses. Accordingly, in preliminary testing operators' psi abilities, averaging results of runs should be replaced

by statistical analysis of the length of a series of correct responses (Lee and Chunovkina, in publication).

5   In experiments on the biofield interaction with other physical fields the experimental error can be easily determined by a metrological analysis of the measuring device for best runs.

The objective of the Symposium and the following research program is not to prove or disprove the existence of the phenomena but to try to understand them.

References

1.   Benor, D. *Healing Research,* Vol.1, Helix, UK, 1992, 366 p

2.   Bischof, Marco. (1998) The History of Biological Holism and Field Theories in the 20th Century. *MISAHA Newsletter,* #22-23, pp.7-11

3.   Bockris, John O'M (1997) Private communication

4.   Boldyrev, L. B. and Sozhina, N. B. (1992) Human's Distant Influence and Quantum Mechanics (in Russian). *Parapsychology and Psychophysics,* # 3(5), pp. 42-50

5.   Denisov, A. (1975) *Theoretical Bases of Cybernetics (the Information Field).* Polytechnic Institute, Leningrad, USSR, (in Russian)

6.   DeRoberts, E.A., E. M. Morita., and Cho, K.W.Y.(1991).Gradient fields and homeobox genes. *Development* 112:669-678

7.   Driesch, H. (1891) Entwicklungsmechanische Studien. *Zeitschrift fur Zoology,* V.53, pp.160-178

8.   Dulnev, Gennady (1995) Methodological Bases for Registering Some Anomalous Phenomena. *MISAHA Newsletter,* # 10, pp. 2-3

9.   Dulnev, Gennady. (1998a) Registration of PK Phenomena: Optical, electrical, and Acoustical Methods. *Consciousness and Physical Reality* (in Russian), V. 3, # 1

10.   Dulnev, Gennady. (1998b) Registering PK Phenomena. *Consciousness and Physical Reality* (in Russian), V. 3, # 3

11.   Dulnev, Gennady. (2002) Registration of Phenomena of Psychokinesis by Means of Magnetic Devices. In *Physicists in Parapsychology,* L. Boldyreva and N. Sotina, Editors, Hatrol, Moscow, pp. 48-51

12.   Filatov, D.P. (1943): Developmental mechanics as a method for study of some of the problems of evolution. *Zh. Obshch. Biol.* 4: 28-46

13.   Ge Rong-chao et al. (1998) Study of ATPasa Activity of Fast-Germinating Sprouts of Wheat and Pea Treated [by Ms. Sun Chu-lin]. *CJSC,* V.8, #4, pp.152-154 (in Chinese)

14. Gilbert, S.F., J.M. Opitz., and R.A.Raff, (1996). Resynthesizing evolutionary and developmental biology. *Dev.Bioi.*173: 357-372

15. Goodwin, B. (1982). Development and Evolution. *J. Theor. Biol.* 97,43-55

16. Goodwin, B. (1995). *"How the Leopard Changed Its Spots: The Evolution of Complexity."* Scribner, New York

17. Gurwitsch, A.G. (1944) *The Theory of the Biological Field.* "Sovetskaya Nauka," Moscow, (in Russian). Extended bibliography is given in Lipkin, M. Application of the Theory of Biological Field by A. Gurwitsch to the Problem of Consciousness. In *Current Development of Biophysics.* C. Zhang, F.A. Popp and M. Bischof editors, Hangzhou University Press, P.R.of China, 1996, pp.223-251

18. Haraway, D (1976). *Crystals, Fabrics, and Fields: Metaphors of Organicism in Twentieth Century Developmental Biology.* Yale University Press. New Haven

19. Hasten, John B. (1979) Paranormal Metal Bending. In *The Iceland Papers*, A. Puharich, Editor. Republished by The Planetary Association for Clean Energy, Ottawa, Canada, 1996, pp.95-110

20. Huxley, J. and Debeer, G.R. (1934) *The Elements of Experimental Embryology.* Cambridge University Press, Cambridge

21. Jahn, Robert, et al. (1997) Correlations of Random Binary Sequences with Pre-Stated Operator Intention: A Review of a 12-Year Program. *JSE* V. 11, # 3, pp.345-367

22. Kmetz, John M. (1981) Cell Culture Experiments with Dean Kraft at Science Unlimited Research Foundation. Appendix in *Dean Kraft: Portrait of a Psychic Healer.* Berkley Books, NY, pp.169-174

23. Kokubo, Hideyuki et al. (1999) Review of Recent Measurements of Anomalous Bio-Magnetic Fields. *ISLIS*, V.17, # 1, pp.20-25

24. Krieger D. (1973) The relationship of touch with the intent to help or heal, to subject in-vivo hemoglobin values: a study in personalized interaction. *Proc 9th Amer Nurses Assoc Research Conf.* New York: American Nurses Association

25. Krieger D. (1973) *The Therapeutic Touch: How to Use Your Hands to Help or Heal.* Englewood Cliffs, NJ: Prentice Hall.

26. Mitman, G. and Fausto-Sterling, A. (1992). Whatever happened to Planaria? C.M.Child and the physiology of inheritance. *In The Right Tool for the Job: At Work in Twentieth-Century Life Sciences.* (Eds.A. E. Clarke and J. H. Fujimura). Princeton University Press, Princeton

27. Opitz, J. M. (1993). Blastogenesis and the primary field in human development. *Birth Defects: Orig. Art. Ser. 29* (1): 1-34

28. Opitz, J.M. and S.F. Gilbert (1997) Commentary to Lev Beloussov's „Life of Alexander G. Gurwitsch and His Relevant Contribution to the Theory of Morphogenic Fields" *Int.J.Dev.Biol.* V.41, pp.771-779

29. Parkhomov A.G. (2002) Experiments and Thoughts. In *Physicists in Parapsychology*, L. Boldyreva and N. Sotina, Editors, Hatrol, Moscow, pp. 15-38

30. Puthoff, Harold and Russel Targ. (1979) Direct Perception of Remote Geographical Locations. In *The Iceland Papers*, A. Puharich, Editor. Republished by The Planetary Association for Clean Energy, Ottawa, Canada, 1996, pp.17-47

31. Pyatnitsky, L. N. and Fonkin, V. A. (1995) Human Consciousness Influence on Water Structure. *JSE,* V. 9, # 1, pp.89-106

32. Rein, Glen. (1992) *Quantum Biology: Healing with Subtle Energy.* Quantum Biology Research Lab., Palo Alto, CA

33. Rein, Glen. (1995) The In-Vitro Effect of Bioenergy on the Conformational States of Human DNA in Aqueous Solutions. *International Journal of Acupuncture and Electrotherapeutics.* V.20, pp.173-180

34. Rubik, B. (1966) Volitional Effects of Healers on a Bacterial System. In Rubik, B. *Life at the Edge of Science.* Institute for Frontier Science, pp.1-20

35. Savva, Savely (1997) A Systems Approach in Biology and Biophysics. *MISAHA Newsletter*, #18-19, pp.2-9;

36. Savva, Savely (1998) Toward a Cybernetic Model of the Organism *Advances in Mind-Body Medicine*, V.14, # 4, pp. 292-301

37. Savva, Savely (1999) Alternative Biophysics: Investing in the Study of the Biofield. *MISAHA Newsletter*, #24-27, pp.2-10

38. Schmalhausen, I.I. (1938). *Organism as a Whole in Individual and Historical Development.* Acad. Sci. SSR Press, Moscow.

39. Schmidt, Helmut. (1992) Progress and Problems in Psychokinesis Research. In *The Interrelationship Between Mind and Matter.* B. Rubik, Editor.Temple University, pp.39-56

40. Shen J. and Sun C. (1991) The Magnetic Effect Generated at the Points of Human Body under the Qigong State (in Chinese). *CJSS*, V.1, # 5, pp.208-210; Referred to in: Zhu Ran-long and Zhu Yi-yi The Latest Progress in Somatic Science. *Journal of ISLIS,* V. 17, # 2, 1999, pp.244-256

41. Song, Kongzhi. (1999) The Extence and Significance of Parapsychological Functions. *ISLIS*, V.17, # 1, pp.198-210

42. Stepanov, A. M. and A. M. Mozhaisky. (1997) Distant Informational Interaction Between an Organism and Solutions of its Biological Components. *Proceedings of the III International Conference: Altered*

States of Consciousness—Experimental and Theoretical Studies into Parapsychology. Moscow, Russia, April 18-20, p.35; see also a brief review in *MISAHA Newsletter # 16-17*, 1997, p.14

43. Stern, C. M. (1954). Two or three bristles. *Am. Sci. 42*:213-247

44. VanWijk, R. (2001) Bio-photos and Bio-communication. *JSE*, V.15, # 2, pp.183-197

45. Volchenko, V. N., G. N. Dulnev, G. N. Vassilieva, et al. (1992) Study of the K-Phenomenon (in Russian). *Parapsychology and Psychophysics*, # 5(7), pp. 35-51

46. Weiss, P. (1935). The so-called organizer and the problem of organization inamphibian development. *Physiol. Rev. 15*,639-674.

47. Weiss, P. (1939*). Principles of Development.* Cambridge University Press, Cambridge

48. Wirth D.P. (1992) The Effect of Non-contact Therapeutic Touch on the Healing Rate of Full Thickness Dermal Wounds. *Subtle Energies, #* 1(1):1

49. Yan Xin, Lu Zuyin, et.al. (1988a) The Effect of Qigong the Polarization Plane of a Laser Beam. *Nature Journal* (in Chinese), V.11, # 8, p. 563; see also *MISAHA Newsletter*, # 13, 1996, pp. 4-7

50. Yan Xin, Lu Zuyin, et.al. (1988b) The Hyperchromic Effect on Nucleic Acid Solutions Induced by Qigong. *Nature Journal* (in Chinese), V.11, # 9, p. 647; see also *MISAHA Newsletter*, # 13, 1996, pp. 4-7

51. Yan Xin, Lu Zuyin, et.al. (1988c) The Effect of External Qi on the Rate of [241]Am Radioactive Decay. *Nature Journal* (in Chinese), V.11, # 11, p. 809; see also *MISAHA Newsletter*, # 13, 1996, pp. 4-7

52. Yan Xin, Lu Zuyin, et.al. (1996d) The Effect of Qigong on Raman Spectra of Tap Water, Saline and Glucose Solutions. *Nature Journal* (in Chinese), V.11, # 8, 1988, p. 567; see also *MISAHA Newsletter*, # 13, pp. 4-7

53. Yan Xin, Feng Lu, Hongjian Jiang, Xinqi Wu, Mei Cao, Zhenqin Xia, Hua Shen, Ming Dao,Hui Lin, Runsheng Zhu. (2002) Certain Physical Manifestation and Effects of External Qi of Yan Xin Life Science Technology. *JSE*, V.16, # 3, pp.381-411

54. Ye Z. and Fan, L. (1983) The Piezo Effect of Psychic Function of the Human Body (in Chinese). *RTGY*, # 1(2), pp. 61-62: Sited from Zhu Ran-long and Zhu Yi-yi The Latest Progress in Somatic Science. *Journal of ISLIS*, V. 17, # 2, 1999, pp.244-256

55. Yount G.L., Qian, Y. (1997) External QI and Cultured Human Cells. Presented at the 16th Annual Meeting of the Society for Scientific Exploration, Las Vegas, Nevada

ENERGY—THE MISSING LINK TO HEALTH

New Effective Energy Medicine Tools

Yury Kronn, Ph.D.
drkronn@earthlink.net

> *"Our physical structures do not first exist and then radiate energy; our energy determines our physical structures."* Dr. RM Chin, M.D. [1]

The subject of this presentation is Subtle Energy called 'Chi" or "Prana" in Traditional Oriental Medicine, and its relationship to the human body and human health.

First I will speak about the nature and properties of subtle energy and the mechanism of its influence on substances of the physical world and on our (human) physical systems.

The second part is about a technology that is able to generate subtle energy and provide us with new energy medicine tools: namely, a wide variety of subtle energy formulas, infused into substances like concentrated trace minerals and targeted for very specific physiological and psychological applications.

Everybody knows we have gold in our bodies. Too little gold in the body makes us unable to assimilate the entire spectrum of minerals and vitamins; it causes neurological imbalance, arthritis, rheumatism and other problems. Why do we need gold? It is a chemically neutral metal. How can gold influence our biochemistry?

When something is happening without the direct participation of matter, science says it is because of the presence of some kind "energy field". What kind of energy field are we dealing with in this case?

The main known energy of our physical universe is the electromagnetic field (EM field). But there is no measurable EM field around the metal gold and other so called catalysts (Pt and Pd among them) that stimulate chemical reactions without directly participating in them. In search of that immeasurable agent that is the cause of the catalytic effect let us consider something which has been known to Eastern cultures for more than five thousand years: Energy Medicine. The most well known representative of Energy Medicine is acupuncture.

Acupuncturists say that the essence of their method of treatment is in regulating the flow of the so-called "Chi" (Qi) energy, which regulates all life processes in the body. Speaking in the language of modern science this statement means 2 things:

a). There is an energy in the Universe (and in the human body) that is not identical with electromagnetic energy, and

b). That energy plays the role of "software" for human processes on all levels, physiological, psychological and mental. Traditional Chinese Medicine says that Chi (software) can be altered not only with the help of needles, but also with herbs, essential oils, food and special excercises, called Tai Chi and Qi-gong.

The existence of this energy remains outside the paradigm of Western science in spite of five thousand years of experience of Traditional Chinese Medicine practitioners. The question arises: if energy that is so important for life really exists, how come modern science doesn't know about it? The answer is simple: it doesn't know because it doesn't want to know.

Science has some excuse for denying the existence of Chi, as it is not possible to measure this type of energy with regular scientific equipment. Scientific equipment can only measure electromagnetic fields and waves. What if Chi is not electromagnetic in nature? Let us remember that the neutron, one of just three stable particles that make our entire physical world, also cannot be directly detected (because it doesn't have an electrical charge) or observed (because it is too small). Nevertheless, science is sure about the existence of the neutron from observing the properties of atoms and nuclear reactions: in other words, science is satisfied with this indirect evidence of the neutron's existence.

Is there analogous "indirect" but scientific evidence of the existence of Chi and its effect? For the last 50 years a lot of serious frontier scientists in many countries, including Russia, China, US, Germany, France, Czechoslovakia, Bulgaria and others, have conducted and published hundreds of rigorous experiments that have unequivocally proven the existence and powerful influence of Chi on inanimate matter, on molecular and even on nuclear levels, in chemical reactions and on living organisms, including cells, bacteria, plants, animals and humans. Articles and books have been published, often against severe resistance from the ordinary scientific community.

Just listing these experiments would take me more time than I have for this lecture. So, let us look at the main results of that research, results that can help us to guess what this Chi energy is about.

Prof. Joie Jones and his colleagues from the University of California in Irvine used functional MRI to register the signal which comes to the visual cortex of the brain when acupuncture point BL67 (used for eye treatments) was affected by needle or by ultrasound impulses [2]. They found that the image in the visual cortex, registered by fMRI, was similar to the image produced by flashing light into the eyes. If the needle or ultrasound signal were moved several millimeters out of the acupoint position, the signal in the visual cortex disappeared. <u>What is most astonishing is that the signal produced by stimulating the acupoint, located on the small toe, reached the visual cortex more than 1000 times faster than the bioelectric signal produced by flashing light in the eyes!</u> It gives us a hint about the non-electromagnetic nature of Chi, doesn't it? In spite of the rigorous scientific research present in this article, scientific journals resisted publishing it for two years. It was finally published after five Nobel Prize winners insisted on its publication.

Later, using ultrasound, Prof. Jones and his group showed that acupuncture points change their size, and slightly change their positions [3] as is described in Traditional Chinese Medical literature. This research shows, along with the unusual properties of Chi, the reality of the human body's subtle energy network (acupuncture meridians).

Dr. Hiroshi Motoyama in Japan developed an instrument called the AMI for monitoring the status, not only of all 12 acupuncture meridians, but also energy centers in the body, called chakras by the Indians [4]. He has an organization called the "Human Science Institute" in Encinitas, CA.

In Russia, Dr. Konstantin Korotkov made the GDV (Gas Discharge Visualization) device based on different principles, known as Kirilian Photography [6], for direct analysis of the human energy field. The GDV makes it possible to analyze conditions of the energy centers (chakras) as well as the energetic status of the organs and systems of the body.

There is another set of experiments we need to mention: this is the change in the absorption spectrum of various substances, including water, observed by scientists in the US, China, Russia, and other countries. A prominent Chinese physicist, Prof. Lu, published his observations on changes in the vibrational-rotational spectra of liquids, the so-called Raman Spectra, under the influence of Chi emitted by Qigong master Dr. Yan Xin [7].

We observed changes in the absorption spectrum of water in different ranges of wavelength under the influence of subtle energy generated by Vital Force™ Technology that we will discuss later. Why is this change in the absorption spectrum of substances under the influence of Chi so essential? <u>Because this indicates that subtle energy, Chi, is able to change the structure of physical matter.</u> Molecular rotational and/or vibrational frequencies and amplitudes (for instance, water—a triangle shaped molecule) can be changed only if the position of atoms in the molecule is changed. What is especially important: our experiment has shown that different subtle energy patterns produce different changes in the absorption spectrum of water. In other words, changes in the structure of the water molecule depend on the information imbedded in the subtle energy. (For detailed charts look at our web site www.energytoolsint.com under "Research".)

So, what we have learned from all this?
• Subtle Energy ("Chi", "Qi", "Prana") is non-electromagnetic in nature
• It is able to influence the molecular structure of physical matter
• This influence depends on the type of energy pattern
• It influences the human body through the body's sophisticated energetic structure, which is no less sophisticated than the physical body itself (see [4,8,9]).

Now, how do we get a hint about the nature of this mysterious subtle energy, Chi?

For that purpose let us have a look at another experiment published by the Chinese nuclear physicist Professor Lu in his book "Scientific Qigong Exploration": *Emission of Chi by Qigong Master Dr. Yan Xin changed radioactive decay rate of Periodic Table element #95 Americium (Isotope Am with atomic weight 241)* ([10] p.379.)

Modern science doesn't have the energetic means to change the decay rate of radioactive elements. You can heat or cool them, put in extra-strong electrical or magnetic fields, expose them to electromagnetic waves, and the decay rate will be the same. But Chi emissions change it! To change the decay rate, you need to change the structure of the atomic nucleus, consisting of protons and neutrons. Chi doesn't interact with protons: otherwise it could be detected in the same way as EM energy.

And what are protons and neutrons made of?

According to our science, each proton and neutron is made up of three quarks (subatomic particles) of two different types. The existence of quarks was confirmed in 1990, only 13 years ago. If we name one of these quarks #1, and the other #2, then a proton consists, let us say, of two of #1 and one of #2, and a neutron consists of one of #1 and two of #2. The only logical way to explain the fact that Chi influences the decay rate of a radioactive nucleus is to assume that this type of energy interacts with quarks or the even more elementary subatomic particles, which compose the quarks.

If so, we can draw the following conclusion: *subtle energy, called Chi by TCM, is the energy type belonging to the world of subatomic particles or the subatomic world.*

And it is logical: just as our matter has an electromagnetic energy field that defines all physical and chemical interactions of substances, the subatomic world should have a specific energy field that defines the laws of interactions in that world.

Now, several words about the subatomic world: how many of these subatomic particles exist in our Universe besides those that are already bonded in protons and neutrons? Go on the Internet and search for the words "Dark Matter". You will find an overwhelming number of articles about the phenomenon called "Dark Matter" by our science. You will find these kinds of statements:

As published in the "National Geographic", February, 2003 in *The Invisible Grip of Dark Matter*: *"The most persuasive theory about the origin of galaxies depends on the behavior of particles no one has ever seen. Known only by its gravitational force, mysterious dark matter pulls ordinary matter into its web, amassing enough gas for galaxies to form. Ordinary matter accounts for only 10 percent of the universe; the rest is dark matter."*

In the L.A. Times, April 30, 2001[11]:

"The observations provide a new basis for calculating the contents of the universe, confirming mounting evidence that ordinary matter—all the shining stars and galaxies, plus people, computers, cats and so on—accounts for less than 5% of it all. The rest takes the form of mysterious "dark matter" (30%) and an even more enigmatic "dark energy" in space (65%) that is causing galaxies to rush apart from one another at an accelerating rate with unknown consequences for the cosmic future."

Some scientists suggest that this "Dark Matter" consists of known and unknown subatomic particles and "beyond-atomic", meaning those not participating directly in the creation of our physical matter [12].

If Chi interacts with at least some of these particles, it could be an "energetic range" from that "enigmatic dark energy", like light is a range inside the spectrum of electromagnetic energy!

One more question for science: does it know where these subatomic particles come from and how they are made? The only hint science has on this topic is a theoretical one: it is the so called "Superstring Theory" which suggests that everything in the universe is made of infinitesimally small string-like "primal particles" existing in at least a 10-dimensional space. This theory is still far from answering the question of how all the known and unknown subatomic particles are made from these strings.

Thus after a hundred years of research and many billions of dollars spent, the only thing we know for sure is that our scientific equipment is capable of measuring processes happening in only 5% of the universe. But the good news is that science now recognizes the idea that the universe can be more than 3-dimensional.

From this position, it is very arrogant for modern science to refuse to recognize the wealth of knowledge about the structure and energies of the universe that has been collected by ancient and more modern but "unofficial" sciences.

Ancient scientists knew very well about the subtle structure of the universe and its subtle energies and about the crucial role of these energies in human life. The giant of ancient Chinese philosophy and science, Lao Tzu, said in his book "Hua Hu Ching" written 500 years before Christ:

> "There are numberless energy rays in the Universe...All rays...come from the subtle nature of the Universe...The interwoven energy net influences the lives of individual human beings, whole societies and entire races...A virtuous individual who responds to the high, pure, harmonious subtle energy rays and integrates them with the positive elements of his own inner being may strengthen his life, enhance his health and power, and lengthen his years [14]."

Now let us briefly outline the results of more recent extra-sensory research on the process of creation of physical atoms from subatomic particles. This research was conducted over the course of 38 years from 1895 until 1933 by two extraordinary personalities Annie Besant and Charles W. Leadbeater, who were trained by Indian Yogi teachers to "see", using extra-sensory perception, the microstructure of matter. Beginning in 1895 they published in the journal "The Theosophist" their observations on the nuclear structure of all the Periodic Table Elements [15]. They described the existence of isotopes of the elements five years before they were discovered by official science. And think about this: they described many elements with correct atomic weights that were not known to science and were only discovered years later!

Elements Discovered By Besant and Leadbeater Years
Before Western Science

Element#	Scientific Name	Year Publ. By B&L	Year Disc. by Science
87	Francium	1932	1939
85	Astatine	1932	1940
43	Technetium	1932	1937
61	Promethium	1909	1945

What is astonishing is that in 1895 Besant and Leadbeater described three particles making up the nucleus of Hydrogen, which is a proton. These sub-atomic particles, named quarks, as we discussed, were discovered by our science in 1990: and the proton is made from three of them. More than that, Besant and Leadbeater also described the smaller particles, which make up the quarks.

The authenticity of their representation of the nuclei of periodic table elements was mathematically examined and confirmed by an open-minded physicist from England, Dr. Stephen M. Phillips, a graduate of Cambridge University. Dr. Phillips developed a whole theory of subatomic particles based on Besant's and Leadbeater's research [16]. He published two books, the latest of which is the "ESP of Quarks and Superstrings". As you can guess, this work is almost completely ignored by our scientific community.

Now let us consider a concept regarding the construction of the universe and the role played by subtle energy according to the research of Besant and Leadbeater. This will help us to understand why subtle energy is present in all substances of the physical world, including those which make up the human body. We will look at the role it plays and how it can be harnessed using the knowledge and technology of modern physics combined with the ancient knowledge of the properties of subtle energy.

Besant and Leadbeater described the basic "particle" of the physical world, which they called the "Anu" [15]. The "Anu" is actually kind of a sophisticated vortex of string-like streams of energy-matter from the world much subtler than physical. The "Anu", or the "ultimate physical atom" as Besant and Leadbeater called it, exists in two forms, positive and negative, or clockwise and counterclockwise vortexes.

"Anus" combine with each other in different combinations like ++-,—+, etc., and these combinations create more sophisticated structures, which science now calls "subatomic particles". This process ends with the formation of basic atomic particles, which make up the atoms of the Periodic Table of Elements (Fig.1). These, in turn, make up all substances of the physical world including those that make up our bodies.

What is interesting is that all subatomic particles and substances of the preceding world, which make the "ultimate physical atom," are subjected to gravitational force, and the Ancients knew about it! Dr. Henry Pullen-Burry, another open-minded English scientist, who deeply researched ancient knowledge about the construction of the Universe, wrote about it in his book "Qabalism" in 1925.

If modern scientists would read this book, the enigma of "Dark Matter", first discovered in 1933 via astrophysical observations of the movement of galaxies, would be answered the day it was discovered. But, it is still an enigma for our science.

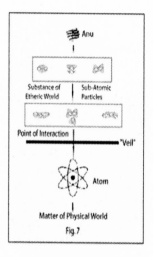

Fig. 7

Dr. Pullen-Burry asked scientists:

"Look out, O chemist into space, peer at the atom, O physicist, and read for yourselves the lessons discovered by your ancestors. Open your eyes, ye blind." *([18] p.34)*

When someone is blind, things look dark for him. Probably that is the reason why our science named the invisible part of the Universe "Dark Matter".

Now, looking at the picture of the formation of physical matter according to Besant and Leadbeater, we can answer the question of how subtle energy can influence inanimate matter and living organisms, and everything in the physical world (Fig.2). Remember, subtle energy doesn't interact directly with physical matter and, as a result, our scientific equipment cannot measure it. That is why it is so important to answer this question

First of all, looking at the vortex-like nature of the ultimate physical atom, we see that the process of the creation of physical matter is a continuous, dynamic process.

Do you remember the expression: "God creates the world every moment"? So, it is literally true. If the energy of the subatomic world, interacting with the ultimate physical atom (or other subatomic particles), slightly changes the "vortex" of this atom, and consequently our physical atoms comprised from it, the chemical molecules in the physical world will be also changed (Fig.2). Using scientific terminology, chemical isomers could be created in this way. Of course, taking into account the quantum nature of the subatomic world, it is a very sophisticated process, but the general idea is clear.   We saw confirmation that Chi produces this kind of effect on physical matter when we discussed changes in the absorption spectrum of substances under the influence of Chi.

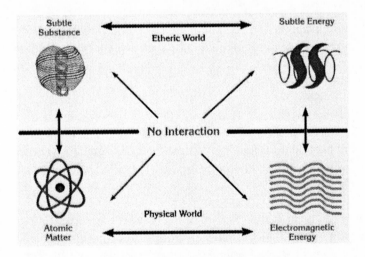

Now, we have come to the point where we can ask: "Is it possible to harness this subtle energy, the energy of the subatomic world, using the achievements and knowledge of modern physics?" Obviously it would be a benefit, since we could use Chi generating technology for the enhancement of many healing modalities.

I asked myself this question more than twenty years ago after being shocked and impressed by what I saw during experiments with the Russian equivalent of Qigong Masters in the Radiotechnic and Electronics Institute in Moscow, where I worked at that time. You probably guessed where I went for advice on how to create subtle energy technology (which we now call Vital Force™ Technology). Of course, I went to ancient science. And there I found the following statements:

- First, the energies of the physical and etheric (or subatomic in modern language) worlds are connected (see Fig.2)
- Second: there is a "point of connection" between the physical and etheric/subatomic world, where the energies of both worlds communicate the most effectively. It is like a phenomenon of resonance: if you are "out of resonance", the interaction between the energies of two worlds is weak, but if you are "in resonance" the interaction is very strong.

After years of experimentation I found this point of connection (which is, of course, proprietary information) and created a generator of subtle energy or Chi. It is plasma based computerized equipment that is able to generate an almost unlimited variety of subtle energy or Chi patterns. I found specific plasma configurations that if manipulated by electrical and magnetic fields are able to emit Chi patterns with qualities described by Traditional Chinese Medicine as the Five Elements (water, wood, fire, earth, and metal) and also with Yin and Yang properties.

I am sure many of you know about the Five Elements [14,19]. The classical diagram of the Five Elements actually states that there are five main kinds of Chi in the Universe, each with distinctively different qualities. Thus, while the Yin-Yang concept determines the difference in the state of Chi movement, the Five Elements define the differences in Chi qualities. The interaction of different elements of Chi can be supportive or restrictive (controlling). There are an infinite number of Chi patterns of various subtleties in the Universe; however, all of them can be presented as containing the qualities of the Five Elements in various proportions. The existence of both supportive and controlling qualities in the Five Elemental energies makes possible what we call "Dynamic Balance", a state of balanced movement of energies, named in Chinese Medicine and philosophy as Tai-Chi. This state is considered paramount in achieving true well-being and harmony. "If the energies are circulating correctly, no evil can attack successfully", said the classical book of Traditional Chinese Medicine, *Lin Shu*.

When I say that my Vital Force™ Technology (VFT) is able to generate Chi patterns with any of the Five Element properties, people usually ask: how do you know? The answer is: it was confirmed in blind experiments by measuring the effect of energy patterns created for all 12 acupuncture meridians using 3 different types of computerized electro-acupuncture devices. (The principle of these devices was first developed in Germany by Dr. Voll). Energies flowing through the 12 major acupuncture meridians have different "elemental" qualities; experiments have shown that each particular meridian was influenced by the energy pattern, created by VFT, with the "elemental" quality exactly corresponding to the "elemental" quality of the meridian.

In addition to the Five Element properties of energy patterns generated by my equipment I found a way to reproduce the energetic blueprint of any of the Elements of the Periodic Table, which is the base of all substances in our physical world. These two features make it possible to create subtle energy patterns targeted for specific biological functions whether physiological or psychological.

On top of this: since any generator can also work as an amplifier, my equipment is able to reproduce the energetic blueprint of any substance, including herbs and essential oils. And, of course, the equipment can tremendously amplify the energetic blueprints. As they are produced, these formulas can be stored by a special part of the equipment and amplified again when needed.

We call all these patterns Vital Force™ Formulas. How can we deliver these energy formulas to people? Experimentation has shown that Vital Force™ Formulas can be infused into organic substances including herbs, oils and into inorganic concentrated trace minerals, which hold this energy for years.

One of the possible explanations for this phenomenon can be the ability of subtle energy to create isomer-like changes in substances, which we discussed earlier.

Now I would like to mention some experimental results observed with various Vital Force™ formulas. First, I will talk about experiments where the so-called "placebo effect" is not in question.

1. The influence of Vital Force™ Formulas infused into water on the germination and growth of wheat, pinto beans and carrot seedlings: compared with the control, energy infused water produced highly significant changes in seedling germination and development with ranges from +77% to—35%. Results were dependant on the specific energy pattern introduced in the water, and on concentrations required for old and new seeds (Dr. William C. Levengood, Pinelandia BioPhysics Lab, MI).

2. Excitation of the visual cortex in the brain by oils infused with subtle energy patterns formulated for the Bladder acupuncture meridian:

3. When applied to the vision-related point BL67, infused oil activated the occipital lobes as registered by functional MRI similar to the excitation produced by acupuncture needles or ultrasound and reported in [2] (Dr. J.P. Jones, University of California, Irvine). The result suggests that the nature of subtle energy generated by VFT is identical to that of the energy referred to as "Chi".

4. Revitalization of HeLa cells subjected to gamma radiation:
5. The Vital Force™ formula "Rejuvenation" infused into liquid trace minerals revived over 80% of radiated cells in comparison with 50% of the cells that survived in control samples. (Dr. Joie P. Jones)

6. Over a period of 1 1/2 years, Vital Force™ formulas infused into concentrated trace minerals, topicals and water have been tested on small animals having various health problems in Dr. Gary Tran's Emergency Animal Clinic in Louisville, KY. Vital Force™ Formulas in trace minerals in combination with other supplements like Noni Juice, played a significant role in curing serious diseases like <u>Canine Parvoviral Infection, Congestive Heart Failure, Insecticide poisoning with seizures, Hepatic Encephalopathy, Closed Head Injuries, and Chronic Masticatory Myositis</u>, which is conventionally an incurable autoimmune disease. Energy infused topicals were successfully used for pain relief, swelling reduction, and enhancing the healing process in severely injured animals

7. The effect of Vital Force™ Formulas on the autonomic nervous system in patients with different conditions was measured with the Heart Rate Variability Test "Nerve-Express" on more than 600 patients (Dr. Jeffrey L. Marrongelle, DC, CNN, Pennsylvania). Electro-acupuncture (Dr. Voll method) was used to determine which Vital Force™ formula was appropriate in each particular case.

    a. Positive shifts were observed in most of the Heart Rate Variability (HRV) parameters, particularly in the relationship of the Sympathetic (SNS) and the Parasympathetic (PSNS) response (see examples on our web page). Positive shifts in heart rate, myocardial response, high frequency and low frequency neurological function, and vascular compliance were observed repeatedly. Improvement in reserve capacity and physical fitness were seen consistently. It needs to be stressed that these changes were often observed very shortly (less than

30 min.) after taking 10-15 drops of energy infused minerals in a glass of water.

b.   Observations on the use of Vital Force™ Formulas over time demonstrate their ability to enhance the biological actions of all other therapeutic modalities.

An example of the kind of enhancement produced by Vital Force™ formulas is presented in the report from a group of health practitioners including two MD's who observed significant improvement in two patients with Lyme Disease using Tetracyclic Oxindole Alkaloid free "Cat's Claw" infused with Vital Force™ energy patterns. After using energy infused "Cats Claw" for 3 months both patients tested negatively for Lyme Disease in Immunoglobulin M and G and Western Blot tests. Patients previously treated with the same type of "Cat's Claw" without the energy infusion did not experience improvement in their conditions.

I would like to mention one more way of exploring the synergistic effect of herbal remedies and energetic formulas. Some Vital Force™ formulas don't have an analogy in nature; they are created experimentally using the rules of ancient medicines. For instance, we have the Stress Relief formula in concentrated trace minerals. Drinking 10 drops of this formula in a glass of water usually takes away anxiety in minutes. When about 3% of a Magnolia tincture is added, it works for depression and when you add 3% Jujube, it works for improving sleep.

How well does it work? Dr. Steven Davis from Redding, CA, reported that all 7 of his patients with insomnia began to sleep normally after using "Jujube Sleep Aid" for a few days.

One more example: when the Stress Relief energy pattern is infused in MSM cream, the cream acquires significant new properties: it relieves the pain of soft tissue traumas in minutes, prevents or significantly diminishes bruising and swelling and accelerates healing.

Why do remedies work significantly better and faster when enhanced with subtle energy?

There are at least two reasons that can be suggested.

1.   On a systemic level, infused subtle energy directly enhances the functioning of the energetic system of the body. The energetic system, in turn, regulates the Autonomic Nervous System, including the Parasympathetic part of it, which is responsible for 99% of all functions of the body, such as heartbeat, digestion, breathing, excretion etc. The connection between the body's energy system, the ANS, and

the organs of the body was very well researched and published with details by subtle energy researchers like Leadbeater [8], Dr. Motoyama [4], Dr. Sankey [9], Reid [19].

2.   On the cellular level: cells have receptors that are responsible for detecting signals from a remedy's molecules to distinguish which molecule the cell needs to absorb. Energetically weak transmitters or receivers can prevent cells from effective absorption and assimilation. Obviously, the better the information encrypted in the energy pattern and the stronger the energetic signal of the (remedy) molecule, the better the cell will recognize it. Thus, energetic patterns work in two ways: they stimulate the Autonomic Nervous System and they improve the communication of the therapeutic remedy with the cells, thereby enhancing the process of assimilation and absorption. That is why 3% of Jujube in the Stress Relief energy pattern works better than 100% Jujube without the energy infusion.

In conclusion I would like to say that in our opinion, Vital Force™ Technology establishes a bridge between traditional Eastern and modern Western medicines. It also provides tools for regulating the body's energy system, which is still a missing component in Western medicine's concept of health.

For a full graphic presentation and added research go to our web page at www.energytoolsint.com.

References

1.   Chin RM (1995) The energy within. Marlowe and Company, New York

2.   Cho ZD, Chung SC, Jones JP, Park JB, Park HJ, Lee HJ, Wong EK, Min BI (1998) Proc Natl Acad Sci USA 95: 2670

3.   Jones JP, Wilson L, Bae YK, So CS, Kidney DD (2002) Soc for Sci Expl Explr 18:381

4.   Motoyama H (1981) Theories of the chakras: bridge to higher consciousness. Theosophical Publishing House, Wheaton

5.   Motoyama H (1991) Correlation between psi energy and ki. Human Science Press, Tokyo

6.   Konstantin K, Leigh G (2001) 11th Ann ISSSEEM Conf Abst, Boulder

7. Lu Z (1997) Laser raman observations on tap water, saline, glucose, and medemycine solutions under the influence of external qi. In: Hui L, Ming D (eds) Scientific qigong exploration. Amber Leaf Press, Malvern, p 325

8. Leadbeater CW (1927) The chakras. Theosophical Publishing House, Wheaton

9. Sankey M (1999) Esoteric acupuncture gateway to expanded healing vol 1. Mountain Castle Publishing, Los Angeles

10. Lu Z (1997) The influence of external qi on the radioactive decay rate of Am 241. In: Hui L, Ming D (eds) Scientific qigong exploration. Amber Leaf Press, Malvern, p 373

11. Washington Post (2001) Studies shed light on universe in the moments of creation. In: Los Angeles Times, Los Angeles, p A9

12. Trefil J (1993) Smithsonian 24: 27

13. Barbree J, Caidin M (1995) A journey through time. Penguin Books USA Inc., New York

14. Lao Tzu (1997) The complete works of lao tzu (Hua Ching Ni, Trans). Seven Star Communications, Santa Monica

15. Besant A, Leadbeater CW (1951) Occult chemistry, 3rd edn. Kessinger Publishing Company, Montana

16. Phillips SM (1980) The extrasensory perception of quarks. The Theosophical Publishing House, Wheaton

17. Phillips SM (1999) ESP of quarks and superstrings. New Age International Press Limited, New Delhi

18. Pullen-Burry HB (1925) Qabalism. The Yogi Publication Society, Chicago

19. Reid D (1995) The complete book of chinese health and healing. Shambala, Boston

20. Powell AE (1953) The etheric double. The Theosophical Publishing House, London

EFFECTS OF INTENT AND MENTAL STATUS ON BIOLOGICAL SUBJECTS:

A Review and Its Implications for Medical Research

Kevin W. Chen, Ph.D., MPH.
UMDNJ-Robert Wood Johnson Medical School
chenke@umdnj.edu

Lian Sidorov, DDS
The Journal of Non-Locality and Remote Mental Interactions
jnlrmi@hotmail.com

ABSTRACT

Because the source of most chronic diseases remains poorly understood and modern medicine knows very little about the roles of mental status and human intent in disease and healing, this study presents scientific evidence that demonstrates the impact of human intent and mental status on biological subjects in many in-vivo and in-vitro experiments. These studies include: a) acceleration of plant, bacteria or cell growth, or with a different pre-determined intent, inhibition of bacteria or cell growth—which reflect changes in the DNA synthesis and cell mitotic rates; b) changes in the rates of transcription (mRNA synthesis) and translation (protein synthesis); c) changes in the substructure of bio-molecules or cell cultures in terms of their conformation, functional activity and other characteristics; d) mutagenesis or mutation in cells or bacteria, even generating new forms of biological species; and, e) cell differentiation (from revitalization of compromised genetic material to apoptosis).

This evidence demonstrates the important roles that intent and mental status play in health and healing, and suggests that mental influence may produce pathological or genetic changes in biological subjects. It suggests that the most common impact of mental status and intent on our health and healing is self-implemented, and may be much stronger, longer lasting and more powerful than what we observed in lab experiments. Therefore, the sources of many diseases that modern medicine tries to identify at the gene level may not be original, but only the consequence of the radical or long-term effect of these unseen sources—human intention and/or mental status.

In a follow-up to this paper (see "Biophysical mechanisms of genetic regulation: Is there a link to mind-body healing?" included in this volume) we will focus our attention on some of the most promising theoretical models that have been proposed to account for mind-body and nonlocal healing—as well as on the remarkable biophysical evidence that has been accumulating over the past three decades with surprisingly little coverage in the mainstream medical literature. Unfortunately, due to lack of substantial data and research funding in this area, none of these models can be fully validated at this stage. Hopefully the current review will generate more interest from a broad spectrum of researchers and funding resources in this direction of scientific exploration, so that we can produce meaningful evidence and make additional progress in understanding of mind-body interaction and bio-energy healing in health and medicine.

Key Words: Intent, mental status, biological growth, conformation, mutagen, in-vitro, in-vivo

Introduction

Modern medicine is a system of knowledge based on our understanding of the human body (organs, tissues, cells, genes, DNA, RNA and so on) and of visible etiological factors like viruses and bacteria. Unfortunately, this tradition of medicine dismisses other significant aspects of human life and health, such as mental status or intent, because these elements cannot be easily quantified or standardized within the framework of known pathological mechanisms. From ordinary layman to top scientist, everyone is aware of the existence of his/her own consciousness or mood, and recognizes that his/her emotion and mental status affects his/her own body function and health. However, we know little about how these emotions and mental status coexist and interact with body and health (Sternberg, 2001). There is no systematic knowledge of mind-body interaction and no medical or anatomy textbook diagramming the roles of human mind or intent.

In laboratory-based experiments and clinical studies, researchers tend to exclude the effects of intent or expectation (such as placebo or experimenter effects) in most medical research. However, as the sources of most chronic diseases remain unknown, and mind-body therapies that take human mind or intent into consideration have achieved increasingly successful and widespread results, more and more scientists have started to explore the potential roles that mental status and intentionality play in human disease and health. In addition to the exploration of placebo effects, studies in psychoneuroimmunology, bioenergy medicine, distant healing and parapsychology and distant mental interaction with living systems (DMILS) have generated a lot of data to support the effect of human mind or intent on our environment and on our own health.

There are many potential confounding effects in self application of mental power or intent, such as those observed in somatic symptoms of mental disorders or placebo effects. In addition, most scientists tend to consider the results from laboratory experiments more convincing than clinical studies. Therefore, the current study systematically reviews the scientific evidence that demonstrates the impact of human intentionality and mental status on biological subjects in in-vivo and in-vitro experiments. This should lower the opportunity to attribute the potential power or effect to other known physical or biological sources. We hope the studies of human intent and mental power will gradually become part of mainstream medical research, and the knowledge of mind-body interaction will be applied more widely in healing and preventive medicine.

Method Issues

The literature in this field is relatively scarce, with little representation in the mainstream medical journals. There are a number of reasons for this. On the one hand, there is a general lack of funds and support for this type of research in science and medicine, as most scientists do not consider this a legitimate research subject. On the other hand, those reports based on carefully conducted research are rarely granted publication in the mainstream journals as it is very difficult to convince biased reviewers or editors to consider these scientific findings. Therefore, it may not be practical for us to conduct a high-quality systematic review of all sources available with the traditional criteria in literature selection and comparison due to lack of publication channels and lack of access in this area. With a non-traditional way of literature review, we intend to include some good literatures in each area of interests to point out the significance and implications of these studies, and to raise a serious concern of why there was not more research being done.

The primary sources of literature in our review include: 1) the popular medical literature indexes such as Medline and Pubmed; 2) the accumulated publications in para-psychology literature that are rarely listed in the major indexes or search engines; 3) Qigong Database by the Qigong Institute (Sancier, 2001), which collected more than 2,000 abstracts and publications of qigong research from various conference proceedings and journals; 4) personal collections and related literature review, such as Benor's (2001) "*Spiritual Healing: Scientific Validation of A Healing Revolution*," as well as some accessible publications in Chinese journals and books.

What exactly is the intent, mental status or mind power we are referring to here? There is no concrete definition on mind power, intent or consciousness power. In Chinese it is called "*nianli*" (power of intent or mental state). We tend to use these terms exchangeably to catch the common meaning of the non-physical power or bioenergy from human intent and consciousness. We have cited many studies from qigong literature in Chinese, where external Qi therapy (EQT) is a popular form of "*nianli*" (intent power) therapy in qigong healing. EQT refers the process whereby a q*igong* practitioner uses his intention to direct his bioenergy to help patients break the qi blockage and to regain qi balance or health. This therapy is practiced through the use of q*i* (vital energy) or y*i* (intent or mind), or in most of cases a combination of the two (Lin & Chen, 2002). As the qi in EQT is supposed to have the same characteristics as the qi flowing within human body and EQT would not work without yi or intent, we consider EQT the result of intent or consciousness power, instead of just bioenergy. Although to an outside observer it might appear similar to the Western "therapeutic touch", only with more distance between the healer and the patient, it is more complicated.

This review will present scientific studies of intent or mental state in the following effect categories: a) Acceleration of plant, bacteria or cell growth, or with a different pre-determined intent, inhibition of bacteria or cell growth—which reflect changes in the DNA synthesis and cell mitotic rates; b) changes in the rates of transcription (mRNA synthesis) and translation (protein synthesis); c) changes in the substructure of bio-molecules or cell cultures in terms of their conformation, functional activity and other characteristics; d) mutagenesis or mutation in cells or bacteria, even generating new forms of biological species or bacteria; e) cell differentiation (ranging from revitalization of compromised genetic material to apoptosis).

Major Results

Accelerating or Decelerating the Growth of Biological Subjects

It is generally assumed that all biological entities have their own "internal clock" regulating the timing of growth, development and death; and that the human mind or intent cannot affect this natural cycle. However, evidence from an increasing number of laboratory experiments challenge this assumption, and suggests some impact of human intent on the biological growing process.

Growth of Plants

Studies of mental influence on seed germination are well documented in both Eastern and Western literatures. For example, Scofield and Hoges (1991) reported that intent-treated cress seeds showed double the rate of germination than the controls. In two blind-placed experiments, Saklani (1988, 1990) found that the wheat seeds treated by an Indian Shaman showed greater height and greater rate of germination. Nicholas (1977) studied radish plants treated with "loving attention", and found a significant increase in the weight of plants but not the height. Miller (1972) reported the effects of distant intent (prayer) on grass growth, an 840% increase in growth rate starting exactly at the time of intent transmission. Grad (1965) reported that the emotional status of the subjects who hold the barley seeds for 30 minutes had significantly effect on the growth of the plant. Many other researchers reported that the effects of conscious intent or mental status could significantly accelerate the germination and growth of various plant seeds, such as rice, wheat, peas, beans, peanuts and flowers (Hu et al. 1989; Jin et al. 1994; Zhou et al. 1989; Pan 1995; Haid & Huprikar, 2001).

Ms. Chulin Sun is a well-known psi subject from the Chinese Geology University. After reading the Tompkins and Bird (1973) book "*The Secret Life of Plants*," she started to learn how to communicate with various plants, and soon discovered her capability to talk with the plants for revitalization and acceleration of growth (Sun 1998). She has worked with dozens of scientists around the world in the past 16 years to explore and verify how human intent or mental power can revitalize fully denatured seeds and accelerate sprouting of various seeds in minutes. With hundreds of successful trials, scientists have reported her success in revitalization of fried peas or cooked peanuts (Lee et al. 1999; Shen & Sun, 1998, 2002), and in acceleration of sprouting of peas (Bai et al. 2000), wheat (Ge et al. 1998), corn, watermelon seed, bean, flower seed and peanuts (Shen & Sun, 1996, 1998). For example, in one study, peanuts were microwaved and specially processed, with a resulting 0% sprouting rate under optimal conditions. Each peanut was then marked with several secret signs on the skin before giving it to Ms. Sun. Witnessed by experimenters and a camera, Sun put her hand over the plate containing one such peanut, revitalized the seed and produced a 3.8 cm sprout in 8 minutes (Lee et al. 1999). This type of study was replicated many times by various scientists in China, Hong Kong, Taiwan, Japan, Malaysia and Thailand. However, the involved scientists had a hard time publishing their data in Western scientific journals as the editors or reviewers simply did not believe what had actually occurred, or refused to publish it because they lacked a scientific explanation for the effect.

Haid and Huprikar (2001) explored the possible effect of meditation on the germination and growth of green pea or wheat by imbuing them with the intent to stimulate or inhibit them. In a series of double-blind experiments, the plant seeds were cultivated by the tap water treated by either acceleration or deceleration intent through meditation. After 7 or 8 repeated trials for each design, they found that the germination rate of the 504 green pea seeds receiving treated water with simulating intent was significantly higher than the 504 in the control (60.3% vs. 51.8%; $p < .01$); while the germination rate of 2970 wheat seeds receiving treated water with inhibitory intent was 70.7% versus 74.9% for 2970 controls ($p < 0.001$).

Growth of Cancer Cells

Accelerations or decelerations of the growth of laboratory-prepared cell cultures (*in vitro*) are more widely carried out and accepted by the scientific community. We have found many documented successes in the literature, especially with respect to various cancer cell lines (e.g. Shah et al. 1999). There is a lot of literature in Chinese that reported the inhibitory effects of EQT on various cancer cells. The typical *in-vitro* study involved randomly dividing laboratory-prepared cancer cells or other cultures into groups with at least one group being treated with intention or external bio-energy (like EQT), plus one or two control groups. Sometimes, one group was treated by a sham healer (person without training of bioenergy healing). For example, Chen and her colleagues were involved in many of these studies (Chen et al. 1990). In one of their studies, a qigong healer conducted EQT toward the human nasopharyngeal carcinoma cell line (CNE-2). Compared with the non-treatment control, the inhibitory rates of EQT on CNE-2 growth in four separate experiments were 43%, 33%, 60% and 36% ($p < .05$). The H3-TdR incorporation inhibition rates by EQT in 6 different experiments ranged from 22% to 53% (p < .01). They have subsequently repeated this line of cancer research both *in vitro* and *in vivo*, and have had similar findings (Chen et al. 1995; Chen et al. 1997). Cao et al. (1993) replicated Chen's findings with the same CNE-2 cells. They compared the number of CNE-2 cells cloned after three types of treatment: EQT only, Gamma (G) ray only, and EQT plus G ray; and found that the number of cells cloned in the G-ray + EQ group (9.2) were significantly lower than the G-ray alone group (15.8; p < .001).

Many other cancer cells were studied in this type of in-vitro experiment with EQT or intent therapy, including human breast cancer cell lines, lung cancer cells (SPC-A1), liver cancer cell line (BEL-7402), erythroleukemia (K562), promyelocytic leukemia, CNE-2, SGC-7901 gastric adenocarcinoma, spleen cells of mice, lung tumor cell line (LA-795), etc. Most studies used randomization to create the treatment or control groups, and reported statistically significant inhibitory effect of intent or EQT on cancer growth (see Chen & Yueng 2002 for a review).

One of the authors (KC) was involved personally in an *in-vitro* study to explore the inhibitory effects of EQT on Preprotachykinin-I (PPT-I) expression in four types of breast cancer cells. In our study four breast cancer cell lines (BC-123; BC 125; BC-HT-20; BC-T47D) were grown to confluence in four 6-well plates, one plate for each treatment condition: external qigong treatment, sham treatment, incubator control, room temperature control. The qigong healer put his hand over the cell culture plates at a distance of 15 to 20 cm for 10 minutes. Meanwhile, the "incubator control" plate was kept in an incubator, and the "room temperature" plate was placed on the lab bench in the same lab, but not treated; while the sham treatment was performed by an individual who had no training in qigong but imitated the gesture of the qigong healer. After the designed treatment, all plates were re-incubated for 16 hours. Total RNA was extracted by using the standard procedure and then it was used in quantitative RT-PCR to determine the levels of beta-PPT-I. The technician who did the extraction and counted the cell growth was blinded to the plate identity. The results showed a consistent and obviously downward trend among the BC cells treated by qigong (as much as 40% slower growth than the control). Compared to sham-treated cells, the cells treated by EQT in all 8 observations (4 different BC cells in two separate trials) had the slowest growth. This could have occurred by chance only at p = 0.0038 in a cumulative binomial probability distribution.

Bi-directional Effect on Bacterial Growth

Feng and her colleagues conducted a series of studies on the possible bi-directional effects of EQ on the growth of bacteria (E-coli)—inhibition or acceleration—depending upon the intent of qigong healer (Feng et al. 1982). When the intent of the qigong healer was to destroy the bacteria, the rate of the E-coli growth of the EQ group ranged from 45% to 91%of the control groups growth rate. Under the same condition, when the intent of qigong healer was to accelerate the growth of the bacteria, the rate of E-coli growth in the qigong group was 2.3 to 6.9 times faster than that of the control group. She repeated the studies 20 times before publishing the results. This study confirms that EQT is not just a bioenergy therapy, but also a therapy of intent and highly related to healer's consciousness or intention.

At about the same time, Nash (1982) in the United States conducted a similar study on the same bacterium, with ordinary students instead of a specially trained healer. Nash attempted to determine if the growth of e-coli could be psychokinetically accelerated or decelerated during a 24-hour period. Each of 60 subjects was tested in a single run consisting of a set of 3 tubes of bacteria culture to be growth-promoted by intent, a set of three to be growth-inhibited by intent, and a set of three to serve as controls. The results show that the growth was significantly greater in the promoted tubes than in either control or inhibited tubes (p < .05), and there was significant difference between promoted and inhibited tubes (p < .001).

Rauscher and Rubik (1983) conducted the similar studies on human volitional effect on a model bacterial system (salmonella typhimurium), and reported that the healer treatment (laying on hand, buy no touching) produced significant growth and motility increases over control cultures in the presence of a variety of chemical inhibitors.

In Vivo Studies of Tumor Growth

In addition to the in-vitro studies of acceleration or inhibitory effect of intent or mentality on cell and bacteria growth, another well-replicated area of study is on the effects of EQT or intent on tumor growth in mice. The typical study of this type involved the injection of tumors or cancerous cells into mice; then randomly dividing the tumor-infected mice into various groups with one group being treated by EQT or other energy or spiritual therapies for a set period of time. The control group could be either non-treatment or sham treatment. Then tumor size and the survival time were measured as the outcomes. Chen and Yueng (2002) reviewed 18 *in vivo* studies of EQT in Chinese literature, and found that most studies reported significantly reduced tumor growth and/or longer survival lives among the cancer-infected mice in the treated group, compared to the sham-treated or non-treatment controls.

The same finding was also reported in the western literature. For example, Onetto and Elguin (1966) examined the potential of psychokinesis (PK) to inhibit tumor growth in mice, and found that a group of 30 tumorogenic mice treated with "negative PK" showed significantly less growth of cancer mass (weight and volume, $p < .01$) than that of non-treatment control. Bengston and Krinsley (2000) assigned the mice injected with fatal breast caner into two groups, "laying-on of hand" treatment versus non-treatment control with the same normal feeding and watering, and found that, while all mice in the control died, all mice in the treatment survived the fatal breast cancer. What is more interesting is, those mice exposed to the laying-on hand developed the immunity to the same breast cancer and survived the repeated breast cancer injection in the late trials without further laying-on-hand healing.

Following is a brief description of a well-replicated Chinese study of EQT on tumor growth in mice. Thirty nude mice injected with human hepatocarcinoma were randomly assigned into three groups: the control (no-treatment), the sham (non-healer imitating EQT movement) and the EQT group. The qigong treatment involved EQT towards the mice at a distance of 10-15 cm for 10 minutes from day 3 of transplantation, every other day, for a total of four treatment sessions (40 minutes EQT). The mice were then sacrificed on day 10 or 11, the liver cancer was separated out, measured and weighed in a blind fashion. The same protocol was replicated three times. Compared with the control group, the tumor growth-inhibitory rates of EQT group were 70.3%, 79.7%, and 78.7%, respectively ($p < 0.0001$); while the inhibitory rates of the sham treated group were not significant (Chen et al. 1997).

Benor (2001), Crawford et al (2003) and Braud & Schlitz (1991) have systematically reviewed literature in this area and revealed abundant evidence for the acceleration and inhibitory effects of human intent or distant healing on biological subjects in laboratory experiments (including bacteria, yeast, fungi, mobile algae, plants, animals, and humans). These studies suggest the possibility that human intent or mental power may alter biological parameters like cell membrane permeability, or the rate of enzyme activity or DNA synthesis in order to modulate the growth of biological subjects. This suggests the potential role of intent for healing by inhibiting bacterial/virus or malignant growth in the body.

Transcription/ Translation and Differential Gene Expression

Chien et al. (1991) looked at the bi-directional effects of external qi on FS-4 human fibroblasts and found that "facilitating" qi produced a 1.8% increase in cell growth rate in 24 hrs, 10-15% increase in DNA synthesis and 3-5% increase in cell protein synthesis in a 2 hr period. With "inhibiting" qi, cell growth decreased by 6% in 24 hours, while DNA and protein synthesis decreased respectively by 20-23%, 35-48%.

Zhang et al. (1990) studied the effect of emitted qi on the nucleic acids of chick red blood cells and found a two-fold increase in DNA and 12-fold increase in RNA content.

Li et al. (1992) examined the effect of EQT on gliomas in mice (G422) and their immune response. In their studies, tumor-implanted mice were divided into 4 groups: normal control, tumor control (no treatment), and two qigong treated groups (once a day or once every other day). Eight different qigong healers did qi healing to different mice 10 minutes each time daily or every other day. After 11 days of EQT, mice were sacrificed to weigh the lymph nodes and spleens; blood samples were obtained, lymphocytes suspensions prepared, and the activities of NK and K cells were measured. They found that the tumor growth in EQT groups were significantly slower than that in the control (p < .05); and that the NK cell and K cell activities in the normal control (normal cells instead of tumor cells) and the EQT groups were significantly higher than the tumor control group.

Jia et al (1988) examined the effect of EQT on ultra-structural changes of overstrained muscle of lab rabbits. Twelve healthy male rabbits were randomly assigned into two groups after passive contraction of quadriceps muscles of the thigh was given by designed stimulation. The EQT treatment was given to one group for 6 sessions of 3 minutes each. Under the microscope, they found that the quality and quantity of both fibrous and bony callus in the EQT group were superior to those in controls. EQT increased the number of osteoclasts in the process of both absorption of necrotic bone in the early stage and bony callus remodeling of the later stage. This study partially explained why EQT has a good therapeutic effect on fractures of both humans and animals.

These studies suggest that conscious intent may act by increasing cell differentiation and/or recruitment, as well as cell-specific transcription/translation responsible for specialized functions.

Structural Changes Caused by Intent or Mental Power

Another notable area of research on human intent or mentality documented changes in the structures of biomolecules or cells in terms of activities, conformation and other characteristics. The findings in this area provide partial explanation of the mechanisms of mind healing and bio-energy therapies; meanwhile, they posit great challenge to the current scientific views on consciousness and intent.

Changes in the Conformation of Biomolecules

Chu of Peking University tested more than 20 qigong healers in controlled studies to explore the effects of EQT on the conformation of bio-molecules (Chu et al. 1998). In her study, a circular dichroism (CD) spectrum was used to monitor the conformation of various bio-molecules, such as poly-glutamic acid, poly-lysine, metallothionein, and some RNAs. After more than a hundred trials were repeated by different healers and controls, she found that the CD spectra of bio-molecule samples were changed significantly after exposure to EQT in comparison with both controls and the baseline. In general, the changes of the CD characteristic elliptisity were over the range of $1\text{-}10 \times 10^3$ dgr·cm2·dmol-1, and the maximum was 93.9×10^4 dgr·cm2·dmol-1. The change of elliptisity could be positive or negative depending on the intent of the qigong healer. Here again, bi-directional effects of intent were reported. She concluded that qigong healers might change the conformation of biomolecules by making them more orderly or converting them into greater disorder.

The National Science Foundation in China formally funded the continuation of this project in 1999. In addition, the study was repeated in the U. S. when she visited the U.S. in 2000 and it yielded similar findings (Chu et al. 2001).

In a blind study of "the ability of healers capable of generating coherent heart frequencies to influence a DNA sample", Rein and McCraty (1994) reported a 250% change in DNA conformation, directly correlating with the intent of a healer from a distance. The directional winding-unwinding of DNA under specific intent has been repeatedly demonstrated by Rein and his team over a number of years and experimental set-ups, with some samples showing more denaturation than could be obtained via normal heating or mechanical means (Benor 2001). Similar changes in the conformation of DNA and RNA samples have been found under the effect of conscious intent (external qi) by Lu Zuyin (1989) and Sun et al. (1988) as indicated by changes in the samples' ultraviolet absorption curve.

Effect on Cell Membrane

Braud examined the effect of PK on red blood cells (RBC) with both a PK healer (Braud et al. 1979) and ordinary subjects (Braud 1990) in the blind-control studies, and found that the rate of hemolysis (bursting) of RBC could be slowed significantly by either the PK healer ($p < .001$) or a group of ordinary persons from a distance ($p < .0001$).

Sun et al (1990) examined the effect of qigong intention on the RBC as well, and found that the RBC from the rats exposed to EQT have the following characteristics in comparison with non-treatment controls: 1) decreased content of plasma fibrinogen ($P<0.05$); 2) decreased osmotic fragility of erythrocyte ($P<0.01$); 3) increased fluidity of erythrocytic membrane ($P<0.001$); 4) suppressed activity of Na+, K+ of erthrocytic membrane ($P<0.001$).

Effect on cell colony architecture

In a replicated, controlled, double-blind study, Chen X et al (1996) reported that in-vitro cultures squamous nasopharyngeal carcinoma (CNE-2 line) treated with external qi was poorly differentiated and showed a 43-45% reduction in DNA synthesis, as well as an inability to form colonies and agglutinate in the presence of PHA—with normal colony formation and thriving in the control and sham treatment groups.

A similar reduction in the degree of agglutination and survival rates of in-vitro cancer lines has been reported by Chen (1993, 1998) for pulmonary ade-nocarcinoma (SPC-A1 line); and for human liver cancer cell (BEL-7402). In general these effects correlated with a change in the types of glycoproteins expressed on the cell membrane surface, so may be a result of alterations in the specific genes expressed under the effect of external qi.

Intent-induced Mutation or Intent as Mutagen

Research has also documented some demonstrations that human intent or bio-energy may produce, to various degree, mutagenesis or mutation in cells under laboratory conditions. Although the following results need to be repli-cated, they make us want to start rethinking the possible sources of some observed genetic mutation for various diseases.

Gu et al (1990) of China Pharmaceutical University applied the directional feature of qigong healer's intent, as a novel physico-mutagen in industrial pro-duction of antibiotics, and investigated the effect of EQ on mutation to the mydecamycin producing strain (streptomyces mycarofarieus nov.sp.10204) in comparison with conventional uv method. With a goal of producing mutants with high productivity of MDM, the qigong healer used intent to isolate the mutants EQ0002 and EQ0022 from the parent strain (S.10204). They found that production of MDM from the mutant strains was greatly increased, 45.6% and 49.5% respectively. The pharmaceutical company supported their research continuously in this area and applied this technique in the new antibi-otic production.

Li et al (1990) of Tsinghua University used EQ and intention as a new means of mutagenesis technique. They found that EQT can affect molecules such as amino acids, proteins, pyrimidines, RNA and DNA. Their experiment on fish sperm DNA shows that the EQ effect is not only powerful (it changed over half of the intensity 257nm UV absorption peak), but also versatile as it could change in either positive or negative direction. They concluded that EQT or healer's intention could be used as industrial producer for kanamycin and ribostamycin, as EQT affects the growth ability of the producer, and could greatly increase the productivity. They actually have a long-term collaboration with North China Pharmaceuticals, Inc. by using this technique in the phar-maceutical production.

In one of the extreme cases, Luther Burbank (1849-1926), a nurseryman with psi abilities, reportedly developed 800 new varieties of fruits, vegetables, flowers, cacti and trees in just a few generations, by selecting plants with desired characteristics and cross-breeding them.

Although it usually takes several decades to produce a stable hybrid with normal methods, Burbank produced his new varieties in an average of 2-4 years, by claiming to "communicate" with plants (Benor, 2001).

Instead of using healer or psychically gifted persons, Nash (1984) randomly assigned 60 ordinary subjects (not known to be psychically gifted) into three groups: one group mentally promoted mutation of lac-negative strains of *e-coli* to lac-positive strains in three test tubes, one group mentally inhibited mutation in three test tubes, and the rest 20 subjects worked as control. All tube conditions were carefully blinded to the lab technicians. He found that the mutation ratio of lac-positive to total bacteria was greater in the promoted tubes than that in the inhibited tubes ($p < .005$); and less in the inhibited tubes than in the control ($p < .02$). This implies that everyone's intent may have the potential to produce the mutation change in biological subjects.

There are many more studies in this area that we will not discuss in detail here. For example, Liu et al (1993) applied EQT as mutagenesis for micromonospora echinosal, and found that EQ has the ability to kill micro-organisms and change strains properties. Pei et al (1994) reported that muta-tion of E-coli C311 occurred after exposure to EQ. Shan et al (1990) also used the intent of qigong healer as mutagenesis to select various antibiotic-produc-ing strains in the pharmaceutical production, and had some success. Bai et al. (2000) reported that the seeds mentally induced to germinate rapidly were apparently genetically altered with significant differences in DNA extraction and Polymerase chain reaction.

Morphological Alterations and Cell Differentiation

In their study on the inhibitory effect of EQT on human hepatocarcinoma in mice, Chen et al (1997) used an electron-microscope to analyze the struc-tural differences between cancer cells treated by EQT and those in the controls, and found some morphological alterations in qigong treated mice, which include decreased cell volume of most cancer cells; nuclear condensation, nuclear fragmentation; decreased ratio of nucleus and cytoplasm; swollen mitochondria with poorly organized mitochondrial cristae, some vacuolated; many apoptotic bodies in the extracellular space.

Shao et al. (1990) examined by electronic microscopy the pathological changes in morphology of mice with implanted S180 sarcoma, including changes in numbers of nucleolar organizing regions (NOR) in the sarcoma, using the argyrophil (Ag-NOR) technique. They compared EQT treated mice with control mice,. It was reported that the averaged diameters of cells and nuclei, the ratio of nucleus to cytoplasm and the number of tumor cells division phase and Ag-NOR counts in nuclei in the sarcoma of EQT treated mice were all much less than those in the controls (P < 0.001). They also found that in the EQT treated mice, a great number of sarcoma cells showed atrophy, degeneration, and pyknosis or karyolysis, especially some membrane structures such as mitochondria appeared to be injured. All these occurred after intention-guided EQT without any physical touch.

Li et al. (1992) studied the effects of emitted qi on G422 neurogliomas implanted in mice. They divided the subjects into normal, cancer and qigong groups. 11-14 days after tumor transplantation, the mice were sacrificed and a comprehensive set of parameters were measured and compared across the three groups. The results showed that 4 of the 13 Qigong masters used in the study achieved a 40% reduction in the size of the gliomas; in those samples, the mitotic rates were reduced and the differentiation of the glioma cells tended to be reversed and the activity of NK and K cells was increased significantly compared to the tumor control.

In addition, we have noticed that many of these laboratory effects were actually produced by the conscious intent or healing effort from a distance, some as far as thousand miles away in the form of remote viewing or intercessory prayer (Benor, 2002; Hrading, 2001; Chibnall et al. 2001). For example, in a prospective, double-blind randomized trial, Cha et al (2001) reported that the successful implantation rate among women in Korean treated with *in vitro* fertilization-embryo transfer was significantly affected by the prayers in the United States. Among the in vitro group treated with the intercessory prayer from the Unites States, the fertilization rate was significantly higher than that in the non-treatment control (16.3% vs. 8%, P< .001). This phenomenon increased the difficulty applying any of the existent theories to explain the observed biological or healing effects.

Discussion
What Have We Learned?

The studies listed above are just examples, with many more independent experiments available to support these results. As remarkable as they are, their sheer number and the technical expertise with which they have been conducted force us to accept the very strong hypothesis that the mind can indeed intervene at a molecular level to produce major alterations in when and how genetic material is expressed.

This scientific evidence supports the hypothesis that human intent and mental status play important roles in health and healing. Human intent and mental status represent more than just non-specific, stress-reducing "positive thinking"; as the reviewed studies suggest. Conscious intent seems capable of producing highly specific, pathological and beneficial changes in biological subjects at the deepest levels of genetic regulation. Thus we will argue that the elimination of mental influences from the current program of medical research in areas like cancer and HIV was a major historical mistake, which continues to handicap the development of modern medicine.

In order to avoid potential confounding effects in self-application of intention or mental power, we have purposely selected only in-vitro and in-vivo laboratory studies—to confirm that this is an objective, powerful and measurable effect. In reality, the most powerful and most frequent impacts of intent and mental status on health and healing are self-implemented. The self-implemented effects of intent, emotional status and suggestions are much stronger, longer lasting and more powerful than the external effects.

From these studies, we could postulate that the growth of viruses or bacteria, the progress of disease and healing, and the mutation capabilities of normal genes, tumors or viral and bacterial agents may all be influenced by human intent or mental status, or even initiated by our consciousness. Many studies were conducted with the help of well-trained healers or psychically gifted individuals in order to achieve observable and significant results in a limited time period. Nonetheless, some studies did use ordinary people as subjects and proved that everyone's consciousness and intent has potentially the same power, with variations in the magnitude of the effect, which may be a function of training and length of application.

These studies present a compelling body of evidence with deep implications to our understanding of human health and healing. Thus, we are forced to ask why the medical research community has not been more interested in verifying their claims. The medical field spends hundreds of billions of dollars to explore the source of many chronic diseases at a biochemical and genetic level (which most often compensates in a mechanistic way for functional errors, without addressing the cause of those errors), but very little (almost none) is spent on study of human intent or mental status in the complex life processes. The source of many diseases that modern medicine tries to identify at the level of proteins or DNA may not be the causal, but actually the consequence of radical or long-term effects of these unseen sources—human intent and/or mental status. We seem to have imbalanced science, and desperately need more attention focused on the research of human intention and mental power in health and healing.

Problems and Concerns

When we reviewed the literature, we were confronted with many limitations and problems in the field as a whole and in these studies in particular; as in any area of study, no research can be validated without replication and collective effort. To recognize these problems is a necessary step to begin a more in-depth investigation into the roles of human intent and mentality in disease, health and healing.

There is plenty of room for improvement in research protocol and design. Lack of sophisticated research design undermines the results of some studies although the lack of resources and support may be one of the reasons behind simplified protocols. Few double-blind randomization methods were used in these exploratory studies, which may greatly discount the results or conclusions, because the experimenter effect and measurement bias might become part of the observed results. However, in terms of overall quality of the research, studies of human intent or consciousness power, mostly by parapsychologists and energy medicine researchers, are quite competitive with, if not better than, most of the mainstream scientific research. According to a recent review by Sheldrake (1998), among the publications in the major British scientific journals in 1996-97, the proportion of studies implementing blindness design to avoid experimenter effects is lowest in the so-called mainstream physical science (0%) or biological studies (0.8%), moderate in medical studies (5.9%) and psychological studies (4.9%), but by far the highest proportion (85.2%) was in parapsychology. However, it has been very difficult for these well-designed parapsychological studies to be published in the mainstream scientific journals due to prejudice barriers stemming from the belief system of mainstream scientists.

The belief system of the involved scientists could significantly limit the type of research design and the quality of studies being done. Most scientists simply do not believe in the kind of power or potential that human mind or intent possess, and require replicated confirmations of the observed effects again and again. They cannot accept research approaches to explore the mechanism and/or applications of such human potential. These simple "proof-of-existence" replications, which only confirm well-known facts, end up frustrating those gifted individuals who are involved in the research. For example, the revitalization of denatured peanuts by Ms. Sun (Sun 1998) and the PK effect on red blood cells by Matthew Manning (Braud et al. 1979) have been repeated so many times, that he became bored and frustrated when the positive results produced in various laboratories never convinced the scientists. Sometimes the gifted individuals started to refuse further collaboration with scientists; as Manning stated, "They kept asking me to produce the same effects over and over again; we didn't seem to be getting anywhere." (p. 350 in Benor, 2001). This requires us to open up our belief system, and start thinking of mechanisms and implications instead of stagnating at verification stage.

In general, the studies of human intent and mental status still lack integrated theoretical guidance and the necessary resources. These short comings make it difficult for research findings to be accepted by the mainstream scientific community, or to be incorporated into the broader medical research field. In a separate paper we will try to outline several critical new experimental findings in the area of nonlocal genetic regulation, as well as some major working hypotheses that attempt to explain the possible mechanism of intention and mental influence in healing. The role of coherent electromagnetic fields associated with genetic material; the significance of liquid crystals as major components of the body; the wave-transfer of genetic information and experimental evidence of wave-hybridization; and the possibility of quantum entanglement between separate biosystems will be discussed in turn, with the available experimental support. However, due to lack of substantial data and research funding in this area, none of these models can be fully validated at this stage. Hopefully the current review will generate more interest from a broad spectrum of researchers and funding resources in this direction of scientific exploration, so that we can produce meaningful evidence and make additional progress in understanding of mind-body interaction and bio-energy healing in health and medicine.

Since none of the existent scientific theories or assumptions can completely explain these phenomena and healing power, the study of intent or mentality has long been lacking basic support from scientific community. For any scientific study of a new phenomenon, a large amount of time and resources are needed for an accurate account of existence, effectiveness, dose response and limitations. However, most studies in this area have been done by scientists who were confronted with the long-term problem of lacking necessary support and resources. Our review suggests that these phenomena should be seriously examined and be considered as an important subject of scientific exploration and medical development.

What's Next?

There are many unanswered questions that need further attention. How far can the reductionist, biochemical models of the human body take us in understanding health and healing, since they completely ignore the role of intent and mental status? On what level of genetic regulation does consciousness or intention interact with the DNA? The bi-directional feature of intent has been supported by two decades of laboratory studies at Princeton University (PEAR Lab, Jahn et al. 2000): how can we interpret this remarkable finding and what kinds of specific bioenergy does human intention produce? What are physical correlates of bio-information? How do they interact with our body and health?

Science should not be based on a rigid belief system that merely defends what is already known. Good science should be able to acknowledge new information and explore better explanations for, and application of, this information. We have presented some solid evidence and data on the potential effects of human intent and mental state on various biological subjects. What should scientists do next? We believe that it is time to benefit from this knowledge by integrating it into our overall medical research program. If we applied 10% of current resources and funding for biomolecular research into the study of human intent and mental state in disease and healing, the entire field of medicine and human health would likely witness a dramatic improvement.

References

1.   Bai F, Sun CL, Liu ZY, Shen JC, Shen YZ, Ge RC, et al. (2000). "Seeds induced to germinate rapidly by mentally projected 'qi energy' are apparently genetically altered." *American Journal of Chinese Medicine.* 28(1): 3-8.

2.   Bengston WF, Krinsley D. (2000). The effect of the "laying on of hands" on transplanted breast cancer in mice. *Journal of Scientific Exploration.* 14(3):353-364.

3.   Benor DJ, (2001). *Spiritual Healing: Scientific Validation of a Healing Revolution,* Southfield MI: Vision Publications

4.   Benor DJ. (2002). Distant healing. *Subtle Energies and Energy Medicine.* 2002; 11(3): 249-264.

5.   Braud, WG (1979). Conformance behavior involving living systems. In Roll WG et al. (eds), *Research in Parapsychology 1978,* Metuchen, NJ: Scarecrow Press, 111-115.

6. Braud, WG (1990). Distant mental influence of rate of hemolysis of human red blood cells, *Journal of the American Society for Psychical Research*, 1990, 84(1): 1-24.

7. Braud WG, Schlitz MJ. (1991) Conscious interactions with remote biological systems: anomalous intentionality effects. *Subtle Energies.* 1991;2:1-46.

8. Cha KY, Wirth DP, Lobo R. (2001). Does prayer influence the success of in vitro fertilization-embryo transfer? Report of a masked, randomized Trial." *J. Reproductive Medicine.* September 2001; 46(9): 781-787.

9. Chen K, & Yeung R, (2002). "Exploratory studies of qigong therapy for cancer in China." *Integrative Cancer Therapies. 1(4): 345-370.*

10. Chen XJ, Gao QY, Jao XR, Zhang JM. (1990). Effects of emitted qi on inhibition of human NPC cell line and DNA synthesis. *Third National Academic Conference on Qigong Science*; 1990; Guangzhou, China.

11. Chen XJ, Li YQ, Liu GC & He BH, (1997). "The inhibitory effects of Chinese Taiji Five Element Qigong on transplanted hepatocarcinoma in mice." *Asian Medicine,* Issue 11 (1997): 36-38.

12. Chen XJ, Yi Q, Liu KL & Zhang JM, (1995). "Double-blinded study of the effect of qigong external qi on the human nose cancer cells in nude mice." p. 288 in Lin ZP (ed.) *Understanding of True Qi Cultivation and Sublimation.* Beijing: Chinese Publisher of Constructive Materials.

13. Chen XJ, Yi Q, Li YQ, He WM, Zhang JM, and Chen YS, (1996). Observations on the effect of the emitted qi on the reversion of nasopharyngeal carcinoma cell line; p.108 in the *Proceedings of the Third World Conference on Medical Qigong,* Sept. 1996, Beijing, China

14. Chen YF (1993). Effect of emitted qi on agglutinating reaction of human pulmonary adenocarcinoma cell (SPC-A1) mediated by ConA; Beijing, China. 1993: 102.

15. Chen YF. (1998). Molecular biology study for the effect of qigong—outgoing qi with labeled biochemical factors on human body cancer cells the BEL—7402 and SPC—A1; 7-th Int Sym on Qigong, Shanghai, China. 1998: 96.

16. Chibnall JT, Jeral JM, Cerullo MA. (2001). Experiments in distant intercessory prayer: God, science, and the lesson of Massah. *Archives of Internal Medicine.* 161(21):2529-2536.

17. Chien CI; Tsuei JJ; Lee SC; Huang YC, and Wei YH (1991). Effect of emitted bioenergy on biochemical functions of cells.. *American J. of Chinese Medicine*; 19 (3-4):285-92;

18. Chu DY, He WG, Zhou YF & Chen BC, (1998). "The effect of Chinese qigong on the conformation of biomolecule." *Chinese Journal of Somatic Science.* 8(4): 155-159.

19. Chu DY, Wang WZ, He BH & Chen, K. (2001). The effect of external qi of qigong on bio-molecular conformation (III). Pp. 132-137 in Chez RA (ed.) *Proceedings: Bridging Worlds and Filling Gaps in the Science of Healing.* Hawaii, November 29-Dcember 3, 2001.

20. Crawford CC, Sparber AG, Jonas WB. (2003) A systematic review of the quality of research on hands-on healing: clinical and laboratory studies. *Alter Therap in Health and Meds.* 2003. 9(3): in press.

21. Feng LD, Bao GW, Qian JQ, Li SY. (1982). "Observation of the effect of external qi on the Glen's bacteria." *The Nature Journal (Chinese),* 5(9): 36.

22. Ge RC, Liu ZY, Shen YZ, Bai F & Sun CL, (1998). The study on the ATPase activity of the fast germinating sprouts of the wheat and pea whose seeds were somatic psychic ability, *Chinese Journal of Somatic Science,* 8(4): 152-154.

23. Grad BR (1965) Some biological effects of laying-on of hands: A review of experiments with animals and plants. *Journal of the American Society for Psychical Research.* 59:95-127.

24. Gu Jf, Wang YW, and Wu J, 1990. Effect of emitted qi on mutation to streptomyces mycarofarieus nov. sp.10204; *Third National Academic Conf on Qigong Science,* Guangzhou, China. 1990:113.

25. Haid M & Huprikar S. (2001) Modulation of germination and growth of plants by meditation. *American J Chinese Med* 2001;29 (3-4):393-401

26. Harding OG. (2001) The healing power of intercessory prayer. *West Indian Med J* 2001 Dec;50(4):269-72

27. Hu G, Yi J et al. (1989). "The effects of external qi on the germination of rice and wheat." P.91 in Hu HC & Wu QY (eds) *Paper Collections of Qigong Science. Vol I.* Beijing: Beijing University of Technology Press.

28. Jahn R, Dunne B, Bradish Y, Dobyns Y, Lettieri A, Nelson R, et al. (2000). Mind/machine interaction consortium: PortREG replication experiments. *Journal of Scientific Exploration.* 14(4): 499-555.

29. Jia L, Jia JD, Lu DY (1988). Effects of emitted qi on ultrastructural changes of the overstrained muscle of rabbits. P.14 in The First World Conf Acad Exch Med Qigong, Beijing China.

30. Jin AW et al. (1994). "Biological effect of external qi on the germination of rice seed." *Chinese Journal of Somatic Science,* 4(4): 167-70.

31. Lee SC, Shen JC & Sun CL, (1999). The revival of peanut by psychic, *Chinese Journal of Somatic Science,* 7(1):3-7, 1997.

32. Li CX et al. (1992). "Preliminary exploration of the effect of external qi on the immune functional of mice with tumors." *Chinese Journal of Somatic Science,* 2(2): 67-71.

33. Li SP, Sun MY, Yan X et al. (1990). "Basic research on the feasibility of a bacteria treatment method using qigong." In *Proceedings of the 3rd National Academic Conference on Qigong Science.* Guangzhou, China.

34. Lin ZP & Chen K, (2002). Exploratory studies of external qi in China." *Journal of International Society of Life Information Science.* 20 (2): 457-461.

35. Liu ZR, Ren T, Ren JP, Zhang, ZX, (1993). Comparative study of emitted qi and physical-chemical factors on the protoplasmic mutagenesis of micromonospora echinospord; 2nd World Conf Acad Exch Med Qigong. Beijing, China. 1993: 97.

36. Lu ZY, (1997). *Scientific Qigong Exploration: The Wonders and Mysteries of Qi.* Malvern PA: Amber Leaf Press.

37. Lu, ZY (1989). The effects of qi on biomolecules; 2nd Int Conf on Qigong, Xian, China. 1989: 359.

38. Miller RN, (1972). The positive effect of prayer on plants. *Psychic,* 3(5): 24-25.

39. Nash, Carroll B. (1982). Psychokinetic control of bacterial growth. *Journal of Society for Psychical Research.* 51:217-221.

40. Nash, Carroll B., (1984). Test of psychokinetic control of bacterial mutation. *Journal of the American Society for Psychical Research.* 78(2):145-152.

41. Nicholas C, (1977). The effects of loving attention on plant growth, *New England J. of Parapsychology,* 1977, 1:19-24.

42. Onetto B & Elguin GH, (1966). Psychokinesis in experimental rumor-genesis, *J. o f Parapsychology,* 30: 220.

43. Pan XK, (1995). "The effect of external Qi on the seed of wheat." P.313 in Lin ZP (ed.) *Understanding of True Qi Cultivation and Sublimation.* Beijing: Chinese Publisher of Constructive Materials.

44. Pei HS et al. (1994). "Preliminary observation of the effect of external Qi on the E-coli (C311)." *Chinese Journal of Somatic Science.* 4(2): 83-85.

45. Rauscher EA and Rubik BA (1983). Human volitional effects on a model bacterial system. *Psi Research.* 1983, 2(1), 38-48.

46. Rein G and McCraty R, (1994), DNA as a detector of subtle energies. Proceedings of the 4th annual conf. of the ISSSEEM, Boulder, CO.

47. Rein G and McCraty R, (1995), Structural changes in water and DNA associated with new physiologically measurable states. *Journal of Scientific Exploration.* 8(3), 438-439

48. Saklani A. (1988). Preliminary tests for psi-ability in shamans of Garhwal Himalaya. J. of the Soceity for Psychical Research. 55(81), 60-70.

49. Saklani A. (1990). Psychokinetic effects on plant growth: further studies. In: Roll W, Morris R, Morris J, eds. *Research in Parapsychology 1989.* Metuchen, NJ: Scarecrow Press; 37-41.

50. Sancier KM. (2001). Search for medical applications of qigong with the Qigong Database. *Journal of Alternative & Complementary Medicine.* 2001 Feb: 7(1): 93-95.

51. Scofield, AM and Hodges, RD, (1991). Demonstration of a healing effect in the laboratory using a simple plant model. *Journal of the society for Psychical Research.* 57, 321-343.

52. Shah S, Ogden AT, Pettker CM, Raffo A, Itescu S, Oz MC. (1999). A study of the effect of energy healing on in vitro tumor cell proliferation. *J Altern Complement Med.* 5(4):359-365.

53. Shao XM, Liu GC, Zhou QJ, Yu F, Xu HF, Xue HL, et al (1990). Effect of qigong waiqi (emitted qi) on the growth and differentiation of implanted tumor cells (in mice); 3rd Nat Acad Conf on Qigong Science, Guangzhou, China. 1990: 85.

54. Shan LY, Sun Y, Zhang LY, Hu YJ, Li SP, Sun MY et al. (1990). Studies on the selection of antibiotic producing strains by treatment with qigong. 3rd Nat Acad Conf on Qigong Science, Guangzhou, China. 1990: 20.

55. Sheldrake R (1998). Experimenter effects in scientific research: How widely are they neglected? *Journal of Scientific Exploration,* 12(1): 73-78

56. Shen JC and Sun CL, (1996). "Confirmation and thinking of energy-gathering phenomenon under the deeper conscious state." *Chinese Journal of Somatic Science,* 6(1): 10-15.

57. Shen JC and Sun CL, (1998). "The experiments and thinking on the directional effects of human consciousness on plant growth." *Chinese Journal of Somatic Science,* 8(1): 51-60.

58. Shen JC and Sun CL, (2002). "Solid evidence of psychic power: Materiality of consciousness (Sixteen years research of Psi phenomena). Journal of International Society of Life information Science. 20(2):549-554.

59. Sternberg EM, (2001) *The Balance Within: The Science Connecting Health and Emotions.* New York: W.H. Freeman and Co.

60. Sun CL, (1998). My life experience on communicating with plants. *Chinese J. of Somatic Science,* 8(2):51-60.

61. Sun CL, Liu CM, Shen ZQ, and Li XM (1990). Effect of Xiantian-ziran qigong on red blood cells; 3rd Nat Acad Conf on Qigong Science, Guangzhou, China. 1990: 48.

62. Sun MY, Li SP, Meng GR, Cui YH, and Yan X, (1988). Effect of emitted qi on trace examination of UV spectroscopy on the DNA solution of fish sperm; 1st World Conf Acad Exch Med Qigong. Beijing, China. 1988: 172.

63. Tompkin P & Bird C, (1973). *The Secret Life of Plants,* New York: Harper & Collins Publication.

64. Wilkinson DS, Knox PL, Chatman JE, Johnson TL, Barbour N, Myles Y, Reel A (2002). The clinical effectiveness of healing touch. *J Altern Complement Med.* 8(1):33-47.

65. Zhang FD, Zhao J, Yue HQ, Liu GQ, and Liu, A (1990). Study of molecular biology of functional mechanism of emitted qi on proteins; Guangzhou, China. 1990: 62.

66. Zhou RH, Wu QY, Xie HZ, (1989). "A Study of the effect of external Qi on the growth of plants." P. 82 in Hu HC & Wu QY (eds) *Paper Collections of Qigong Science. Vol I.* Beijing: Beijing University of Technology Press.

A System for Monitoring the Health Condition of Qigong Trainers as Computer Users in Real Time

Chao LIU[1]
Yoshio MACHI[1]

[1]Department of Electronic Engineering
Tokyo Denki University
Chiyoda-ku, Tokyo 101-8457 Japan
Tel: +81-3-5280-3360, Fax +81-3-5280-3567
E-mail: l_chao@d.dendai.ac.jp
        machi@d.dendai.ac.jp

Abstract

Our goal is to create a system, which monitors and informs Qigong Trainers of their mental and physical state in real time. Such a system would allow individual users to adjust their work and rest rate, posture, and other factors, which affect their general condition and their efficiency in each interaction. This system takes a number of physiological indices (such as GSR, SpO2, Pulse and Temperature etc.), which are used to monitor the qigong effects and the general well being of qigong trainers. We performed an experiment not only to test the effectiveness of this system but also to establish a model to represent the basic healthy state of a user's body and mind in a specific interaction situation in real time. Our experiment confirmed that this system is effective in monitoring the stress and strain and providing feedback in real time.

Introduction

Computers have become indispensable for office work and they are now commonplace in the home. Following the explosive development of information technology and the global reach of the Internet, people of all ages have regular contact with some kind of computer for business and/or domestic purposes. We developed a system for monitoring the state of the user's body. Thus computers can use certain physiological indices to monitor a user's condition, compare it to the basic model, and indicate to the user when a rest or health care action are needed.

Method

The system included both hardware and software. We designed and made a sensor, which gets the physiological information via simple contact with the user's skin. The software analyses the state of the user's body based on this physiological information and shows the user the result on the computer display. When necessary, the computer can deliver a warning indicating to the user his/her deteriorating condition. The analyses are based not only on physiological information but also on psychological factors.

Eight university students (age from 22 to 24, all of them familiar with mouse operations) were asked to perform a dragging task i.e. drag a blue circle into a similar icon, which was a round target. We connected the array sensor to the subject's left thumb; the sensor monitored the physiological indices when using a mouse. To compare the degree of effort applied in different computer tasks, we designed two procedures; in the first procedure the dragging task was performed 72 times and in the second it was performed 144 times. There were five steps: (1) close your eyes and be quiet, (2) do the dragging task 72 times, (3) do the dragging task 144 times, (4) close your eyes and be quiet again, (5) The subjects then answered questions regarding their subjective responses." (PSRS-50R). The computer recorded the subjects' physiological indices as well as the performance results (reaction times, dragging times, error rates, and scores). The circle appeared randomly in eight directions, three sizes and three distances from the target point (see **Figure 1**). We recorded the recognized response time (RRT) from the instant the circle appeared on the screen until the subject pointed at it with the mouse. We also recorded the concentration reaction time (CRT), from the moment the user clicked on the circle until the instant it was correctly released inside the target.

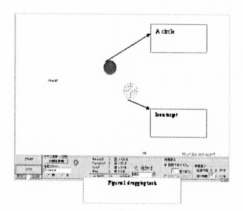

Figure 1 dragging task

The score was automatically recorded along with the level of concentration. The average RRT was calculated thus: $\{\sum_{n=1}^{n}d(RRT)\}/n$, ("n" is the number of times the circle was caught, n=72 or 144). The CRT: $\{\sum_{n=1}^{n}d(CRT)\}/n$, ("n" is the number of times the circle was "caught", n=72 or 144). First the circle was placed 72 times (3 sizes x 8 directions x 3 distances). To increase the workload the subject did the exercise a further 144 times (n=144).

The physiological indices used in the experiments were GSR (Galvanic Skin Response), SpO_2 (the ratio of O_2 Saturation Level in a non-invasive fashion), Pulse (waveform) and skin Temperature using a thermistor transducer. These were used to indicate the level of individual effort and the level of attention applied in the tasks.

Results

The psychological analyses

We recorded scores from the two processes (point and drag 72 times, and point and drag 144 times). The average score for the second test (144 times) was lower at 22.4 points compared with 24.7 points for the shorter task (72 times). For six of the subjects the score decreased, and for two the score increased. The maximum score of all eight subjects was 32.5 points and the minimum score was 16.4 points. The average concentration reaction time was slower in the longer test, 2.51sec (for 72 times) to 2.74sec. (for 144 times). Six subjects became slower and two became faster. The maximum time was 3.83 sec., the minimum time was 1.68 sec.

The physiological analyses

The average GSR increased during the dragging task when compared with the users quiet condition before and after the experiments, and it increased further in the longer test. The average GSR reading for the subjects was greater in the longer task than in the shorter task. The maximum GSR was 1.07 and the minimum was 1.00. The average SpO_2 ratio in both cases did not change significantly (the difference being just 0.001), but, considered individually, half increased (maximum 1.026) and half decreased (minimum 0.978), see **Figure 2**. The average maximum PULSE ratio did not vary much, but six increased and two decreased when compared with their relaxed states before and after the tasks. The maximum was 1.004 and the minimum was 0.997. The temperature changes were obvious, compared with their original quiet state. The average ratio for the shorter test was lower for all subjects (0.82) than it was in the longer test (0.98). Individually, three increased and five decreased.

Discussion

The dragging task was considered to be a typical basic computing task.

The system is designed to monitor the general health condition for computer operators. Computer tasks influence the subject's body and mind in various ways. For a quantitative analysis regarding various workloads, we needed to define some physiological and psychological indices relevant to computer users. We supposed that dragging tasks are basic computer operations. We felt that the physiological and psychological data from a dragging task would be typical and representative of computer work and the computer environment. Thus this approach can be applied to more complicated tasks and environments or interactions.

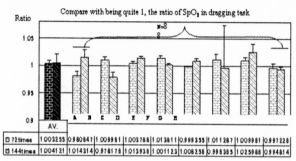

Figure 2 SpO₂ of ratio for 72 and 144 with every subject

The expression of physiological and psychological indexes

From the results we considered that continuous work on computers effects individuals' bodies and minds in different ways. Concentration generally tends to slowly subside, and the movements of most subjects become slower (from 2 to 9 minutes). We concluded that as a subject continues to work on a computer the level of concentration and the speed of physical actions and reactions tends to decrease slowly. Statistics can be used to represent the common user elements and we have here used average values to establish a basic model. For example **Figure 2** shows us the SpO_2 average (AV) and the differences between the individuals. The physiological and psychological indices in our system will also account for various demographic e.g. older people whose basic standard condition may be expected to be different to young persons. From the dragging task results we found the correlation between the scores and CRT was r=0.81 (result of correlation parametric) N=8 (amount of subjects) (p<0.05)?which shows that the results were significant. Since the score decreased and the CRT became slower for most subjects, we concluded that the level of workload has a significant effect.

Conclusion

We confirmed that the system incorporating these physiological indices could monitor a user's state of stress and strain under different computing workloads and action states. The experimental results also reveal differences in various individual performances, even though the subjects did the same task. Thus the system will therefore also indicate personal characteristics while a task is being performed and refer not only to a universal average (model) but also to the individual's normal rest state. According to these experimental results we can use the indices as a reference point in real time computing. Our future research will include other useful indices, which will give an even fuller picture of the user's condition including attitudes and responses to various kinds of computer images, information and tasks for the health condition of qigong trainers.

Reference

1. Rie SHINNA, "The measurement of stress response: psychological test" CLINICAL NEUROSCIENCE, 12, 530-533, 1994 (in Japanese)
2. Qi-wei MA, The psychology of exercise and sport: The Board of Public of Education in ZHEJIANG Province, p342-360, 1998 (in Chinese)
3. Ark, W., Dryer, C.E., Lu, D.J., "The emotion mouse" Human-computer Interaction Ergonomics and User Interfaces Vol.1 p818-823 Proceedings of HCI International '99, Munich, Germany (August 1999).

Biophysical Mechanisms of Genetic Regulation: Is There a Link to Mind-Body Healing?

Lian Sidorov, DDS
jnlrmi@hotmail.com

Kevin Chen, Ph.D.
chenke@umdnj.edu

Abstract

Over the past several decades, pioneering biophysics work has shown that living tissues interact with electric and magnetic fields in unexpected and dramatic ways: from initial anecdotal accounts of enhanced healing under electromagnetic stimulation, research in this field has progressed to a sophisticated arsenal of investigative tools and theoretical models which include polarized light microscopy to study the liquid crystal properties of living cells and laser-excitation of DNA to induce hybridization through non-molecular information transfer. In almost all cases, the results point to a set of remarkable properties of living tissues, and in particular of genetic material: the emerging picture is that of biosystems as sources and domains of coherent electromagnetic fields, which account for practically instantaneous inter-cellular communication and a highly efficient mechanism of energy utilization, and which seem to reflect very closely the developmental and patho-physiological state of the organism. In addition, a wide spectrum of genetic mechanisms now appear to be under the influence of surrounding electromagnetic fields.

At the same time, an impressive number of studies in the areas of parapsychology and mind-body medicine converge to show that conscious intent can affect practically every single type of genetic program, as well as many physiological parameters [1]. These studies also show that such effects can be produced from great distances, and that occasionally they are accompanied by unusual energy signatures.

Is there a correlation between the effects of electromagnetic fields and those of mental intent on genetic regulation and living tissues? This paper will discuss the major experimental evidence and proposed mechanisms of these interactions, as well as the principal obstacles lying in the way of a viable, comprehensive theory. At the same time, we will attempt to formulate several preliminary hypotheses based on this evidence and to sketch some possible directions for future research in this field.

Keywords: genetic control architecture, EMFs, coherence, liquid crystals, interference grids, photon polarization, psycho-physiological remodeling, nonlocal communication, topological geometrodynamics

Introduction

The history of mind-body medicine in the modern era has been one of continuous struggle against both the derisive attitudes of a scientific mainstream firmly embedded into a reductionist, materialistic mind frame and the conceptual difficulties of studying something as elusive as the contents of consciousness. While gradual correlations with general factors such as stress have lead to the acceptance of psychoneuroimmunology as a legitimate field of study, there is very little material in the medical literature about other, more specific effects that mental intent might have on the body.

This unfortunate state of affairs, we hope, is about to change. Over the past decade, thousands of studies have been conducted all over the world, looking at the interactions between conscious intent and living systems—from biomolecules and single celled organisms to human beings—and describing statistically significant effects in very concrete, histological and physiological terms. These studies, reported in the scientific parapsychology literature as well as in some physics and biomedical publications, are part of a rapidly growing body of "human potential science" projects—frontier programs funded by governments such as Japan and China to look at exceptional human abilities and harness their implications. Similar studies have also been carried out in the US, Russia, Germany and other Western countries, unfortunately under less supportive conditions which are generally reflected by their more conservative protocols. A large proportion of this material is now available in abstract format through English-language publications such as D. Benor's "Spiritual Healing: Scientific Evidence of a Healing Revolution" (Vision Publications, 2001 Edition) and the Qigong Institute's Database CD-ROM, updated yearly.

In another paper presented at this conference [1], we have reviewed the main classes of studies described in this literature, with a focus on genetic functions—showing how practically every major genetic program (from DNA replication and cell division rates to gene-specific transcription, translation and mutagenesis, to cell differentiation and apoptosis) can be modulated by intent under experimental conditions. In this follow-up article, we would like to take the discussion one step further and begin to look at a possible mechanism that might account for these startling experimental findings.

The present model of genetic control, based on chemical messengers, transcription factors, molecular feedback loops, enzyme conformation, promoter regions and other forms of cis-/trans modulatory regulation is restricted to describing these all-important programs at a primarily intra-cellular level which fails to fully account for the astounding degree of synchronization between the billions of cells comprising the human body. It has been shown that on average four to eight different transcription factors service each gene's regulatory module and that many hundreds to thousands of genes must be coherently expressed in order to create any given tissue or multicellular structure [2-p. 9]. Thus higher-level aspects of growth and development, as well as pathological and healing processes, such as the differential spatio-temporal expression of DNA in specialized cells and the emergence/loss of complex architecture during embryogenesis or malignant growth, are still a matter of heated debate and speculation [3,77]. How does the DNA material in each cell respond to its variable environmental circumstances in a way which reflects the cell's lineage, internal clock and also the activities of thousands of cells in its immediate vicinity? Are chemical messengers sufficient to account for the speed and accuracy of this large-scale orchestration, or are there higher levels of genetic control architecture yet to be discovered? We believe that sufficient evidence has already accumulated to support the existence of such nonlocal, non-molecular controls. We also believe, along with a growing number of biophysical research scientists, that the key to the most effective preventive and therapeutic health interventions lies in the understanding of genetic regulation at the top levels of the control hierarchy—that is, in the way cells communicate with each other, their environment and, possibly, with the poorly-understood physical correlates of mental intent.

We have therefore divided this article into several parts: in the first section we will try to challenge the strict biomolecular approach to medicine by presenting a number of studies which clearly demonstrate that electromagnetic fields play a major role in genetic expression; the second part will briefly review the main characteristics of mind-matter interactions with respect to living systems; finally the discussion will attempt to draw parallels between the biophysical and consciousness-mediated mechanisms and point to theoretical models that might account for the effects of intent on targeted biological structures in a nonlocal framework.

The Effects of Weak EM Fields on Genetic Programs
CELL DIFFERENTIATION IN ADULT, EMBYONIC AND MALIGNANT STATES
The work of Rose and Becker (1940s-1970s)

It was known as early as 1958 that applying a small, polarity-enhancing external current to an injured plant increased its regeneration rate by as much as 300% [4-p. 61]. In 1961, Becker and his team found that negative electrodes applied directly to the marrow cavity of dogs' thighbones had stimulated considerable amounts of bone growth, compared to controls. But nothing prepared them for the magnitude of their next discovery: following up on preliminary experiments done by German researchers in the 1920s, they found that applying a very weak current (in the order of a billionth of an ampere) to a culture of nucleated frog red blood cells induced complete dedifferentiation in the cells, which reactivated their nuclei, lost all hemoglobin and became primitive (unspecialized) in the space of four hours [4-p. 143].

These changes, which were later found in the RBCs of fish and other reptiles, suggested a *reactivation of the DNA*—for once the staining characteristics of the nucleus shifted, the process continued even if the current was interrupted. All the changes involved paralleled those found in the salamander limb blastemas, demonstrating that the process of regeneration was initiated by an endogenous "current of injury". Applying this knowledge to wound healing in mammals, in 1971 Beckers's team stimulated the bone marrow of rats' amputated forelegs with a 1 nanoampere current and managed to obtain partial regeneration of the limb, including new, well organized bone, cartilage, muscle, blood and nerve tissue: at least ten types of cells had differentiated from the blastema, and some specimens even demonstrated the rudiments of finger cartilage. [4-p. 153]

Beyond the exhilarating prospect of organ and nerve regeneration (which Becker explores at length in his book), *the observation that mature cells can dedifferentiate and redifferentiate opens up what is perhaps the most extraordinary possibility yet: a mechanism for understanding otherwise inexplicable healing accounts, such as "spontaneous" cancer remission.*

Observing that three major characteristics of malignant cells (cell simplicity, mitotic speed and metabolic priority) were also typical of embryonic growth and regeneration, in 1948 Meryl Rose conducted a landmark experiment designed to test whether the physiological environment of regeneration could take over the controls of tumor cells. After transplanting pieces of frog kidney tumor to the limbs of salamanders and watching them grow, he amputated the leg just below or, in some cases, right through the tumor mass. As opposed to controls, where the tumor metastasized and ended up killing the host, these specimens demonstrated a remarkable phenomenon: the tumor cells dedifferentiated more fully as the blastema formed, then redifferentiated along with the blastema—thus proving a monumentally important point: "the regeneration's guidance system could control cancer, too" [4-p. 217]. Furthermore, replicating experiments conducted in 1962-1963 by F. Seilern-Aspang and K. Kratochwil at the Austrian Cancer Institute showed that, in cases where the primary tumor was in the tail, amputation of the tail below that level (ie leaving the primary tumor intact) resulted in total disappearance of both the primary mass and all its distant metastases as the tail regenerated [4-p. 220]—thus complete healing of two aetiologically-distinct injuries (incidentally, a claim not uncommonly found in the alternative healing literature). Although this result was obtained only when the amputation was close to the site of the primary tumor, it demonstrated beyond doubt that the key to such "spontaneous regression" was a shift in the tumor's immediate environment—most probably the electrical currents in the neuroepidermal junction, which Becker had proven were the initiators of regeneration.

What is the nature of this endogenous current which preoccupied Becker for over three decades? Far from being restricted to areas of injury, as originally believed, Becker showed in a series of ingenious experiments that the entire body of a living organism was permeated by a weak DC current, which furthermore appeared to reverse its polarity as the organism's state of consciousness changed from awake to deep sedation/anaesthesia. By demonstrating the Hall effect in the leg of a salamander as it regained consciousness [4-p. 101], Becker showed that this DC potential was a semiconductor current—in other words, that the carrier were electrons in a semiconducting lattice. But to admit the existence of a semiconductor current permeating and regulating the brain-body continuum, one must be ready to look for an appropriate substrate. Semiconduction requires an ordered molecular structure, such as crystals, in which electrons can exist in a delocalized fashion and flow coherently across large distances with minimal dissipation of energy—a very different model from the type of conduction associated with neurons. In the wet, warm, perpetually-fluctuating environment which is the living organism, what could possibly constitute a proper matrix for this type of phenomenon?

INTERACTIONS BETWEEN EMFs AND DNA
EVIDENCE FROM BIOELECTROMAGNETICS LABS (1990s-2003)

Before addressing the nature of semiconduction in living tissues, let us review a few more interesting studies which look at the effects of electromagnetic fields on DNA regulation.

In a 2002 study, Tofani & al. found a statistically significant inhibition of tumor growth (40%) and increase in survival time (31%) when mice bearing a subcutaneous human colon adenocarcinoma (WiDr) were exposed to 70min/day 5.5mT magnetic fields with 50 Hz modulation for 4 weeks; a decrease in tumor cell mitotic index and proliferative activity and increase in apoptosis were also observed—with no adverse or abnormal effects [5]

In a similar study reported by Simko & al. [6], extremely-low frequency EMFs (0.1-1mT, 50Hz) applied continuously for 48-72 hrs resulted in increased micronucleus formation and apoptosis in transformed cell lines (human squamous cell carcinoma SCL II), but no adverse effects in normal, non-transformed cells.

Cell death induction consistent with apoptosis was reported in two transformed cell lines (WiDr human colon adenocarcinoma and MCF-7 human breast adenocarcinoma) that were exposed to 1mT magnetic fields modulated by 50Hz ELFs). Cells with daily exposure of 70 min. for 4 weeks showed significant tumor growth inhibition (up to 50%) by the end of treatment. No toxic morphological changes were observed in renewing, slowly proliferating or static normal cells. [7]

In a Holandino & al. study [8] human multidrug resistant leukemic cells (K562 and K562-Lucena1) exposed to direct current (DC) demonstrated significant inhibition of tumor growth, with cell lysis, alteration in shape, membrane extraction or discontinuity and intense vacuolization.

Zhou & al [9] have shown that a 72 hr exposure of HL60 cells to 50Hz, 0.1-0.8 mT magnetic fields resulted in an increased transcription level for tumor necrosis factor receptor p75 and interleukin Il-6Ralpha mRNA expression.

Zhao [10] examined the promotion of DNA synthesis in PDL fibroblasts under exposure to 0.14T magnetic field for 10,40,60,120 min/day x 1week, comparing these to similar treatments every other day. Remarkably, he found that the the cellular DNA contents increased proportionally with exposure time in the daily-treated samples, while no significant changes were found if the treatmets occurred on alternate days. He concluded that the magnetic field had a cumulative, threshold-dependent and time-delayed effect on DNA synthesis.

Eichwald & Walleczek [11] found that ELF (extremely low frequency) EMFs controlled calcium uptake regulation in T lymphocytes: a bi-phasic response (stimulation/inhibition) was identified depending on the degree of cellular activation. The authors also noted that this, in turn, may affect other cellular processes that are Ca dependent—ie DNA synthesis

Sontag & Dertinger [12] reported that human promyelocytes (HL-60) exposed for 5 minutes to an amplitude-modulated, 4000 kHz interferential current (25, 250 and 2500 microA/cm^2) showed windows of significant stimulation and depression in intracellular cAMP within the range of frequencies studied (0-125 Hz).

In a study by Kubinyi & al., t-RNA synthetase activity isolated from the brain and liver of mice exposed to microwave radiation (2.45 GHz) during gestation showed a decrease after continuous wave exposure, and an increase in activity after amplitude-modulated irradiation [13]

It is interesting to note that many of these studies specifically report finding no adverse effects on normal cells exposed to the same EM fields.

Finally, Blank and Soo [14] reviewed evidence that EM fields interact with the activity of the cell membrane enzymes Na,K-ATPase and cytochrome oxidase in a frequency-dependent manner—but argued that, in addition, large electron flows known to exist within the stacked base pairs of DNA could interact directly with EM currents and lead to gene activation [15]. One finding that supports this contention is that DNA transcription in cell-free solutions can be activated by electromagnetic fields [16].

ENDOGENOUS COHERENT FIELDS: BIOSYSTEMS AS DYNAMIC HOLOGRAMS
EVIDENCE FROM THE INTERNATIONAL INSTITUTE OF BIOPHYSICS (1970s-2003)

All living systems emit light spontaneously: these ultra-weak emissions range from a few up to several hundred photons per second per square centimeter of surface area. The distribution spectrum ranges from infra-red to ultra-violet and is nearly flat (does not depend on the wavelength), which indicates that the energy is emitted from a wide range of excited molecules and stored in a delocalized manner within the system. This broad spectral distribution persists when the organism is stimulated with monochromatic light ("delayed luminescence"), in which case a hyperbolic decay rate is observed. It has been argued by Popp and others [17, 18] that these characteristics are necessary and sufficient to demonstrate that the source of biophotons is a coherent photon field within the organism. Furthermore, it has been shown by Popp [19] that the flat distribution results in an optimization of the signal-noise ratio over all wavelengths and minimal entropy.

Cells undergo an average 10^5 reactions per second. Cilento has shown [20] that most biological reactions take place when a photon is borrowed from the surrounding electromagnetic bath, exciting the transition state complex, then is returned to the surroundings to become available for the next reaction. Since the average reaction takes 10^-9 seconds, Popp has argued that one photon (or an extremely low photon intensity) may be all that is needed to supply the required activation energy for all cell reactions. In fact, given that in 10^-9 seconds the electromagnetic wave packet travels over a distance of 10 cm (or 10^4 times the diameter of a cell), it is impractical to even speak of single photons inside a cell: instead, we must envision a field of electromagnetic wave amplitudes which can localize and delocalize according to the interference patterns and non-equilibrium dynamics of a field whose coherence volume may range from nanometers to meters.

Photon fluxes play a remarkable number of biological roles as either carriers of information (in enzyme activation, phototropism, photomorphogenesis, phototaxis, regulation of gene expression, vision) or as a driving energy for biological processes [21]. Furthermore, it is known [22, 23] that both the intensity and the spectrum of the biophoton emission are strongly correlated with the physiological and developmental state of the organism, and with the actions of the environment upon it (especially stressors, which tend to cause an increase of bioluminescence intensity). The dominating role of source and sink for the biophoton field is the DNA molecule [17, 24] (in fact the mammalian red blood cells, which do not have active chromatine, are the only cells which do not emit biophotons). There are definite correlations between the intensity of biophoton emission and conformational states of DNA during meiosis [24]. For example, increased levels of ultraweak luminescence (BPE) have been observed during cell division in frog eggs, the germination of seeds and during early stages of differentiation of *Dictyosteluim discoideum* [25, 23]The same papers report significantly higher level of photon emission from surgically removed tumors compared to normal tissues, a non-linear correlation between BPE and growth rate, and further correlations between the UWL from the fingertips of patients and their age and certain physiopathological states. These findings offer ample support to the thesis that biophotons are intimately related to the regulation of critical biological functions.

Noting correlations between optical properties of molecules and their carcinogenic activity, Popp has suggested that cancer induction is related to the loss of coherence of a photon field in the living tissues, originating from excited states of DNA [26, 27]. Growth regulation is based on the death rate of cells, with sudden cell death and mitosis having to balance each other perfectly. With 10^7 cells dying every second in the human body, this information has to travel a distance of at least 10^{-3} cm in 10^{-7} seconds, which is much faster than the velocity of messenger molecules, approaching the velocity of sound. If it is assumed that the message is holistic and "communicated" to the entire body, then the scale becomes 1 meter, and the speed of transmission reaches electromagnetic values. Thus cancer can be seen as an imbalance between cell growth and death due to a deterioration of intercellular and full-body communication systems [17]—and indeed, research has shown [25] that the characteristics of biophoton emission curves are different for normal versus tumor tissues.

The spatio-temporal coherence of biophoton fields means that complex electromagnetic (EM) interference patterns are created throughout the organism: the more coherent the light, the sharper the interference patterns. It has been suggested by Popp, Gariaev and others that these patterns may be the basis of morphogenesis and structural/biochemical regulation of the organism throughout its life—an EM blueprint guiding the development, repair and even social behavior of organisms. The phase information within and between cells is hypothesized to act as a biological control parameter regulating the growth and differentiation of cells, with constructive interference domains intracellularly and destructive interference in the extracellular matrix [24]. Experimental evidence such as the phantom leaf effect [28] the delayed luminescence function of tumor cells and the distribution of *Daphnia* larvae [29, 30, 18]certainly seem to support this hypothesis.

One of the most remarkable findings to shed some light on the possible mechanism of biophoton control comes from Ho's laboratory: in 1993, she and Lawrence discovered that, under polarized light microscopy, the extraordinary level of molecular coherence makes organisms appear crystalline. This dynamic coherence is a continuum that extends from intracellular molecules to the cytoplasm, extracellular matrix and the connective tissues throughout the organism [18]. The lipids in cellular membranes, the cytoskeletal and muscle proteins, collagen and other connective tissue macromolecules, as well as the DNA in chromosomes—all these essential and ubiquitous molecules of living systems are liquid crystals [31, 32]. Consequently, the organism may be seen as a solid state possessing many of the physical characteristics of these highly interesting materials.

Liquid crystals (LCs) are mesophases—states of matter between the solid and liquid phase. While they possesss long range orientational order, they are highly mobile and responsive, undergoing orientation changes (phase transitions) when exposed to a wide variety of stimuli, including electromagnetic fields, temperature and pressure changes, hydration, pH, concentrations of inorganic ions and other psysicochemical parameters [31, 32]. LC can convert information about minute changes in pressure, temperature and light into electrical currents (they are piezoelectric, pyroelectric and photoelectric). Lastly (but, as we shall see, very significant for our main proposal) they are **permanently modified (sensitized)** by the passage of electrical currents so as to facilitate the future passage of such currents [4-p. 257).

Considering these arguments, Mae-Wan Ho suggests that the LC matrix may act a quantum holographic medium which records interference patterns between local events and the global body field—an idea which finds full agreement with Gariaev's experimental work [33].

EVIDENCE FROM THE RUSSIAN ACADEMY OF SCIENCES
GARIAEV's DNA-wave BIOCOMPUTER (1990s-2003)

Since the early '90s, Peter Gariaev's team has been developing a new theoretical and experimental approach to the study of genetic material encoding and expression. In a pioneering series of papers [28, 34, 35, 36, 37, 38], he and his colleagues challenge the limits of the genetic code triplet model and propose instead a dual, substantive/wave basis for the encoding and expression of genetic material. The wave-like, non-local aspect of genetic regulation is recorded at the polarization level of DNA-associated photons, and the genome is seen as a quasi-hologram of light and radio waves which create the background necessary for the appropriate expression of genetic material.

Some of the experimental evidence cited in support of this new model is listed below:

1. The existence of homonymous-synonymous ambiguities of genetic texts;
2. The virus-like strain specificity of prions in the absence of nucleic acid material;
3. The role of introns: statistical analysis using the Zipf-Mandelbrot law reveals that DNA non-coding sequences, which account for 95-98% of the genome, have more in common with natural languages and demonstrate more long-distance correlations than coding sequences; this, according to the authors, is a strong indication that non-coding

areas are the basis for one or more biological languages and represent "a strategic informational content of chromosomes".

4.   The ability of DNA and chromatin in vitro to be pumped as a laser-active medium for subsequent laser light generation;

5.   Dzang Kangeng's experiments: successful wave transmission of genetic information from donor biosystem to an accepting one via split laser beams fed repeatedly through the optically-active donor biosystem, then delivered to the receiving biosystem in early developmental stages. Mixed characteristics of these non-molecular hybrids (seeds and chicks) were transferred to the next generation without need for further irradiation. (Although Kangeng provides no theoretical interpretation of the operational device, the authors' previous work with laser mirrors closely parallels his protocol, leading them to conclude that the polarized laser beam split into orthogonal waves which, by repeated passing through the optically active donor DNA and multiple interference with itself, lead to the phenomenon of photon field localization and information recording).

6.   The authors' similar experiments with polarization-laser-radio-wave (PLRW) spectroscopy, whereby they used orthogonally polarized EM beams to repair the genetic information of old radioactively-damaged seeds from the Chernobyl area (1987).

The authors argue that the genome emits light and radio-waves whose delocalized interference patterns create calibration fields (blueprints) for a system's space-time organization. This holographic-type information is being constantly and simultaneously read in billions of cells, accounting for the quick coordinated response typical of living systems. Gariaev and his team suggest that the genome operates like a "complex multi-wave laser with adjustable frequencies", able to produce light and radio waves which regulate the biosystem's space and time organization. This complex background is the basis for the correct expression of genetic material (peptide codes) during embryogenesis and adult life, accounting for the elusive self-regulation and specificity of DNA function in various tissues and under various conditions. Various solitons (optical, acoustic, conformational, rotable-oscillating, etc) excited in polynucleotide areas, and transmitted over large distances significantly exceeding the hydrogen-bond length, "become the apparatus for continual (non-local) reading of context RNA sequences on a whole".

On the basis of this model, the authors suggest that the activation of oncogenes and xenobiotic HIV sequences is dependent on genome holographic processes and therefore that future research in these high-profile areas should focus on the factors modulating such EM field characteristics (such as external artificial modified fields) in addition to local, molecular biology approaches. Given that the expression (onset) of oncogenes and retroviruses such as HIV is known to vary widely among individuals and be largely context-specific, the authors suggest that external artificial modified fields may, in the future, help us modulate this apparent cellular context (environment) and thus keep such noxious genetic material dormant for indefinite periods of time. Another interesting suggestion made by Gariaev is that phenomena such as cellular apoptosis might be connected with an abnormal compression of photons by cell nuclei, which are accumulated to a maximal value and then destroy the nuclei.

Since apoptosis has been demonstrated in healer-treated cancer cultures, and unusual electromagnetic signals are also commonly observed during such healing sessions (see reviews in [1, 39]), we would like at this point to turn our attention to this phenomenon and discuss some of its basic characteristics.

The Effects of Healer's Intent on Living Tissues

In a different paper presented at this conference [1] we have described a series of experiments which demonstrate that human intentionality can produce a statistically significant effect on the following genetic programs:

1. **cell division** (studies of plant, yeast, bacterial, cell culture growth rate)—reflecting **DNA synthesis and mitotic rates**
2. **transcription** (rates of mRNA synthesis); **DNA conformation** studies
3. **translation** (studies on protein synthesis, expression of different membrane surface receptors)
4. **cell differentiation** (reversal of cancer features/ seed revitalization)
5. **mutagenesis** (Burbank case; Nash, Pei E-coli studies; Qigong industrial mutagenesis)
6. **apoptosis** (Qigong in-vitro studies on cancer cell lines)

Furthermore, conscious intent has been shown capable (at statistically significant levels) of producing the following structural and physiological effects:

1. conformational changes in cell membrane, chromatin, proteins [1, 78]
2. distant influence on target's EEG, heart rate, galvanic skin response, finger blood volume, blood pressure, as well as fish orientation and algae motility [40, 41, 42-p. 336]

These several hundred studies, conducted over the past 3 decades by a large number of university and independent laboratories in countries like the US, England, China, Japan, Russia, Germany and others, represent a pioneering body of work whose importance cannot be overstated. Although not all of them have been conducted under ideal methodological conditions of blindness and control, and the reporting style is far from consistent across the field (see [42] for an outstanding synopsis and analysis of experimental quality in these different categories), the overall evidence is much too compelling and significant to ignore. Replicating these studies under proper, uniform academic standards is of course a necessary first step. However, many of the results obtained by independent laboratories appear to reinforce each other, to a degree that certain general observations about the effect of mental intent on biological targets can already be drawn:

Specificity of Intent

The effect of intentionality appears to be directional and target specific. For example, Achterberg and Rider showed that training patients in cell-specific visualization of either T lymphocytes or neutrophils resulted in statistical increase in cell blood levels correlating with the type of imagery employed [43].

Chien & al. found the following when studying the influence of a qigong master's "facilitating" qi on a culture of human fibroblasts: 1.8% increase in cell growth rate in 24 hrs, 10-15% increase in DNA synthesis and 3-5% increase in cell protein synthesis in a 2 hr period. With "inhibiting" qi, cell growth decreased by 6% in 24 hr, while DNA and protein synthesis decreased by 20-23%, respectively 35-48%. Additionally, the respiration rate of boar sperm was increased by 12.5-13% after a 5 minute exposure to "facilitating" qi, and decreased by 45-48% by a 2 minute exposure to "inhibiting" qi. The qi was emitted from the palms of the master and measured using a III-V compound semiconductor InSb detector—as an increase, respectively decrease in the temperature of the environment. [44] Additional studies showing an increase/decrease of target culture viability with opposite intents are described in [1].

Deyin Chu of Peking University found significant conformational changes in the circular dichroism (CD) spectrum when external qi was applied to biomolecules (poly-glutamic acid, poly-lysinec, metallothionein and RNA).

Changes were directional and varied with the intent of the master emitting the qi. [75, 76]

Becker used hypnotized subjects to demonstrate that they could decrease or increase the DC potential of specific areas of the body depending on the suggestion given (a suggestion of numbness in the left arm resulted in no response to a pinprick stimulus and a drop to zero in the DC potential, while the pinprick response/DC potential remained almost unchanged for the right arm; the change in voltage was "exactly the same as that seen in standard chemical nerve block" [45-p 90-91]

Rein & McCraty found that winding and unwinding of the DNA reflected the directionality of intent; in one protocol involving three identical aliquots of DNA, two samples were denatured to different degrees while the third one was left unchanged, as intended. In distant-effect protocols, similar effects were noted, but the onset time varied from immediate to a 60-minute delay. [46-p. 303, 406]

Both Qigong application and simple "concentration" experiments with cell cultures have shown that we can achieve either accelerated culture growth or death, and influence the rate of bacterial and plant mutagenesis in the direction dictated by intent [42, 46, 47].

Electromagnetic Windows of Healing and Intent

Studies by Zimmerman and Beck show that healers' hand and brain frequencies measured during active "healing states" sweep a 0.3-30 Hz range, with most activity in the 7-8 Hz area. These frequencies, which show an uncanny consistency across a remarkable number of cultures and healing traditions, appear to closely overlap the electromagnetic specificity windows used in clinical and laboratory applications to enhance neural regeneration (2 Hz); bone growth (7 Hz); ligament healing (10 Hz) and capillary and fibroblast proliferation (15, 20 and 72 Hz) [48].

Both local and distant mental interactions have been shown to produce unusual EM signatures. Magnetic signals up to 105nT were found by Wu & al.during Qi emission by qigong practitioners [49]. Unusually high static charges (up to 221 volts) from the bodies of healers and psi-gifted people were reported by Watkins, Hochenegg, Shallis and Green [42 p157]. Nakamura measured an increase in biophoton emission intensity from the hands of practitioners in the qigong state [50]. Wallace found that human biophoton emissions could be increased by subjects at will and measured up to 100 time stronger emissions from the hands of gifted subjects compared to controls

[51]. High surges in the magnetic field surrounding healers, or significant effects on distant magnetic sensors, have been published by Ullman, Watkins, Puthoff and Targ, Zimmerman and Ostrander and Schroeder, Sergeyev, (52; 42 p 168; 39]. Photographic film exposure in association with healing or clairvoyance experiments has been demonstrated in independent studies by Watkins, Turner and Zhao Yong-Jie [42 p 157, 169]. Radin reports that the background ionizing radiation could be decreased in accordance to task instructions (p<0.05), only to suddenly increase above control levels 20 seconds after the treatment period [53]. In a series of experiments involving therapeutic touch practitioners and their subjects, gamma radiation levels significantly decreased in 100% of the subjects and at every body site tested [54, 55].

Finally, it is highly interesting to note the close parallel between the genetic-level effects of healing intent as described in [1] and those of weak electromagnetic fields as discussed earlier in this paper (i.e. altered levels of mRNAs and proteins, increased enzyme activities, decrease in tumor growth and cell mitotic index, tumor cell alterations in shape and membrane discontinuity, increase in apoptosis and micronucleus formation, tumor cell lysis and vacuolization, accelerated differentiation—as well as seed revitalization and hybridization with the Gariaev/Kangeng techniques). Furthermore, the fact that many of these bioelectromagnetics studies found no adverse EMF effects on normal cells also seems to mirror the regulatory influence of healing intent [42, 78].

Is there a link between effective mental healing intent, or the altered state of consciousness required to produce it, and these unusual EM emissions? Are characteristic frequencies/spectra required for particular healing effects? And do these unusual EM signals play an active role in healing (perhaps by entrainment and frequency synchronization with the patient, as Oschman suggests)—or are they merely by-products of a deeper interpersonal communication mechanism we have yet to discover?

Finally, we should also ask ourselves what such capabilities tell us about the healer's metabolic status. We know, for example, that advanced practitioners of Qigong can enter a special state (Bigu) in which they can subsist for weeks, sometimes months, on only 2-300 calories per day, while carrying on with normal activities. [56, 57] This "super-efficient state", as Prof. Roy has described it, has been shown to be metabolically different from that of normal fasting—which suggests that the body somehow switches over to a different way to process and conserve energy. Is there a link between Bigu and the energetic phenomena described above?

Distant Mental Interactions with Living Systems (DMILS)

DMILS include a wide range of variables, from physiological parameters like EEG and galvanic skin response [40, 58, 59, 60] to the denaturation of DNA in solution [42, 61] to affecting the morbidity and mortality rates of HIV/AIDS patients by remote prayer groups [62] Typically in these experiments the sender is isolated from the experimental group by distances ranging from a few meters (an adjacent room) up to thousands of kilometers and the subjects are blind to the sending period, so that a comparison can be made with the "non-influence" windows.

The statistical significance of these remote effects across dozens of independent studies is highly consistent despite the subjects' inability to consciously "guess" the sending window. Some studies have shown a lag time to onset of effect in the order of seconds [59,60], while in others, paradoxically, an anticipatory effect has been demonstrated [58]—consistent with decades of parapsychological retro-pk evidence, but a clear shock for the field of medicine.

Such evidence of space and time non-locality is probably the single greatest reason for which spiritual healing continues to encounter major resistance as a legitimate research subject from the scientific establishment. And yet at a physics theoretical level there is nothing that prohibits such effects from taking place: indeed, if there is one salient observation to be made on the basis of our foregoing discussion, it is that modern medicine seems to have almost entirely disassociated itself from the biophysical bases of life: our current thinking appears to stop mysteriously at the biomolecular level, completely oblivious to the physics that lie beneath. Our challenge is to take this next step and place the current, biomolecular understanding of genetic regulation into a broader context—hoping that some of the answers which have eluded us so far, such as the onset criticality and reversal of malignant programs, will become more obvious at this level of the control hierarchy.

A New Perspective of the Genetic Code
A Hierarchy of Genetic Regulatory Mechanisms

Even a brief survey of the literature, such as we have undertook, suggests that there are at least three main levels of control mechanisms dictating the unfolding of genetic programs:

1. THE BIOCHEMICAL LEVEL: this includes, but is not limited to, the triplet genetic code and the newly discovered histone code; mechanisms such as the availability of cellular chemical messengers, molecular feedback loops and cis-/ trans-regulation work on this level, controlling to at least some degree the sequence of different genes' expression.

2. THE BIOPHYSICAL LEVEL: this can further be divided into local and non-local effects.

    2A. LOCAL control refers to the conformational effects of electromagnetic fields on chromatin, enzymes and cell membranes—which in turn affect the exposure of given genes and the rate of transcription/translation, plus possibly the rate of DNA sysnthesis and cell mitosis.

    2B. NON-LOCAL effects include endogenous field coherence, electromagnetic interference grids, superconduction, photon localization phenomena and the possibility of non-material, wave-based genetic hybridization and regeneration, as demonstrated by the experiments of Gariaev and Kangeng.

3. THE CONSCIOUS LEVEL. As we suggested before, it is difficult to tell at this point whether consciousness and mental intent act both locally and non-locally, although the existence of DMILS and anticipatory effects is a strong indication that we need to look beyond simple electromagnetic entrainment between healer and patient.

Once we recognize that genetic programs are continuously modulated by all these different parameters, we need to ask ourselves a new set of questions. For example:

1. What is the correct order of these elements in the hierarchy?
2. How do level 1 and 2 mechanisms interface with conscious intent? (EM or other physical substrate?)
3. How do coherent biophoton fields interact with environmental EMFs?
4. How does conscious intent modulate endogenous EMFs?

5. What is the power/frequency/polarization profile of biophoton emissions under different states of consciousness and how does it vary with various intentions or forms of visualization?
6. What is the basis of target specificity and bi-directional effects in controlled healing/pk studies?
7. How is information transmitted non-locally?

Preliminary Framework

To begin addressing these questions, it is important to re-emphasize the biophysical perspective on living tissues emerging from the works cited above. According to this view, the coherence of endogenous EM fields and liquid crystal properties of biomolecules account for:

- NONLOCAL COMMUNICATION THROUGHOUT THE ORGANISM/ TISSUE/POPULATION
- SYNCHRONIZED BEHAVIOR OF BILLIONS OF CELLS
- EXQUISITE SENSITIVITY AND SPECIFICITY TO WEAK STIMULI
- HIGHLY EFFICIENT ENERGY UTILIZATION
- POSSIBLE BRAIN-BODY ELECTROMAGNETIC CONTINUUM AND TUNING REGULATORY MECHANISM FOR TISSUE-LEVEL INTERFERENCE EFFECTS

Working Hypothesis
Intent Driven Chromatin Decondensation as a Factor in Transcription

It is generally accepted that the conformation of the chromatin fiber must change reversibly in processes that require the access of regulatory proteins and enzymes to the DNA template (such as in transcription, replication and repair). van Holde and Zlatanova have suggested [63, 64] that one of the major conformational changes that occurs during DNA compaction is a collapse of the angle made between three consecutive nucleosomes (internucleosomal angle), probably mediated by electrostatic changes in histone interactions with linker DNA.

Could such a change in angle be partly controlled by the electromagnetic hologram grid nodes postulated by Gariaev, Popp and others? If electrostatic interactions are responsible for chromatin folding/unfolding, it would be easy to see how changes in the frequency or polarization angle of DNA-associated biophotons could alter the locus of action of such pre-transcriptional decondensation. The demonstrated ability of conscious intent to produce winding/unwinding of in-vitro chromatin and to directionally influence transcription becomes highly significant in this context. One other supporting piece of evidence are the published experiments of Yan Xin [65] in which he repeatedly demonstrated the ability of external qi to alter the polarization of targeted He-Ne laser beams from distances ranging between 7-2000 km. The change in polarization occurred within an hour of the external qi emission, as repeated sharp fluctuations averaging 6-7 degrees and 10-12% change in intensity of the normal beam, compared to baseline. No difference was recorded in the controls.

Meditation as a Psycho-Physiological Remodeling

We propose is that qigong and other **meditative techniques** work by **progressively increasing the overall coherence** ("qi flow"?) of the body's **liquid crystal matrix** via conscious mental driving, in a way not dissimilar to laser pumping or the gradual orientation of ferromagnetic particles in an EM field. Meditation frequencies could engage the thalamic silent periods (as Oschman has suggested) and possibly other frequency-window pacemakers, and thus **drive the configurational states** that the body naturally cycles through, **to sensitize its LC matrix to particular frequencies.** Moreover, the semiconductor nature of living tissues suggests that, with repeated passage of an EM current through them, their sensitivity to subsequent signals should increase—a property which, we believe, is critical to the understanding of **long-term physiological changes** seen in meditators [66, 67]. The maintenance of a mentally-driven, permanent tighter-than-average molecular coherence would, in our model, lead to a gradual increase in tissue liquid crystallinity, more efficient signal detection/transmission and hence greater perceptual sensitivity, energy efficiency (Bigu) and ability to correct local EM "contextual errors".

Do Specific Intents Translate into Characteristic Brain-Body Wave Forms?

As we have seen earlier, Becker has shown that an organism's somatic DC field correlates in very specific ways with its state of consciousness: using salamanders for test subjects, Becker found that under anesthesia, their peripheral voltages dropped to zero, and even reversed in very deep stages [4 p. 111]. Similar instances of reversal in body polarity are reported as occurring in human subjects monitored during deep trances induced in preparation for remote viewing. In Spiritual Healing, Benor reports on a study by Rein and Laskow which found that four different intentions by the same healer produced different body magnetic emissions which correlated with different biological effects on tumor cell cultures [42 p. 159].

Based on the evidence reviewed in this paper, we tend to agree with suggestions by Beck, Oschman and Becker that healers produce characteristic electromagnetic frequencies which can exert specific biological effects on their target. However, we would like to qualify this statement by adding the following observations:

1. Frequency may not be the only parameter involved in modulating the EM signal. In view of Popp's and Gariaev's data, we have reason to believe that the **phase and polarization of endogenous fields are also under the effect of conscious intent**, which may be self-generated or transmitted non-locally by a healer.

    Thus the **specificity of guided imagery may be the result of unique windows of frequency/ polarization** excited at the level of the cerebral cortex, then spreading globally along neural and perineural pathways. It is also possible that concentration on complex sensory modalities (ie the vividness of imagery) synchronizes larger areas of the cortex, resulting in a more powerful signal. Gariaev's contextual holographic paradigm further suggests that a pathologic EM environment may be less stable than that of healthy tissue, and thus more easily modified. (It is interesting to note, in this context, the phenomenon of "qi striking" that commonly takes place during qigong meditation, whereby a patient focusing only on overall "emptiness", suddenly notices pain in the diseased areas; the pain is often very intense, and vanishes as soon as the meditative state is ended. Traditional explanations view this as "qi striking the energy blockage", with the pain diminishing as the blockage is eliminated over weeks or months of practice. Alternatively, we could postulate that the abnormal EM environment leads to an accumulation of charge and the depolarization of local pain fibers under the continued input of "circulating qi", or mentally-pumped frequencies.). Finally, we could also make an argument that stress, or other cronic emotional disturbances, represent a possible source of de-synchronization with partial loss of endogenous field coherence.

2.   Another point that cannot be overemphasized is that **the presence of electromagnetic signatures associated with intent does not necessarily imply an EM transmission mechanism** (i.e. via proximal frequency entrainment or coupling to the Schumann resonance, as previously discussed by Oschman, Becker and Sidorov)—but **simply that these ubiquitous EM signals may be produced as a secondary, local effect of the primary interaction.** While EM coupling cannot be excluded in some situations, we need to realize that the nonlocal characteristics of mental healing (target specificity, distance and time independence) require more than a classical communication framework (see below).

Distant Information Transfer

One of the most remarkable features of distant mental interactions with living and inert systems is that they affect only the target samples, leaving other (control) samples which are within the same radius, statistically unchanged [49]. This strongly suggests that we are dealing with some form of **entanglement between healer and target**, rather than a classical, isotropic field-mediated process. However, it has been repeatedly pointed out by Dossey, Walach, Pitkanen and others that in such case **the definition and exact mechanism of quantum entanglement would have to be expanded** to account for the insertion/extraction of intelligent information and for the notorious problem of decoherence in complex quantum systems.

One comprehensive model that happens to contain such an extended concept of entanglement (together with numerous testable predictions which are supported by Gariaev's spectra and the presence of EM signatures at the target) is Pitkanen's Topological Geometrodynamics—an 8-dimensional cosmology which is the product of 4-D Minkowskian space-time and the SU(3)/U(2) projective space of two complex dimensions [68, 69, 70, 71]. The geometrization of all basic interactions in TGD means that classical fields and matter form a pseudo-Feynman diagram in which the lines representing matter are replaced by spacetime sheets and virtual bosons are replaced by topological light rays ("massless extremals", MEs). MEs generate geometrical supracurrents which serve as a **source of coherent photons** and act as geometrical correlates of entanglement between distant material spacetime sheets (the vertices of the pseudo-Feynman diagram). One of the predictions of TGD is that focused mental intent produces topological field quanta—form-specific MEs which act as **non-dissipative entanglement "bridges"** between sender and target and which create characteristic ionic and electromagnetic signatures at both ends by their interaction with local magnetic flux tubes.

Thus the solution proposed by Pitkanen appears to elegantly connect all the major observations we have discussed in our paper up to this point: a distant healer's conscious intent can be seen as generating form-specific geometrical currents which "propagate" non-dissipatively across arbitrarily large distances and which interact with the intended target by producing characteristic, coherent photon signatures. In turn these photons interact with the organism's endogenous electromagnetic field to modulate specific frequency or polarization parameters as described by Popp and Gariaev, thus altering interference patterns, regulating inter-cellular communication and the contextual environment of DNA/RNA expression inside cells.

Of course, at this point it is difficult to fill in all the details, or indeed feel confident of the absolute validity of such a model. On the other hand, TGD opens experimental possibilities that have generally not been available with other theories of nonlocal healing. In [70] we have made a number of proposals regarding the types of tests that could be conducted as a **preliminary verification of TGD predictions.** Together with additional replications of the Gariaev experiments and of the major histo-molecular qigong studies reviewed in our two papers at this conference, we believe these ideas are well-worth pursuing as part of a future research program in complementary and alternative medicine. As opposed to previous mind-body research proposals, all these suggested protocols are remarkably concrete, objective, quantifiable and compatible with our need to construct a consistent physical theory. Since only innovative experimentation will be able to select the most promising theoretical models, and since in the absence of such models we cannot begin to incorporate this valuable body of evidence into our overall therapeutic strategy, we feel it is imperative that the NIH and other potential sponsors treat these proposals with the attention they deserve.

Conclusion

Where do we go from here? The first step, of course, should be a well-coordinated experimental program replicating the major classes of mental interactions described in these two papers. Protocols could be set up to study the biophysical basis of differential response in normal and abnormal cell populations (target specificity/normalization); to compare the effect size, replicability, side effects and long-term response for biophysical and mind-body therapeutic approaches in specific pathological models; to study the ability of normal human populations to learn and effectively implement such mental techniques (clinical studies); and to investigate the interactions between external EM fields and endogenous currents with respect to genetic regulation. Finally, given the common challenge that nonlocal communication presents to researchers in physics, parapsychology and mind-body medicine, we strongly advocate the establishment of interdisciplinary teams to collaborate on innovative new protocols capable of extracting meaningful conclusions about this fundamental aspect of reality.

From an applications point of view, we should start identifying the most effective meditation protocols for specific effects—i.e. enhancement of immune function, expression of specific genes, suppression of pathogens or reversal of malignant cell behavior/induction of apoptosis. It is also important to start designing and standardizing teaching programs, perhaps through the use of biofeedback methods to evaluate the effectiveness of teachers' and students' meditation on specific biological parameters. Understanding the interactions between mind-body interventions and conventional treatment modalities (such as the demonstrated increase in drug uptake and reduction in chemotharepy side effects with concurrent qigong practice) is another long-term goal, which should allow us to eventually integrate such multi-modality therapies for optimal results with minimal iatrogenic trauma to the organism.

Finally, we would like to take a step back and end this presentation with a philosophical observation. For more than a century, the common assumption in parapsychology research has been that the brain is the primary detection organ for subconscious/ anomalous cognition. However, in spite of this experimental focus, there is a remarkable lack of evidence supporting this contention—in fact we now know that certain peripheral responses to anomalous stimuli, such as the galvanic skin response, are highly consistent in the absence of any conscious awareness of these stimuli. Is the brain the only conceivable transducer of nonlocal information?

Indeed, the literature shows that psi function manifests across the full taxonomic continuum, from humans to animals [41, 58, 73, 74, 77] to plants and individual cells [72, 42]. Since such consistent features are generally attributed to a very successful adaptive mechanism, and Pitkanen's TGD predicts a fractal hierarchy of biological emitters/receivers for nonolocal communication, could it be that the exquisite sensitivity of genetic material (DNA, RNA, protein) to mental intent may in fact reflect a deep evolutionary principle? For these first forms of life, devoid of what we would call a sensory system, chemical and electromagnetic interactions with the environment would have been one, albeit purely random, type of "orientation" response. However, the complex behavior of organisms starting from the very bottom of the taxonomic tree (see virus and prion dynamics, DNA repair and transcription, etc) strongly suggest that behavioral adaptations were set in place, which clearly reflect a directional, self-serving interaction with the environment and that we are at a loss to explain on purely biomolecular grounds. Could the survival instinct of primitive organisms qualify as consciousness—suggesting that the genetic material in our bodies might in fact be the oldest and primary "antenna" for nonlocal conmmunication? While this may at first look like a rhetorical question, the sobering realization that we are still in the dark about the higher-level programs regulating the spatial and temporal expression of DNA [2,3,77], together with the evidence presented in this paper, suggest a positive answer. And if conscious intent has the ability to shape our organism's response to environmental challenges by acting all the way down to DNA, RNA and protein levels, then it is indeed the most versatile and potent therapeutic intervention we could ever conceive of.

References

1. Chen K, Sidorov L. (2003) Effects of Intent and Mental Status on Biological Subjects. 1st Int Conf on the Science of Whole Person Healing, Washington D.C. March 2002
2. Davidson EH (2001) Genomic regulatory systems: development and evolution, 1st ed. Academic Press, San Diego CA
3. Martindale D. (2003) New Scientist 177 [2388]: 32
4. Becker R. and Selden G (1985) The Body Electric: Electromagnetism and the Foundation of Life, 1st edn. Morrow, New York, NY
5. Tofani S, Cintorino M, Barone D, Berardelli M, de Santi MM, Ferrara A, Orlassino R, Rolfo K, Ronchetto F, Tripodi SA, Tosi P (2002) Bioelectromagnetics 23[3]: 230
6. Simko A, Kriehuber R, Weiss DG, Luben RA (1998) Bioelectromagnetics 19[2]: 85
7. Tofani S, Barone D, Cintorino M, deSanti MM, Ferrara A, Orlassino R, Ossola P, Peroglio F, Rolfo K, Ronchetto F (2001) Bioelectromagnetics 22[6]: 419
8. Holandino C, Veiga VF, Rodriguez ML, Morales MM, Capella MAM, Lviano CS (2001) Bioelectromagnetics 22[7]: 470

9. Zhou J, Li C, Yao G, Chiang H, Chang Z (2002) Bioelectromagnetics 23(5): 339

10. Zhao (1994) Chinese Journal of Stomatology 29[2]:75

11. Eichwald C, Walleczek J (1996) Bioelectromagnetics 17(6): 427

12. Sontag W, Dertinger H (1998) Bioelectromagnetics 19[8]: 452

13. Kubinyi G, Thuroczy G, Bakos J, Boloni E, Sinay H, Szabo L (1996) Bioelectromagnetics 17[6]:497

14. Blank M and Soo L (2001) Bioelectrochemistry 53[2]:171

15. Blank M. & Goodman R. (1997) Bioelectromagnetics 18:111

16. Blank M. & Goodman R. (1998) Bioelectromagnetics 19:138

17. Popp FA, Chang J (1998) The Physical Background and the Informational Character of Biophoton Emission. In: Chang JJ, Fisch J, Popp F-A (eds) Biophotons. Kluwer Academic Publishers, Dordrecht p 239

18. Ho, M.-W. (1993) The rainbow and the worm: the physics of organisms, 1st edn. World Scientific Publishing Co., Singapore

19. Ho, M.-W., Popp, F.-A. (1989) Gaia and the Evolution of Coherence. Presented at the 3rd Camelford Conference on the Implications of the Gaia Thesis: Symbiosis, Cooperativity and Coherence.

20. Popp, FA(1999) About the Coherence of Biophotons. In: Boston University and MIT (eds) Macroscopic Quantum Coherence, Proceedings of an International Conference of the Boston University. World Scientific www.datadiwan.de/iib/ib0204e_1.htm

21. Renger G. (1998) Photophysical Reactions in Cells. In: Chang JJ, Fisch J, Popp F-A (eds) Biophotons. Kluwer Academic Publishers, Dordrecht p 1

22. Chwirot BW (1998) Do We Always Need to Know Molecular Origin of Light Emitted by Living Systems? In: Chang JJ, Fisch J, Popp F-A (eds) Biophotons. Kluwer Academic Publishers, Dordrecht, p 229

23. Rubik, B. (1993) Noetic Sciences Review #26

24. Popp, FA Some Features of Biophotons and their Interpretation in Terms of Coherent States. International Institute of Biophysics. www.datadiwan.de/iib/ib0205e_1.htm

25. Chwirot BW (2001) Ultraweak Luminescence as a source of information on biological systems. International Institute of Biophysics. www.datadiwan.de/iib/ib0601e_.htm

26. Popp FA (2002) Basic theory of Cancer Development and Defense, a presentation for the 11th International Conference "Biological Cancer Defense" in Heidelberg, Germany (May 3-5, 2002) International

Institute of Biophysics www.lifescientists.de/publication/pub2002-05.htm

27. Popp FA, Chang J (1998) The Physical Background and the Informational Character of Biophoton Emission. In: Chang JJ, Fisch J, Popp F-A (eds) Biophotons. Kluwer Academic Publishers, Dordrecht p 239

28. Gariaev PP, Vassiliev AA, Grigoriev KV, Poponin BP and Shcheglov VA (1992) The DNA phantom effect (1992) (Short Messages in Physics, FIAN #11-12, 1992; reviewed in MISAHA Newsletter #24-27, 1999)

29. Popp, FA (1986) On the Coherence of Ultraweak Photon Emission from Living Tissues. In: C.W. Kilmister (ed.) Disequilibrium and Self-Organisation. Reidel

30. Chang JJ, Popp FA (1998) Biological organization: a possible mechanism based on the coherence of "biophotons". In: Chang JJ, Fisch J, Popp F-A (eds) Biophotons. Kluwer Academic Publishers, Dordrecht, p 217

31. Ho M-W (1996) Journal of Consciousness Studies 3:231

32. Beal J B (1996) Biosystems liquid crystals and potential effects of natural and artificial electromagnetic fields (EMFs). Second Annual Advanced Water Sciences Symposium, Exploratory Session 1, Dallas, TX http://frontpage.simnet.is/vgv/jim1.htm

33. Ho M-W (1998) Organism and Psyche in a Participatory Universe. In: The Evolutionary Outrider. The Impact of the Human Agent on Evolution, Essays in Honor of Edwin Laszlo (D. Loye ed.) p 49-65, Praeger 1998

34. Gariaev PP, Chudin VI, Komissarov GG, Berezin AA, Vasiliev AA (1991) Holographic associative memory of biological systems. SPIE Vol. 1621 Optical Memory and Neural Networks

35. Reshetnyak SA, Shcheglov VA, Blagodatskikh VI, Gariaev PP, Maslov M. Yu. (1996) Mechanisms of Interaction of Electromagnetic Radiation with a Biosystem. Laser Physics 6[4]: 621

36. Gariaev PG, Kaempf U, Marcer P J, Tertishny GG, Birshtein B, Iarochenko A, Leonova KA (2000) The DNA-wave Biocomputer. The fourth international conference on computing anticipatory systems (CASYS), Liege 2000. http://www.bcs.org.uk/siggroup/cyber/dna.htm

37. Gariaev PP, Tertishny GG, Leonova EA (2002) The wave, probabilistic and linguistic representations of cancer and HIV. J of Nonlocality and Remote Mental Interactions 1[2] www.emergentmind.org/gariaevI2.htm

38. Gariaev PP, Tertishny GG, Iarochenko AM, Maximenko VV, Leonova EA (2002) The spectroscopy of biophotons in non-local genetic regulation. J of Nonlocality and Remote Mental Interactions 1[3] www.emergentmind.org/gariaevI3.htm

39. Sidorov L. (2001) On the Possible Mechanism of Intent in Paranormal Phenomena. J of Theoretics (2001) http://www.journaloftheoretics.com/Links/Papers/INTENT.pdf; J of Nonlocality and Remote Mental Interactions I [1] www.emergent-mind.org/sidorov_II.htm

40. Puthoff EH, Targ R. A Perceptual Channel for Information Transfer over Kilometer Distances: Historical Perspective and Recent Research (2002). In: Tart, Puthoff and Targ (Eds.) IEEE Symposia on the Nature of Extrasensory Perception. Hampton Roads Publishing, Charlottesville, VA

41. Delanoy (1993) Experimental Evidence Suggestive of Anomalous Consciousness Interactions. 2nd Gauss Symposium, Munich, August 1993

42. Benor, D J (2001) Spiritual Healing: Scientific Validation of a Healing Revolution, 1st edn.Vision Publications, Southfield MI 2001

43. Imagery. In: "Alternative Medicine, Expanding Medical Horizons"—a report to the Office of Alternative Medicine in National Institutes of Health on Alternative Medical Systems and Practices in the United States, 1992 http://www.naturalhealthnotebook.com/Alternative_Medicine/Mind-Body/imagery.htm

44. Chien CI; Tsuei JJ; Lee SC; Huang YC, and Wei YH (1991). Am J Chin Med 19 (3-4):285

45. Becker, R. (1990) Cross Currents: the Perils of Electropollution, the Promise of Electromedicine. 1st edn. Tarcher/Putnam, New York, NY

46. Benor D. (2001) Spiritual Healing: Scientific Validation of a Healing Revolution, Prof. Supp. 1st edn.Vision Publications, Southfield MI 2001

47. McGee C, Chow EPY (1994) Qigong: Miracle Healing from China. Medipress, Coeur d'Alene, ID

48. Oschman, JL (1997). J of Bodywork and Movement Therapies, 1[3]:179

49. Lin, Z. and Chen, K. (2002) Exploratory Studies of External Qi in China. J of ISLIS 20[2]:457

50. Nakamura H, Kokubo H, Parkhomtchouk D, Chen W, Tanaka M, Zhang T, Kokado T, Yamamoto M, Fukuda N (2000) J of ISLIS 18[2]: 418

51. Rubik B. (2000) Electromagnetic and Other Subtle Energies in Psi Research. In: Subtle Energies and Uncharted Realms of the Mind: an Esalen Invitational Conference.

52. Wortz EC, Bauer AS, Blackwelder RF, Eerkens JW, Saur AJ. (2002). An investigation of Soviet Psychical Research. In: Tart, Puthoff and Targ (Eds.) IEEE Symposia on the Nature of Extrasensory Perception. Hampton Roads Publishing, Charlottesville, VA

53. (1991) Radin, DI (1991) Beyond Belief: Exploring Interactions Among Mind, Body and Environment. ISSSEEM Journal 2 [3]

54. Benford, M. S. (1999) "Spin doctors": a new paradigm theorizing the mechanism of bioenergy healing. Journal of Theoretics, 1[2] http://www.journaloftheoretics.com/Articles/1-2/benford.html

55. Benford, M. S. (1999) Idiopathic thermogenesis: potential origin and mechanism of action. Journal of Theoretics, 1[3] http://www.journaloftheoretics.com/Articles/1-3/Benford%20IT1-3.pdf

56. The First National Conference on the Bigu Manifestation, Health Effects and Scientific Research of Yan Xin Qigong Pennsylvania State University, June 2000.http://www.clubs.psu.edu/yanxinqigong/report/

57. Huang G, Shen X. and Zhou Z (1988). Experimental Study of Fasting with Qigong Exercises. 1st World Conf Acad Exch Med Qigong; Beijing, China 1988

58. Braud W. (2000) Alternative Therapies in Health and Medicine 6[1]:37

59. Yamamoto M, Hirasawa M., Kokubo H., Kawano K., Kokado T., Hirata, T. and Yasuda, N. (1997). Journal of ISLIS 15[1]:88

60. Yamamoto M, Hirasawa M, Kokado T, Kokubo H, Yamada T, Taniguchi J, Kawano K Fukuda N. Journal of ISLIS 17 [1] : 191

61. Yan X, Zheng C, Zhou G, Lu Z (1988) Nature Journal (Chinese). 11: 647

62. Sicher F, Targ E, Moore D, Smith H. (1998) Positive Therapeutic Effect of Distant Healing in an Advanced AIDS Population. Papapsychology Association Convention, 1998

63. van Holde K, Zlatanova J (1996) What determines the folding of the chromatin fiber? In: Proc. Natl. Acad. Sci. USA, 93: 10548

64. Zlatanova J, Leuba SH, van Holde K (1998) Biophysical Journal 74:2554

65. Yan X, Lu Z (1988) Measurement of the Effects of External Qi on the Polarization Plane of a Linearly Polarized Laser Beam. Nature Journal (Chinese). 11:563

66. Austin, J (2000) Zen and the Brain, 1st edn. MIT Press, Cambridge, MA

67. Murphy M. and Donovan S.(2002) The physical and physiological effects of meditation. IONS Press.

68. Pitkanen M (2003) Macrotemporal Quantum Coherence, Spin Glass Degeneracy and Number Theoretic Information Concept. J of Non-Locality and Remote Mental Interactions II[1]   www.emergent-mind.org/PDF_files.htm/qcohe12.PDF

69. Pitkanen M (2003) Biosystems as Conscious Holograms. J of Non-Locality and Remote Mental Interactions

70. II[1] www.emergentmind.org/PDF_files.htm/conscholo0302.PDF

71. Sidorov L (2003) Entanglement and Decoherence Aspects in Remote Viewing: a Topological Geometrodynamics Approach. J of Non-Locality   and   Remote   Mental   Interactions   II[1] www.emergentmind.org/SidorovII(1).htm

72. Sidorov L (2002) Control Systems, Transduction Arrays and Psi Healing: an Experimental Basis for Human Potential Science. J of Non-Locality and Remote Mental Interactions I[2] www.emergent-mind.org/sidorovI2.htm.htm

73. Stone RB (1995) Cells Caught in the Act of Communication. MIS-AHA Newsletter 11:2

74. Peoc'h R (2002) Psychokinesis Experiments with Human and Animal Subjects upon a Robot Moving at Random. Parapsychology Association Convention 2002

75. Sheldrake R. (2000) J of Scientific Exploration 14:233

76. Chu DY, He WG, Zhou YF, Chen BC (1998) "The Effect of Chinese Qigong on the Conformation of Biomolecules" Chinese Journal of Somatic Science 8[4]:155

77. Chu DY, Wang WZ, He BH & Chen, K. (2001). The effect of external qi of qigong on biomolecular conformation (III). P. 132-137 in Chez RA (ed.) Proceedings: Bridging Worlds and Filling Gaps in the Science of Healing. Hawaii, November 29-December 3, 2001

78. Lemley B. Heresy. Discover 21[8]:60

79. Chen K., Yeung R. (2002) "Exploratory Studies of Qigong Therapy for Cancer in China". Integrative Cancer Therapies 1[4]:345

BIOELECTROMAGNETIC HEALING, ITS HISTORY AND A RATIONALE FOR ITS USE

Thomas F. Valone
Integrity Research Institute, 1220 L Street NW, Suite 100-232
Washington DC 20005, iri@erols.com

Abstract

Bioelectromagnetics (BEMs) is the study of the effect of electromagnetic fields on biological systems.[i] Though electromagnetic fields have sometimes been associated with potential for harm to the body, there are many BEM instruments and devices re-emerging in the 21st century, based on high voltage Tesla coils, that apparently bring beneficial health improvements to human organisms. The Tesla coil class of therapy devices constitute pulsed electromagnetic fields (PEMF) that deliver broadband, wide spectrum, nonthermal photons and electrons deep into biological tissue. Electromedicine or electromagnetic healing are the terms applied to such developments in the ELF, RF, IR, visible or UV band. With short term, non-contacting exposures of several minutes at a time, such high voltage Tesla PEMF devices may represent the ideal, noninvasive therapy of the future, accompanied by a surprising lack of harmful side effects. A biophysical rationale for the benefits of BEM healing a wide variety of illnesses including cancer, proposes a correlation between a bioelectromagnetically restored transmembrane potential, and the electron transport across cell membranes by electroporation, with normal cell metabolism and immune system enhancement. The century-long historical record of these devices is also traced, revealing questionable behavior from the medical and public health institutions toward such remarkable innovations. This

---

i   Bioelectromagnetics Society (founded 1978), 120 W. Church St., Frederick MD
    21701. 301-663-4252 www.bioelectromagnetics.org

report also reviews the highlights of several BEM inventions but does not attempt to present an exhaustive nor comprehensive review of bioelectromagnetic healing devices.

History of Bioelectromagnetic Healing

Historically, as far back as 1890, the American Electro-Therapeutic Association conducted annual conferences on the therapeutic use of electricity and electrical devices by physicians on ailing patients. Some involved current flow through the patient, while others were electrically powered devices. At first, only direct current (DC) devices were utilized in the medical doctor's office for relieving pain and vibrating female patients who were routinely diagnosed with "hysteria."

Nikola Tesla

In 1895, the Niagara Falls Power Company opened for the first time and within a year, sent alternating current (AC) to Buffalo, NY, twenty-five miles away. Cities throughout the world followed suit and made commercial AC power available to the general public, even miles from the power generating station. As a result, Nikola Tesla's high voltage coil devices, which were powered by AC, started to become widely known and applied.

In 1898, Tesla published a paper that he read at the eighth annual meeting of the American Electro-Therapeutic Association in Buffalo, NY entitled, "High Frequency Oscillators for Electro-Therapeutic and Other Purposes."[ii] He states that "One of the early observed and remarkable features of the high frequency currents, and one which was chiefly of interest to the physician, was their apparent harmlessness which made it possible to pass relatively great amounts of electrical energy through the body of a person without causing pain or serious discomfort." Coils up to three feet in diameter were used for magnetically treating the body without contact, though ten to a hundred thousand volts were present "between the first and last turn." Preferably, Tesla describes using spheres of brass covered with two inches of insulating wax for contacting the patient, while unpleasant shocks were prevented. Tesla con-

---

[ii]   Tesla, N (1898) "High Frequency Oscillators for Electro-Therapeutic and Other Purposes," *The Electrical Engineer*, Vol. XXVI, No. 550, Nov. 17, p.477

cludes correctly that bodily "tissues are condensers" in the 1898 paper, which is the basic component (dielectric) for an equivalent circuit only recently developed for the human body.[iii] In fact, the relative permittivity for tissue at any frequency from ELF (10 Hz-100 Hz) through RF (10 kHz—100 MHz) exceeds most commercially available dielectrics on the market.[iv] This unique property of the human body indicates an inherent adaptation and perhaps innate compatibility toward the presence of high voltage electric fields, probably due to the high transmembrane potential already present in cellular tissue. Tesla also indicates that the after-effect from his coil treatment "was certainly beneficial" but that an hour exposure was too strong to be used frequently. This has been found to be still true today with the Tesla coil therapy devices. On September 6, 1932, at a seminar presented by the American Congress of Physical Therapy, held in New York, Dr. Gustave Kolischer announced: *"Tesla's high-frequency electrical currents are bringing about highly beneficial results in dealing with cancer, surpassing anything that could be accomplished with ordinary surgery."*

Alexander Gurvich

In 1922, the Russian doctor and histologist Alexander (Gurwitsch) Gurvich (1874-1954) and his wife discovered that living cells separated by quartz glass were able to communicate vital-cell information. Numerous experiments suggested that this information was transmitted by invisible light waves in a UV frequency spectrum passed by quartz and stopped by window glass. Dr. Gurvich coined the phrase "mitogenic" "mitotic" wave since it was observed during enzymatic reactions and mitosis. "Gurvich determined that muscle tissue, cornea, blood and nerves are all transmitters of this special energy."[v] His work is the first documented evidence of "biophotons," coherent light emitted by animal and plant cells, and became the basis for the design of later bioelectromagnetic therapy devices. It was not until the early 1960's that Leningrad State University succeeded in capturing the mitogenic rays with sensitive photomultipliers.[vi]

[iii] Polk, C, Postow E, (1986) *Handbook of Biological Effects of Electromagnetic Fields*, CRC Press, p. 58

[iv] Fink, DD, (1975) "Dielectric Constant and Loss Factor for Several Dielectrics," *Electrical Engineer's Handbook*, p. 6-36

[v] Manning, Clark A., L. J. Vanrenen, *Bioenergetic Medicines East and West*, North Atlantic Books, Berkeley, 1988, p. 43

[vi] Douglass, W. C. *Into the Light—The Exciting Story of the Life-Saving Breakthrough Therapy of the Age*, Second Opinion Pub., Atlanta, 1996, p. 269

Georges Lakhovsky

In 1925, Georges Lakhovsky published a paper with the explicit title of "Curing Cancer with Ultra Radio Frequencies" in *Radio News*.[vii] His expressed philosophy was that "the amplitude of cell oscillations must reach a certain value, in order that the organism be strong enough to repulse the destructive vibrations from certain microbes." He goes on to say, "The remedy in my opinion, is not to kill the microbes in contact with the healthy cells but to reinforce the oscillations of the cell either directly by reinforcing the radio activity of the blood or in producing on the cells a direct action by means of the proper rays." Lakhovsky's Radio-Cellulo-Oscillator (RCO) produced low frequency ELF all the way through gigahertz radiowaves with lots of "extremely short harmonics."[viii] He favored such a wide bandwidth device so that, "The cells with very weak vibrations, when placed in the field of multiple vibrations, finds its own frequency and starts again to oscillate normally through the phenomenon of resonance." As a result, Lakhovsky's RCO is now more often called MWO (multiple wave oscillator) for these reasons. The MWO uses a Tesla coil and special antenna with concentric rings that induce multiple sparks between them. Details can be found in his US patent #1,962,565 and the compact, portable, screw-in-lightbulb-style-vacuum-tube upgrades seen in his US patent #2,351,055. Lakhovsky's article and patents can be found on line at: http://www.rexresearch.com/lakhov/lakhusps.htm. His book, *The Secret of Life* was first published in English in 1939. In 1949, a review of Lakhovsky's work was published as *Waves That Heal* by Mark Clement. Besides this technical information, the life of Lakhovsky is a study in suppression and summarized below in a paper by Chris Bird:

> The first man I will mention today is the Russian-born Frenchman, Georges Lakhovsky. I learned only yesterday that Lakhovsky seems to have been an associate, or knew, Nikola Tesla. I had not known that and from the point of view of the history of energy medicine, it's a very interesting thing. At any rate, Georges Lakhovsky began to experiment with what he called a "multiwave

---

vii   Lakhovsky, Georges. "Curing Cancer with Ultra Radio Frequencies," *Radio News*, February, 1925, p. 1282-1283.

viii Grotz, Toby, and B. Hillstead. "Frequency Analysis of the Lakhovsky Multiple Wave Oscillator from 20 Hz to 20 GHz," *Proceedings of the US Psychotronics Association Convention*, Portland, OR, July, 1983 oscillator." (In the Library of Congress there are some ten books written by Lakhovsky, all in French.)

This multiwave oscillator (MWO) put out a very broad spectrum of electromagnetic frequencies. The theory, as propounded by Lakhovsky, was that each cell in the body of an organism-be it a plant, an animal, or a human being-is in itself a little radio receiver and works on its own special little frequency. Each cell, in addition to being tissue, in addition to being biology, is also electricity. On that theory, he held that pathology was a not matter of biological concern or intervention, but one of electrical concern and intervention. He theorized that from the bath of electrical frequencies put out by the multiwave oscillator, each cell individually could and would select that frequency which it most needed to restore its equilibrium.

So he began to experiment not with animals or human beings, but with geraniums. These were geraniums which had cancers-plants get cancers too. And, lo and behold, the geraniums were cured of their cancers; which simply began to fall off since they are external in the case of geraniums. The geraniums would just shed the diseased tissues when exposed to the MWO. Lakhovsky then went on to do work on animals and human beings and his work was picked up by doctors in six or seven countries, among them Italy, Sweden and Brazil. Finally, because he was on the "wanted" list of the Nazis, he was smuggled out of France and came to New York during the war, where he worked with a urologist. The record of his treatment of degenerative disease, with what amounts to an early "energy-medicine" device, was remarkable. But the work had to be done in secret because orthodox medicine did not favor this device, and its power, associated with that of the FDA and the AMA and other "control organizations," kept the MWO underground.

The Lakhovsky device is a very effective one. I'm not going to say that it's 100% effective because I don't think any device is, but it is way up there. Georges Lakhovsky died in 1944 or 1945.[ix]

[ix] Bird, Christopher. "The Politics Of Science: A Background On Energy Medicine," *Energetic Processes: Interaction Between Matter, Energy & Consciousness, Volume I*, Xlibris Press, Philadelphia, 2001, p. 226

Royal Raymond Rife

In 1934, the University of Southern California appointed a Special Medical Research Committee to study 16 terminal cancer patients from Pasadena County Hospital that would be treated with mitogenic impulse-wave technology, developed by Royal Raymond Rife. After four months the Medical Research Committee reported that all 16 of the formerly-terminal patients appeared cured.

Rife's high voltage gas tube device was designed, with the aid of his unique microscope, by experimentally witnessing the effects on microbes and bacteria, finding what he believed were the particular frequencies that resonated with their destruction. "In 1938, Rife made his most public announcement. In a two-part article written by Newall Jones of the *San Diego Evening Tribune* (May 6 & 11), Rife said, 'We do not wish at this time to claim that we have "cured" cancer, or any other disease, for that matter. But we can say that these waves, or this ray, as the frequencies might be called, have been shown to possess the power of devitalizing disease organisms, of "killing" them, when tuned to an exact wave length, or frequency, for each organism. This applies to the organisms both in their free state and, with certain exceptions, when they are in living tissues.'"[x]

"He had the backing in his day—this was in the 1930's—of such eminent people as Kendall, a professor of pathology at Northwestern University and Millbank Johnson, M.D., who was on his board, along with many other medical men, when he began to treat people with this new 'ray emitter.'...There were articles written on the Rife technique...in the *Journal for the Medical Society of California* and other medical journals. Suddenly, Rife came under the glassy eye of Morris Fishbein of the AMA and things began to happen very quickly. Rife was put on trial for having invented a 'phony' medical cure. The trial lasted a long time."[xi]

In 1953, Rife published his cancer report in book form, *History of the Development of a Successful Treatment for Cancer and Other Virus, Bacteria and Fungi.*[xii] A turning point occurred in 1958, when the State of California Public Health Department conducted a hearing which ordered the testing of Rife's

---

[x]   Lynes, Barry. *The Cancer Cure That Worked: Fifty Years of Suppression*, Marcus Books, Queensville, Ontario, 1987, p. 103

[xi] Bird, p. 227

[xii] Rife, Royal Raymond. *History of the Development of a Successful Treatment for Cancer and Other Virus, Bacteria and Fungi.* Rife Virus Microscope Institute, San Diego, CA, 1953

Frequency Instrument. The Palo Alto Detection Lab, the Kalbfeld Lab, the UCLA Medical Lab, and the San Diego Testing Lab all participated in the evaluation procedure. "All reported that it was safe to use. Nevertheless, the AMA Board, under Dr. Malcolm Merrill, the Director of Public Health, declared it *unsafe* and banned it from the market."[xiii]

In 1961, after a trial with an AMA doctor as the foreman of the jury, John F. Crane, the new owner of the Rife Virus Microscope Institute, spent three years in jail, ostensibly for using the Frequency Instrument on people, though no specific criminal intent had been proven. In 1965, he attempted to obtain approval from the California Board of Public Health for use of the Frequency Instrument. "On November 17, 1965, the Department of Public Health replied that Crane had not shown that the device was safe or 'effective in use.'"[xiv]

From 1968 to 1983, Dr. Livingston-Wheeler treated approximately 10,000 patients with the Rife Frequency Instrument, at her University of Southern California clinic, with an 80% success rate.[xv] In 1972, Dr. Livingston-Wheeler published *Cancer: A New Breakthrough* in which she "condemned the National Cancer Institute for its misuse of money [$500 million in 13 years], the corrupt handling of public health responsibilities, and its use of people [100,000 cancer patients] as guinea pigs for a 'surgery-radiation-chemotherapy' program dictated by special interests."[xvi] Her last book on *The Conquest of Cancer* was published in 1984 in which she celebrates the European acceptance of the Rife discoveries but complains about the situation in the U.S.

> All these distinguished scientist, back in 1958, had been carrying on significant research in the biological and immunological treatment of cancer for years. It is still only now that the United States orthodoxy is beginning to catch up. Because of the suppressive actions of the American Cancer Society, the American Medical Association, and the Food and Drug Administration, our people have not had the advantage of the European research.
>
> This work has been ignored because certain powerful individuals backed by large monetary grants can become the dictators of

---

xiii   Lynes, p.129
xiv   Ibid., p. 133
xv   Ibid., p. 116
xvi   Ibid., p. 117

research and suppress all work that does not promote their interests or that may present a threat to their prestige.[xvii]

Rife died in 1971, mostly of a broken heart.

Antoine Priore

Antoine Priore's electromagnetic therapy machine was perfected during the 1960's and early 70's as a team of leading French scientists demonstrated "conclusive, total remissions of terminal tumors and infectious diseases in hundreds of laboratory animals...funded by the French Government. The approach employed very complicated mixing of multiple EM signals in a rotating plasma, and modulating the mixed output upon a very strong rippling magnetic field to which the body of the test animal was exposed. Complete remission of the treated diseases was obtained. In addition, the animals' immune systems were also restored to normal...In the mid-70's Priore's work was suppressed, because of hostility of the oncology community, change of the French Government, loss of further funding, and complete inability of the physicists and biological scientists to even hypothesize a mechanism for the curative results."[xviii] This last reason reminds one of the thesis by Thomas Kuhn, who argues that a radical phenomenon in science will be repeatedly treated as an anomaly until a new theory can explain it.[xix]

Chris Bird gives us an interesting insight into his life:

> I will tell you about one more person—still another self-taught genius, Antoine Priore, who began working in 1944-45, right after the war, to develop an electromagnetic device which cured cancer. He got the backing of some very interesting and courageous people, including the world-famous immunologist Dr. Raymond Pautrizel, of the University of Bordeaux II, who did all the animal work.
>
> When Dr. Pautrizel arrived on the scene, because the emotional atmosphere surrounding the cancer cure was so great, he decided to

xvii Livingston-Wheeler, Virginia, and E. G. Addeo, *The Conquest of Cancer*, Franklin Watts, 1984

xviii Bearden, TE, "Vacuum Engines and Priore's Methodology: The True Science of Energy-Medicine" *Explore More*, Number 10, 1995, p. 16

xix Kuhn, Thomas, (1970) The Structure of Scientific Revolutions, University of Chicago Press, 1970, p. 78

take the research in another direction and began to use the machine to treat what he knew best, which was sleeping sickness in animals. Sleeping sickness was of primary concern to Dr. Pautrizel because it is a widespread affliction in tropical countries and, perhaps because he was born and raised in Guadeloupe in the Carribbean, he had become very interested in tropical medicine. When he injected rabbits with the pathogen trypansome, which causes sleeping sickness, the trypanosome would multiply until there were billions of them circulating in the bloodstream and the rabbits would uniformly all die within 72 hours. But, when exposed to the radiation of the Priore device, these same rabbits would live. Yet their blood was still teeming with the trypanosomes, which could be extracted from the radiated rabbits and injected into other control rabbits, which would then die.

This implies that the machine was doing something electromagnetically to the immune system of the rabbits such that they were able to fight off a lethal disease which would normally kill them in 72 hours!

Had it not been for the courage of Dr. Robert Courrier, who at that time was Perpetual Secretary of the Academy of Sciences of France, in the face of great criticism, the scientific data on 20 years of that work might never have been published. Time after time, over 20 years or more, Dr. Courrier personally introduced the papers for publication in the *Comptes Rendues* (Proceedings) of the French Academy of Sciences. There are 28 such papers. Even this could not prevent Dr. Pautrizel from nearly being fired from his post at the University of Bordeaux II, where he finally treated human patients successfully with the Priore device.

When he wrote a paper and sent it this time to the Academy of Medicine, it was refused without explanation. Pautrizel then wrote a long letter, since made public, to the governing offices of the French Academy of Medicine to find out why the paper had been refused and which people on the jury refused it, so that he could consult with them in order to better inform them of the facts. For 3 1/2 years he received no reply.

So then he decided to step outside of normal scientific channels and offered his story to a journalist who wrote an extraordinary book called *The Dossier Priore, A Second Affaire Pasteur?* Because the book has not been translated from French, and may not be (because it was written for a French audience and should really be rewritten in

English) it is not accessible to English readers. But I have written a 50-page paper which is a synopsis of it.

We have discussed the cases of four intrepid researchers. Of these, three had no formal academic training—Priore, Naessens and Rife—and yet they went on to develop the most extraordinary medical tools in energy medicine that I think exist. Two of them were put to trial! One was nearly fired from his position. All this is moving and largely unknown medical history and all of it affords real opportunities for further exciting research.[xx]

Robert Becker

A pioneering medical doctor in the 1960's, Dr. Becker is most famous for his book, *The Body Electric*, which gives an autobiographical account of his life's experiences with bioelectromagnetics.[xxi] Not only did he establish that the Chinese meridians of the body are skin pathways of decreased electrical resistance but he discovered a host of other bioelectric effects within the body as well, such as electrostimulating limb-regeneration in mammals. He also worked on electrically stimulating bone growth with Dr. Andrew Bassett, who along with Dr. Arthur Pilla, developed a very effective PEMF generator to stimulate bone fracture healing, now approved by the FDA with an 80% success rate. Similar PEMF signals recently have been used effectively to prevent osteoporosis even in patients with an ovariectomy.[xxii]

Abraham Liboff

A modern-day physicist and inventor, Dr. Abraham Liboff is the discoverer of electric-field and geomagnetic ion cyclotron resonance, which more reliably explains the resonant interaction of static magnetic fields with endogenous AC

xx   Bird, p. 235

xxi   Becker, Robert O. *The Body Electric, Electromagnetism and the Foundation of Life*, William Morrow & Co., New York, 1985

xxii Chang, K. and W.H. Chang. "Pulsed electromagnetic fields prevent osteoporosis in an ovariectomized female rat model: A prostaglandin E_2-associated process" *Bioelectromagnetics*, V. 24, Issue 3, 2003, p. 189

electric fields in biological systems.[xxiii, xxiv] A physicist with Oakland University, he has introduced significant physics principles into the field of bioelectromagnetics. His "Method and Apparatus for the Treatment of Cancer" (US Patent #5,211,622) tunes an alternating magnetic field, superimposed on a static magnetic field, to maintain a combined effect that has the proper cyclotron resonance frequency so that the neoplastic tissue containing a preselected ion can be treated to bring about a decrease in the proliferation rate of the cancer cells. It also can be combined with a chemotherapeutic agent for a synergistic effect. However, it is noted in the patent disclosure that "up to 100 days of treatment will provide beneficial results."

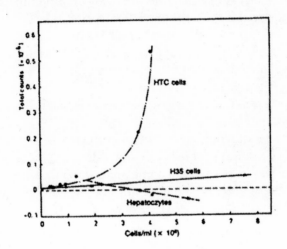

[xxiii] Liboff, A.R. "Electric-field Ion Cyclotron Resonance" *Bioelectromagnetics*, V. 18, Issue 1, P. 85

[xxiv] Liboff, A.R. "Geomagnetic Cyclotron Resonance in Living Cells" Journal of Biological Physics, V. 13, 1985

Stimulated Biophoton Emission

In 1976, Bernard Ruth rediscovered evidence of a very weak but permanent photon emission from living tissue, while doing research for his doctoral dissertation.[xxv] The findings of his research team led by Fritz Albert Popp, subsequently proved experimentally that biophotons exhibit multimode coherent properties akin to laser light and not merely spontaneous chemiluminescence which is chaotic.[xxvi] One example is the unusually high transparency of tissue to biophoton light. It is an interesting phenomenon, which coincides with "light piping" in plant tissues, by which nature apparently ensures that several centimeters of cellular cytoplasm hardly attenuate the amplitude of biophoton intensity. Experimental data of the extinction coefficient of wet sea sand and soya cells at 550 nm from a Guilford spectrophotometer, compared to biophotons emitted by cucumber seedlings passing through the same sand and soya, reveal the lowest value (a <u>constant</u> 0.2/mm value for E/d) for the biophotons passing through 5 cm of soya cell cultures.[xxvii] This biophoton transparency phenomenon has been used to suggest that biogenic, long-distance intercellular communication implies information transmission.[xxviii]

The total number of biophotons emitted by normal cells, when exposed to white light, decreases, not exponentially but with a <u>hyperbolic relaxation</u> of photon intensity after exposure, extending up to an hour. "Under ergodic conditions, hyperbolic decay is a sufficient condition for coherent rescattering."[xxix]

[xxv]   Ruth, Bernard. "Experimenteller Nachweis ultrawacher Photonemission aus biologischen Systemen" *Dissertation*, University of Marburg, 1977

[xxvi] Popp, A. F., "Evolution as Expansion of Coherent States," *The Interrelationship Between Mind and Matter*, Center for Frontier Sciences, Temple University, Philadelphia, 1992, p. 257

[xxvii] Popp, F.A. "Principles of quantum biology as demonstrated by ultraweak photon emission from living cells" *International Journal of Fusion Energy*, V. 1, No. 4, October, 1985, p. 9

[xxviii] Fischer, Helmut. "Photons as transmitters for intra-and intercellular biological and biochemical communication—the construction of a hypothesis" *Electromagnetic Bio-Information*, F. A. Popp, ed., Urban & Schwarzenberg, Munic, 1989, p. 193

[xxix] Ibid., p.259

The emission of biophoton light by cancerous cells when exposed to white light, versus the slow decline in emission levels by healthy cells upon irradiation by white light, demonstrates a remarkable difference (see Figure 1). The HTC cell curve, representing malignant liver cells shows an exponential increase in activity with a linear cell density increase. The weakly malignant cells (H35 cells) show a slight increase, while the normal (Hepatoczytes) display a linear decrease with increasing cell density. One proposed cellular communication hypothesis might correlate the experimental rate of biophoton emission vs. density with stimulating mitosis or proliferation. Normally a cellular colony would reduce such multiplication upon receiving evidence of overcrowding. Instead, cancer cells not only have no such limits, as is well-known, but the evidence suggests a tendency, as seen in Figure 1, for positive feedback, if such a correlation exists. Growth regulation through biophoton emission normally follows a nonlinear (proportional to the square of the number of cells) inhibition, confirmed by experiment, which shows a capacity for coherent superposition of biophoton modes.[xxx]

It is quite possible that the Rife style of Tesla devices stimulate healthful biophotons.

Description of High Voltage Tesla PEMF Devices

While there are numerous other classes of BEM devices, as seen with the Priore machine, the Liboff device, and even pain fighters,[xxxi] this investigation centers on the High Voltage Tesla (HVT) class of BEM therapy PEMF devices. The standard Tesla coil, with a spark gap between the capacitor and high voltage transformer, sets the standard for this class of high voltage BEM devices which are of particular interest. Up until now, the lack of biophysical knowledge surrounding their operation has impeded, in this author's opinion, their widespread acceptance into the medical profession. They are pulsed by virtue of an intermittent high voltage conduction component, which can be a relay,

xxx   Popp, F.A. "Biophotons—Background, Experimental Results, Theoretical Approach and Applications" *Frontier Perspectives*, Vol. 11, No. 1, Spring, 2002, p. 25

xxxi Maloney, Lawrence. "Pain Fighters—Tests help NeuroControl's engineers design an electrical stimulator to ease the suffering of stroke patients" *Test & Measurement World*, April, 2003, p. 30

switch, or simply the spark gap, thus creating PEMF fields, often with square wave characteristics.

Examples of the HVT PEMF devices are the Tesla Coil, Lakhovsky MWO, the Rife Frequency Instrument, and recently, the Natural Energy Institute's Electronic Wind Faser (soliton@optonline.net), the Azure Therapy Device (US Patent #6,217,604), the Vibration Integration Biophotonic Energizing (VIBE) device (www.vibe-machine.com), the Tesla Photon Machine (www.altcancer.com), the Pappas Pulsed Magnetic Induction Device (MID) (US Patent #5,068,039 and #5,556,418), and the Light Beam Generator (www.LightBeamGenerator.com).

Stages and Modality of PEMF Effects

In determining the most likely biophysical reactions, this investigation begins with some bioelectromagnetic statistics. The resistivity, conductivity, dielectric constants, etc. of the human body are all known in the literature. There are many stages and possible modalities of EMF and PEMF interaction with the body. Starting from the exogenous field penetration, known interactions with cellular metabolism are examined.

Skin Depth of HVT PEMF

For example, it has been established that high frequency electromagnetic fields (EMFs) can penetrate several centimeters into tissue, bone, and muscle.[xxxii] Immunological effects of in vivo RF exposure often results an improvement or stimulation when local hyperthermia is induced with continuous wave, gigahertz frequencies of approximately 100 watts per square meter intensity.[xxxiii] However, without local hyperthermia induced, the biophysics of the effects on the tissue is less obvious. At least, it can be reasonably that HVT PEMF's also penetrate deeply into the body. The various effects of the PEMF's inside the body are explored below.

[xxxii] Polk, et al., p. 281

[xxxiii] Ibid., p. 398 (adapted from US EPA, *Biological Effects of RF Radiation*, Elder and Cahill, 1984)

Negative Ion Effects

It is well-known that negative ions and traces of ozone have a wide range of health benefits, including boosting the immune system and killing germs.[xxxiv] Since high voltage Tesla PEMF devices provide an abundance of negative ions and traces of ozone, the hypothetical neuroendocrine cell-initiated reflex arc may also apply to explain neurological benefits.[xxxv]

Transmembrane Potential

Another important aspect of the biophysical effects from HVT PEMF's can be found in analyzing the transmembrane potential (TMP). For example, it is known that damaged or diseased cells present an abnormally low TMP about 80% lower than healthy cells.[xxxvi,xxxvii] This signifies a greatly reduced metabolism and, in particular, impairment of the sodium-potassium (Na-K) pump activity and ATP production.

It is proposed that cell membranes may, in fact, rectify alternating currents since structured proteins behave like solid-state rectifiers.[xxxviii] It is reasonable therefore to conclude, based on these biophysical principles, that any endogenous HV EMF potential of sufficient strength will theoretically stimulate the TMP, normal cell metabolism, the Na-K pump, ATP production and healing. This has already found in the literature: "TMP is proportional to the activity of this pump and thus to the rate of healing."[xxxix]

xxxiv   Valone, T. F. "Fresh Air Curative Effect Related to Ions and Traces of Ozone" *Explore*, V. 7, No. 1, 1996, p. 70

xxxv   Charry, J. and R. Kavet. *Air Ions: Physical and Biological Aspects*, CRC Press, 1987, p. 173

xxxvi   Ceve, G. "Membrane Electrostatics," *Biochim Biophys Acta,* 103(3):311-82, 1990 **Medline 91027827**

xxxvii Malzone, A. et al, "Effect on cellular and tissue metabolism of induced electrical currents" *Arch Stomatology* 30(2):371-82 **Medline 90314754**

xxxviii Szent-Gyorgi, A., *Introduction to Submolecular Biology*, Academic Press, NY, 1960. Also see, *Bioelectronics*, Academic Press, NY 1968, and *Electronic Biology*, Marcel Dekker, NY 1976

xxxix   Jorgenson, W. A. and B.M. Frome, C. Wallach. "Electrochemical Therapy of Pelvic Pain: Effects of Pulsed Electromagnetic Fields (PEMF) on Tissue Trauma," *European Journal of Surgery*, 1994, Supplement 574, p. 86

"Increases in the membrane potential have also been found to increase the uptake of amino acids."[xl] Healthy cells, according to Nobel prize winner Otto Warburg, have cell TMP voltages of 70 to 90 millivolts. Due to the constant stresses of modern life and a toxic environment, cell voltage tends to drop as we age or get sick. As the voltage drops, the cell is unable to maintain a healthy environment for itself. If the electrical charge of a cell drops to 50, a person may experience chronic fatigue. If the voltage drops to 15, the cell often can be cancerous. Dr. Warburg also found in 1925 that cancer cells function best in the absence of oxygen, in effect, living on fermentation rather than respiration.[xli]

Multiple Interactions with EMF

To address some of the complex modalities of interaction with electromagnetic fields, Figure 2 offers a standard set of (1) electronic excitation to a higher energy level following the absorption of electromagnetic energy in the visible or UV spectrum, which is also capable of altering chemical bonds; (2) polarization which, if the dipoles are attached to a membrane, could alter membrane permeability; (3) forces on induced dipoles cause pearl-chain formation for fields above 10 kV/m; (4) heat effects are a "ubiquitous consequence of EMFs" but independent of the details of molecular activity; (5) other processes that have sensitivities as low as one billionth of a microwatt per square centimeter ($10^{-9} \mu W/cm^2$). Such processes include quantum mechanical and classical processes of superconductivity, Hall effect, converse piezoelectric effect, cooperative dipole interactions, and plasma oscillations. The #5 processes are "theoretically capable of serving as the underlying physical mechanism for any known EMF-induced biological effect."[xlii]

[xl]   Bockris, J.M. et al. Modern Aspects of Electrochemistry, No. 14, Plenum Pub., New York, 1982, p. 512

[xli]   Warburg, Otto, "On the Origin of Cancer Cells" Science, V. 123, 1956, p. 309

[xlii]   Becker, R.O. and A.A. Marino. Electromagnetism and Life, State University of NY Press, Albany, 1982, p. 164

High Voltage Effects

Research has shown that simple high voltage electrostatic fields can have many effects on the human body, most of which appear to be favorable. For example, HV fields in the range of 2400 kV/m (2.4 MV/m) were found to have a beneficial effect on mice as measured by their activity, rate of liver respiration, and ability to form antibodies. In contrast, mice which were deprived of any electrostatic fields by being enclosed in a Faraday cage showed opposite results.[xliii] (It is noted that the outdoor, ambient electrostatic field caused by the ionosphere to earth potential is approximately 100 V/m and rises during thunderstorms.) Not only does such research imply a correlation to immunological ability but it also implies another important aspect of BEMs: The <u>endogenous</u> electric field strength, within a few centimeters of bone or tissue, will usually be in the range of only 10 mV/m for an <u>exogenous</u> field of 1 MV/m at 10 Hz or less. (The earth-ionosphere Schumann cavity for example, resonates fundamentally around 10 Hz.) However, the endogenous voltage relationship is a decreasing logarithmic with frequency, so that an exogenous MHz range signal need only be 100 V/m to create the same 10 mV/m internally.[xliv] Higher frequency EMFs thus have correspondingly higher endogenous fields. As an application example, it has been found that a temporal peak electric field magnitude of approximately 150 mV/m averaged within the medial cartilage of the knee, when stimulated by a osteoarthritis therapy, 0.12 mT coil with 260 microsecond pulses.[xlv]

[xliii] Sheppard, A.R. and M. Eisenbud. *Biological Effects of Electric and Magnetic Fields of Extremely Low Frequency*, New York University Press, New York, 1977, Ch. 5, p. 34

[xliv] Polk, et al., p. 10

[xlv] Buechler, D.N. "Calculation of electric fields induced in the human knee by a coil applicator" *Bioelectromagnetics*. V. 22, Issue 4, 2001, p. 224

ADAPTABILITY OF ORGANISMS TO ELECTROMAGNETIC ENERGY

Pulsed electric or magnetic fields are also found to be another recourse, if it is understood that higher endogenous field strengths are desirable. Another example is a 100 kV/m electric field which has been shown to improve the synthesis of macromolecules, such as DNA or collagen (which forms connective tissue). However, if the field is interrupted at least once per second (pulse rate of 1 Hz), DNA synthesis goes up 20% higher than the previous measurement and collagen synthesis by 100%. A dependence on the field strength is also found.[xlvi]

It has been proposed that only one PEMF device operates close to the minimum electroporation gradient of 1 kV/cm (100 MV/m). That is the Pappas Pulsed MID which has reported success in relieving 89% of acute or chronic pelvic pain and explains that, "Electroporation is a universal, non-thermal, bioelectrochemical phenomenon relating to the rate of two-way transmigration of chemical ions through the cell membrane, defining the cell's metabolic rate and hence energy level."[xlvii]

[xlvi]   Sheppard et al., Ch. 5, p. 34
[xlvii] Jorgenson, W.A., et al., p. 83

In perspective, it may be noted that HVT PEMFs such as the Azure device and those like it may not achieve the high endogenous fields for creating electroporation but most likely stimulate membrane permeation through HF effects noted below, confirming the abundance of healing anecdotal reports. Dr. Robert Adair notes that without utilizing pulsed signals, continuous (AC) RF devices need to exceed 10 mW/cm^2 in order to exceed the ubiquitous endogenous noise in biological systems.[xlviii]

Concerns about endogenous HV safety issues have also been addressed in the literature. Recent experiments confirm that a two-minute exposure to 100 kV/m peak electric field, and a pulse duration of 1 ns "does not have an immediate detrimental effect on the cardiovascular system…"[xlix] Also confirmed is that "nonthermal biohazards seem unlikely in the ultra-high frequency range" with the chief physical loss mechanism being ionic conduction and dielectric relaxation.[l]

High Frequency Effects

When studying high voltage, especially with Tesla coils, it is also important to examine the BEM high frequency effects that are also well-known. The average specific absorption rate (SAR) for a human body for example, is measured in watts/kilogram (W/kg) and has an increasing logarithmic dependence with frequency up until 1 gigahertz (1 GHz) where it levels out at about 10 W/kg. The power absorption density for muscle per incident milliwatts per cm^2 also levels out around 1 GHz.[li] This is valuable information for analyzing HVT PEMF devices since they operate in a broadband of frequencies, often with two resonant peaks in the kilohertz or megahertz range but still generating meas-

---

xlviii   Adair, R. "Biophysical limits on athermal effects of RF and microwave radiation" *Bioelctromagnetics*. V. 24, Issue 1, 2003, p. 39

xlix   Jauchem, J. R. et al. "Ultra-wideband electromagnetic pulses: Lack of effects on heart rate and blood pressure during two-minute exposures of rats" *Bioelectromagnetics*. V. 19, Issue 5, 1998, p. 330

l   Pickard, W. F. & E.G. Moros. "Energy deposition processes in biological tissue: Nonthermal biohazards seem unlikely in the ultra-high frequency range" *Bioelectromagnetics*, V. 22, Issue 2, 2001, p. 97

li   Polk, et al., p. 292

lii   Rife Plasma HV Electrotherapy Spectrum Analysis http://www.rifetechnologies.com/Spectral.html

urable energy extending well into the GHz range.[lii] EMFs in the GHz range (1.8 GHz) have been shown to increase the permeability to sucrose of the blood-brain barrier in vitro.[liii]

Also, as noted previously, higher frequency EMFs have correspondingly higher endogenous fields. This has been dramatically confirmed with experiments on human eosinophils in vitro. When 3-5 pulses with electric field intensities of up to 5.3 MV/m and 60 ns (nanosecond) duration were applied to the human eosinophils, intracellular granules were modified without permanent disruption of the plasma membrane. In spite of the ultrashort electrical power levels applied to the cells, thermal effects could be neglected because of the ultrashort pulse duration. "The intracellular effects extends conventional electroporation to cellular substructures and opens the potential for new applications in apoptosis induction, gene delivery to the nucleus, or altered cell functions, depending on the electrical pulse conditions."[liv] It is noted that pulses with nanosecond periods will correspond to frequencies in the gigahertz range by a simple inverse relationship.

Demodulation of amplitude modulated radio frequency (RF) energy has been proposed as a mechanism for the biological responses to these fields. An experiment is also proposed that tests whether the electric and magnetic structures of biological cells exhibit the nonlinear responses necessary for demodulation:

> A high Q cavity and very low noise amplification can be used to detect ultraweak nonlinear responses that appear as a second harmonic of a RF field incident on the sample. Nonlinear fields scattered from metabolically active biological cells grown in monolayer or suspended in medium can be distinguished from nonlinearities of the apparatus. Estimates for the theoretical signal sensitivity and analysis of system noise indicate the possibility of detecting a microwave signal at 1.8 GHz (2nd harmonic of 900 MHz) as weak as one microwave photon per cell per second. The practical limit, set by degradation of the cavity Q, is extremely low compared to the much

[liii]   Schirmacher, A. et al., "Electromagnetic fields (1.8 GHz) increase the permeability to sucrose of the blood-brain barrier in vitro" *Bioelectromagnetics*, V. 21, Issue 5, 2000, p. 338

[liv]   Schoenbach, K.H. et al. "Intracellular effect of ultrashort electrical pulses" *Bioelectromagnetics*, V. 22, Issue 6, 2001, p. 440

brighter thermal background, which has its peak in the infrared at a wavelength of about 17 m and radiates 10^{10} infrared photons per second per cell in the narrow frequency band within 0.5% of the peak. The system can be calibrated by introduction of known quantities of nonlinear material, e.g., a Schottky diode. For an input power of 160 W at 900 MHz incident on such biological material, the apparatus is estimated to produce a robust output signal of 0.10 mV at 1.8 GHz if detected with a spectrum analyzer and a 30-dB gain low noise amplifier. The experimental threshold for detection of nonlinear interaction phenomena is 10^{10} below the signal produced by a Schottky diode, giving an unprecedented sensitivity to the measurement of nonlinear energy conversion processes in living tissue.[lv]

Electron Transport and Free Radicals

Quite possibly the most comprehensive and significant for general disease states including cancer, relates to the science of free radicals in the human body. Free radicals contain an odd number of electrons. An example is a methyl radical or a chlorine radical. It is known that homolytically cleaved covalent bonds break in such a way that each fragment retains one electron of the bond. Oxygen or chlorine are such examples. (Chlorine gas is readily available in small amounts within the home when anyone turns on a water faucet in a metropolitan area throughout the US, without using a charcoal filtration system.) Since molecular chlorine has a rather low bond-dissociation energy (58 kcal/mole) chlorine atom radicals may be produced by light of relatively long wavelength or heating to moderate temperatures. Once chlorine atom radicals are present in a small amount, a chain reaction commences. They can continuously react with another molecule to produce another free radical, going through 10,000 cycles before termination.[lvi] Antioxidants are the most common types of "terminators" for the chain reaction caused by free radicals, since

---

[lv] Balzano, Q. "Proposed test for detection of nonlinear responses in biological preparations exposed to RF energy" *Bioelectromagnetics*. V. 23, Issue 4, 2002, p. 278

[lvi] Stretwieser, A. and C.H. Heathcock. *Introduction to Organic Chemistry*. Second Edition, Macmillan Pub., New York, 1981, p. 105

they offer an extra free electron, which the radical seeks to complete an outer shell. Many types of free radicals exist within our bodies and have been connected with the aging process, most apparent externally by the appearance of skin wrinkling. Antioxidants, donors of free electrons, are used externally to reduce wrinkles on the skin and internally to slow the aging process and halt many disease processes. Coenzyme Q-10 can function, for example, as a coenzyme over and over again as an electron transfer agent or antioxidant.

Looking to a simple analysis of the electron transport chain found in the Krebs cycle, it produces ATP through chemiosmotic phosphorylation.[lvii] It can be proposed that as the high energy electrons are transferred to ubiquinone (Q) and cytochrome c molecules, which are the electron carriers within the membrane, free radicals may interfere with the process before the electrons reach the mitochondron, thus decreasing energy metabolism. In fact, Dr. William Koch found that "polymerizing unsaturated free radicals of low molecular weight stimulated cancer development decidedly...The free radical formed thus at the other pole...continues the polymerization process that supplies the energy for uncontrolled mitosis."[lviii]

It is proposed hypothetically that HVT PEMF devices offer abundant free electrons to the human body, in addition to plentiful negative ions, since they possess a unique static field modulated with a multimode pulsed electric field. Such a flood of free electrons, penetrating through permeable membranes throughout the tissues, muscles and perhaps the bones, not only halt the chain reactions in process, but also most likely force the fermentation production of ATP in the Krebs cycle back into a respiration cycle, in the presence of neoplastic, carcinogenic cells. Any cancer cells thus affected cannot tolerate the respiration cycle, as is well known, with its oxygen abundance and instead, immediately expire. The discharging of toxic residue then may become an important task, requiring only short HVT PEMF exposures and detoxifying interludes.

Light Effects

It has been found that light can offer a photodynamic effect on the body and entire books have been written about the specific therapeutic effects of various frequencies of visible light. Dr. John Ott conducted experiments show-

---

[lvii]   See http://library.thinkquest.org for example, or any biology text.

[lviii] Koch, W.F. *The Survival Factor in Neoplastic and Viral Diseases*. Vanderkloot Press, Detroit, p. 262

ing that mice living under pink fluorescent light were more likely to develop cancer and reproductive problems.[lix] Dr. William Douglass states, "Photonic medicine should soon be used for diagnosis as well as therapy."[lx] Interestingly enough, regarding the HVT PEMF devices which also add Rife gas tubes to the antenna, it has been shown that PEMF and photooxidation together yield "lethal effects on cancer cells."[lxi]

Conclusion

In conclusion, the PEMF devices that are known to utilize a Tesla coil, for the HF and HV PEMF, include the Azure patent assigned to Healing Machines, Inc., the VIBE Machine, the Tesla Photon Machine, the Light Beam Generator, the Lakhovsky multiwave oscillator (MWO), and Natural Healing Institute's Electronic Wind Faser. Several of these also add biophoton-stimulating high voltage gas tubes which appear to have an additional synergistic effect on the body.

[lix] Liberman, Jacob. *Light: Medicine of the Future.* Bear & Company, Santa Fe, 1991, p. 109

[lx] Douglass, p. 33

[lxi] Traitcheva, N. et al. "ELF fields and photooxidation yielding lethal effects on cancer cells" *Bioelectromagnetics.* Vol. 24, Issue 2, 2003, p. 148

0-595-30153-3